PhD

Other books by Jorge Cham:

"Piled Higher and Deeper: A Graduate Student Comic Strip Collection"

"Life is Tough and then You Graduate: The Second Piled Higher and Deeper Comic Strip Collection"

"Scooped! The Third Piled Higher and Deeper Comic Strip Collection"

"Academic Stimulus Package: The Fourth Piled Higher and Deeper Comic Strip Collection"

Adventures in Thesisland

The Fifth *Piled Higher and Deeper* Comic Strip Collection

by

Jorge Cham

Piled Higher and Deeper Publishing, LLC
Los Angeles, CA

Adventures in Thesisland: The Fifth Piled Higher and Deeper Comic Strip Collection

Published by Piled Higher & Deeper, LLC
Los Angeles, California

www.phdcomics.com

First Printing, March 2012
PRINTED IN CANADA

ISBN-10: 0-9721695-5-5
ISBN-13: 978-0-9721695-5-4

Library of Congress Control Number: 2012903955

For Meg, Vahe, Lucie, Roser and the cast and crew: we made a movie, and survived!

and

To Oliver
My favorite son thus far.

Introduction

Excerpt from the screenplay of the PHD Movie

OPENING SEQUENCE AND CREDITS:
EXT. UNIVERSITY CAMPUS -- EARLY MORNING, DAY 1

We see a close-up of a spinning bicycle wheel. An upbeat soundtrack marks a new day in an unnamed Research-One university in California. We see students walking into campus. PROFESSOR SMITH (50s, bearded, wearing a sweater vest and a white helmet) rolls in on his recumbent bicycle. He rides past the new Cahill Center and the women's basketball team taking a jog. We see him go through the Chemical Biology quad and over the Milliken Pond bridge. Then Point of View (POV) from his bicycle as he rides down the Olive walk. Students scatter to get out of his way.

Meanwhile, in a bedroom at the Catalina Grad Student apartments, a bedside alarm goes off, but when the camera pans to the bed, there's nobody there. It keeps panning until we see the Nameless Grad Student at his desk working, haggard from pulling an all-nighter. He throws a book to turn off the alarm, then hits "print" on his computer and his printer starts outputting papers. In an off-campus house in the "Grad Student Ghetto", CECILIA (early-to-mid 20s) starts her day in a chipper mood. She hums a waltz as she carefully arranges her electric toothbrush, toothpaste and washcloth and looks at herself in the mirror, psyching herself up for another day. She is excited about something.

We cut to MIKE SLACKENERNY (unknown age) in bed sleeping, snoring loudly with one leg sticking out the side. He doesn't look like he's going to wake up anytime soon. Back at the house, we see TAJEL (early-to-mid 20s) getting ready for her day. She stands in front of the mirror, pulls out a red lipstick and we follow it to her face, where instead of putting it on her lips, she uses it to draw a big peace sign on her forehead. We pull out and see she is getting ready for a student protest, with signs and banners all around her and slogans written all over her arms and chest.

Back to Prof. Smith, he parks his bike, undoes the reflective straps that hold down his pant legs and takes off his white helmet, leaving his thinning hair in a vertical tuff. He strides into the building, ignoring a student who comes up to him, nearly slamming the door on the student's face.
The screen splits into four panels. The first panel shows the nameless grad student stuffing papers into a red folder, then hurriedly running out the apartment and down the stairs into campus. The second panel shows Cecilia opening her closet, trying to decide what to wear. The third shows Mike sitting up at the edge of his bed, groggy. After a long pause, he throws himself back to sleep. The last panel shows Tajel, looking over her banners, trying to decide which one she'll use today.

FADE OUT.

FADE IN:
INT. UNIVERSITY PROFESSOR'S OFFICE -- DAY, DAY 1
PROF. SMITH and the NAMELESS GRAD STUDENT sit facing each other. The Nameless Grad Student is holding the red folder.

PROF. SMITH:
... (silence)

NAMELESS GRAD STUDENT:
... (silence)

PROF. SMITH:
So.

NAMELESS GRAD STUDENT:
Uh, Prof. Smith, I was hoping to talk to you about your research.

PROF. SMITH:
Why? It's all in my webpage.

CUT TO: COMPUTER SCREENSHOT - PROF. SMITH'S RESEARCH WEBPAGE
We view Prof. Smith's home page which uses an old photo of him from the 1980's. We scroll down past "Recent Publications" to the bottom of the page, which reads "Last Updated April 1993".

CUT TO:
INT. PROFESSOR SMITH'S OFFICE -- CONTINUOUS, DAY 1

NAMELESS GRAD STUDENT:
Y... Yes, I saw that. Well, I'm a first year Master's student, hoping to do a Ph.D. in your research area.

PROF. SMITH:
And you want me to fund you and be your thesis advisor.

NAMELESS GRAD STUDENT:
Y... Yes. (Hands over red folder) Here is all the work I've done. As you can see, I have some ideas for...

PROF. SMITH:
(Takes a glance at folder, then tosses it on top of one of the many piles of papers and documents strewn about his office)
Look, let me tell you how this works. Doing your Ph.D. and working with a Professor is a lot like Marriage. The whole thing typically lasts 5 to 7 years, 50% of them end in bitter divorce and it all culminates in a big ceremony where you walk down the aisle wearing a fancy gown.

NAMELESS GRAD STUDENT:
... (not sure how to respond)

PROF. SMITH: What I'm saying is, maybe you should look around.

The PHD Movie was filmed on location at the California Institute of Technology and stars real grad students, postdocs and faculty. During its release, it was screened at over 420 campuses and research centers worldwide (including Antarctica!).

THE ORIGIN OF THE THESES

COMIC STRIPS
2009–2012

STATE LAW
YIELD
TO
ABSENT-MINDED PROFESSORS
CAUTION
UNDERGRADS ON BIKES
JORGE CHAM © 2009
SLOW
GAGGLE OF GRAD STUDENTS
ST. PHIL
FRUSTRATED POST-DOC
XING

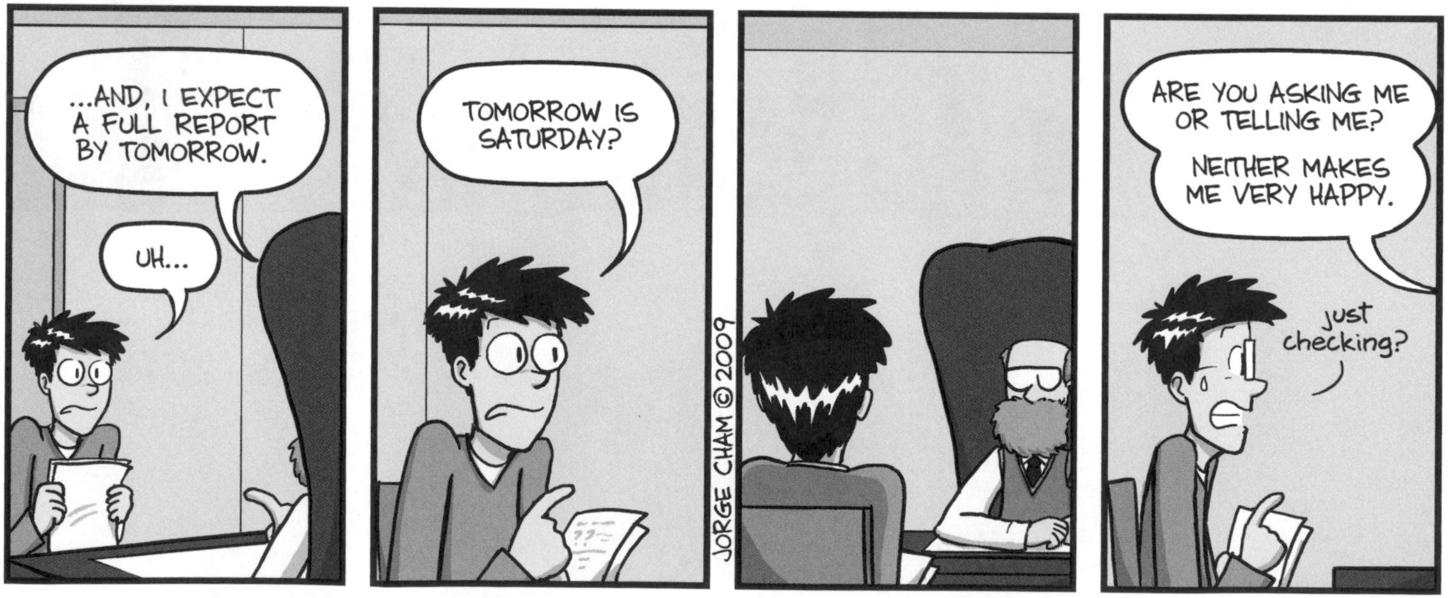
...AND, I EXPECT A FULL REPORT BY TOMORROW.
UH...
TOMORROW IS SATURDAY?
JORGE CHAM © 2009
ARE YOU ASKING ME OR TELLING ME?
NEITHER MAKES ME VERY HAPPY.
just checking?

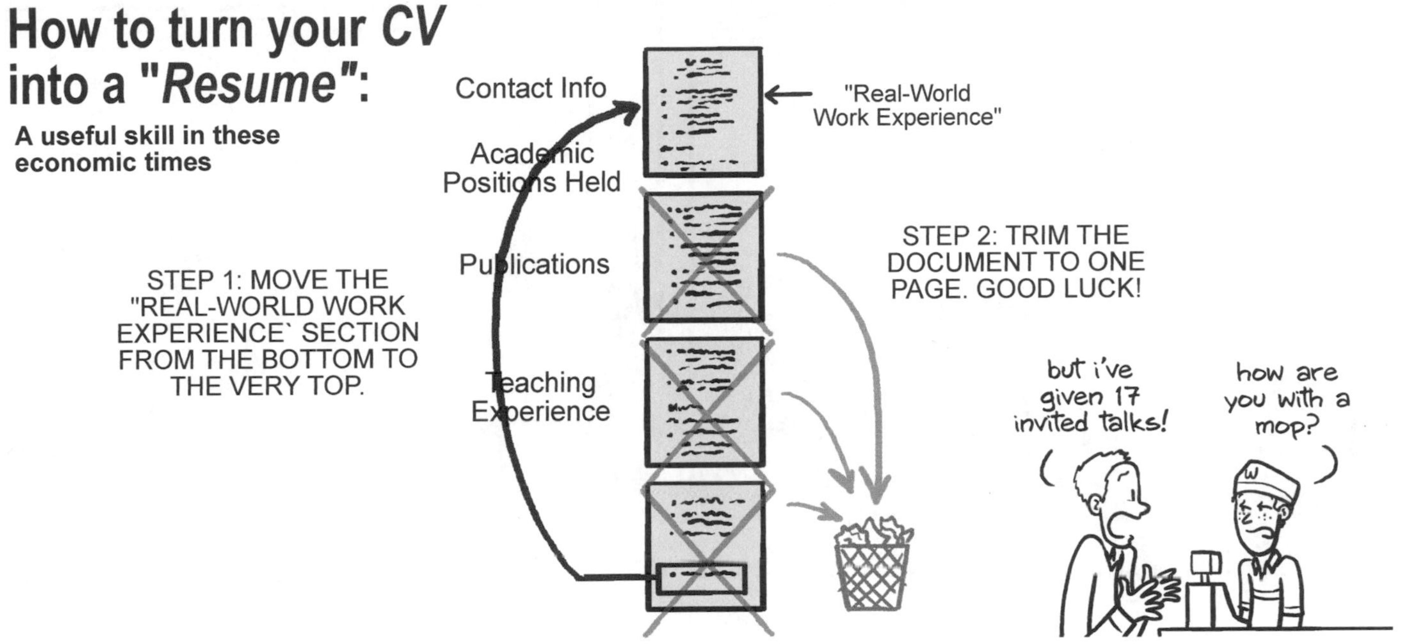
How to turn your *CV* into a "*Resume*":
A useful skill in these economic times
Contact Info
Academic Positions Held
Publications
Teaching Experience
"Real-World Work Experience"
STEP 1: MOVE THE "REAL-WORLD WORK EXPERIENCE` SECTION FROM THE BOTTOM TO THE VERY TOP.
STEP 2: TRIM THE DOCUMENT TO ONE PAGE. GOOD LUCK!
but i've given 17 invited talks!
how are you with a mop?

To: Group list
From now on, I expect everyone in my group to work nights and weekends.
-Prof. Smith
send.
JORGE CHAM © 2009
I mean, *in addition* to days and weekdays.
GROAN...

HONEY? IS THAT YOU?
GUESS WHAT?
DO YOU REMEMBER THAT COMPANY I INTERVIEWED WITH A WHILE BACK?
THEY JUST WENT BANKRUPT! THE WHOLE COMPANY WENT BUST!
JORGE CHAM © 2009
WHAT'S WRONG?
I'VE BEEN LAID OFF!
!
MORE DRAMA!
I'M UNEMPLOYED!
DO YOU REALIZE WHAT THIS MEANS?
JORGE CHAM © 2009
YOU ARE NOW THE SOLE PROVIDER FOR THIS FAMILY, MIKE!
OUR ENTIRE SUBSISTENCE DEPENDS ON YOUR POST-DOC SALARY!
I'M... THE SUGAR DADDY?
PLEASE DON'T GET FIRED.

I DIDN'T HAVE TIME TO READ THE DRAFT PAPER YOU SENT ME...
...BUT I THOUGHT IT LACKED CLARITY AND DEPTH. OVERALL, IT NEEDS VAST IMPROVEMENT.
JORGE CHAM © 2009
WAIT, YOU DIDN'T READ IT, BUT YOU KNOW WHAT'S WRONG WITH IT?
YES, I'M THAT GOOD.
OR YOU'RE THAT BAD.
probably both.

HMM, THAT'S AN INTERESTING PROBLEM.
WHAT DO YOU THINK?
DID... DID HE JUST ASK ME WHAT I THINK?
IS THIS A TRICK QUESTION??
JORGE CHAM © 2009
WHAT IF IT'S A TRAP!? WHAT IF I SAY SOMETHING STUPID?? OH MAN OH MAN..!!
RELAX. I'M ONLY STALLING. I DON'T REALLY CARE.
PHEW?

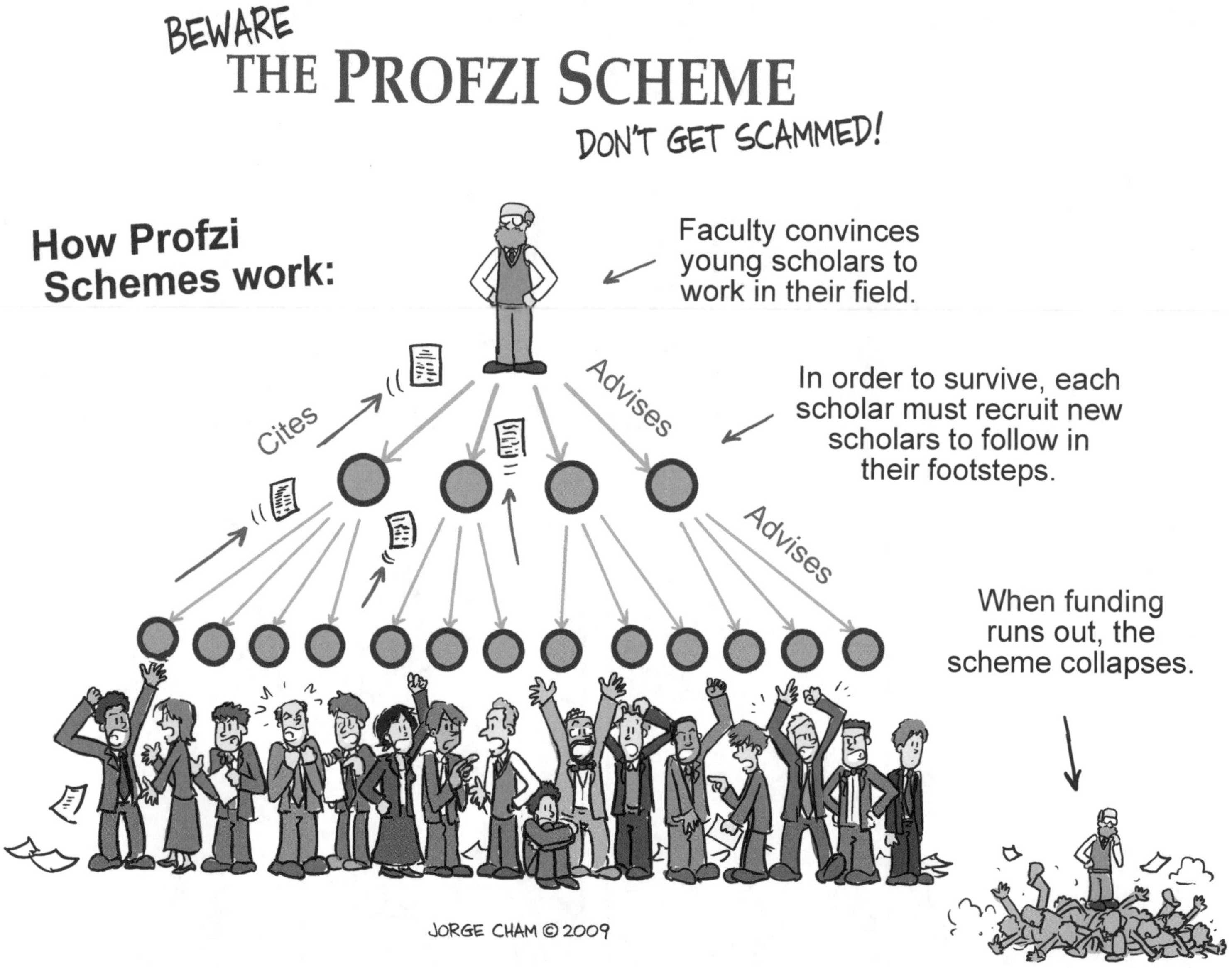
BEWARE
THE PROFZI SCHEME
DON'T GET SCAMMED!
How Profzi Schemes work:
Faculty convinces young scholars to work in their field.
Cites
Advises
In order to survive, each scholar must recruit new scholars to follow in their footsteps.
Advises
When funding runs out, the scheme collapses.
JORGE CHAM © 2009

HOW NORMAL PEOPLE DECIDE WHAT TO WEAR:
HOW SHOULD I DRESS TODAY?
DOES IT MATCH?
JORGE CHAM © 2009
HOW GRAD STUDENTS DECIDE WHAT TO WEAR:
SHOULD I DRESS TODAY?
DOES IT SMELL??

LAID OFF! DO YOU HAVE ANY IDEA HOW THAT FEELS?
TO HAVE SOMEONE TELL YOU EVERYTHING YOU'VE DONE HAS NO VALUE?
TO FIND OUT YEARS OF HARD WORK DON'T MEAN ANYTHING!?
JORGE CHAM © 2009
I WAS A GRAD STUDENT. I HAVE A PRETTY GOOD IDEA.
AT LEAST YOU HAD TIME TO GET USED TO IT.

YES, MICHAEL, YOU ARE NOW...
THE SUGAR DADDY
JORGE CHAM © 2009
THOUGH, GIVEN YOUR SALARY, IT'S MORE LIKE "SWEET 'N LOW" DADDY.
POSTDOC IS A VALID JOB SUBSTITUTE!

OK, THIS IS IT. I AM GOING TO GRADUATE.
NO IFS, BUTS OR MAYBES!
JORGE CHAM © 2009
THE HOW, WHEN AND WHY WOULD BE NICE, THOUGH.

DUDE, PROF. SMITH JUST SIGNED AN EMAIL TO ME WITH HIS FIRST NAME, "BRIAN".
DOES THAT MEAN WE'RE ON A FIRST NAME BASIS NOW?
JORGE CHAM © 2009
HAVE I FINALLY EARNED HIS RESPECT ENOUGH TO OVERCOME THAT BARRIER OF FORMALITY??
WHAT DOES HE CALL YOU?
USELESS, MOSTLY. IT'S A ONE-WAY BARRIER.

CAN WE CALL PROF. SMITH BY HIS FIRST NAME?
LET'S ASK THE PERSON WHO'S BEEN HERE THE LONGEST...
HEY MIKE, WHAT DO YOU CALL PROF. SMITH?
WHAT DO I CALL HIM? "DR. S".
JORGE CHAM © 2009
THAT WAS THE FIRST FEW YEARS. THEN IT WAS "DOC SMITH", THE "DOC MAN", "B-DOC", "SMITH-MEISTER", THE "SMITH MACHINE", "SMITHEREENO"...
MAYBE HE'S NOT THE BEST PERSON TO ASK.
YOU MEAN TO HIS FACE, RIGHT?

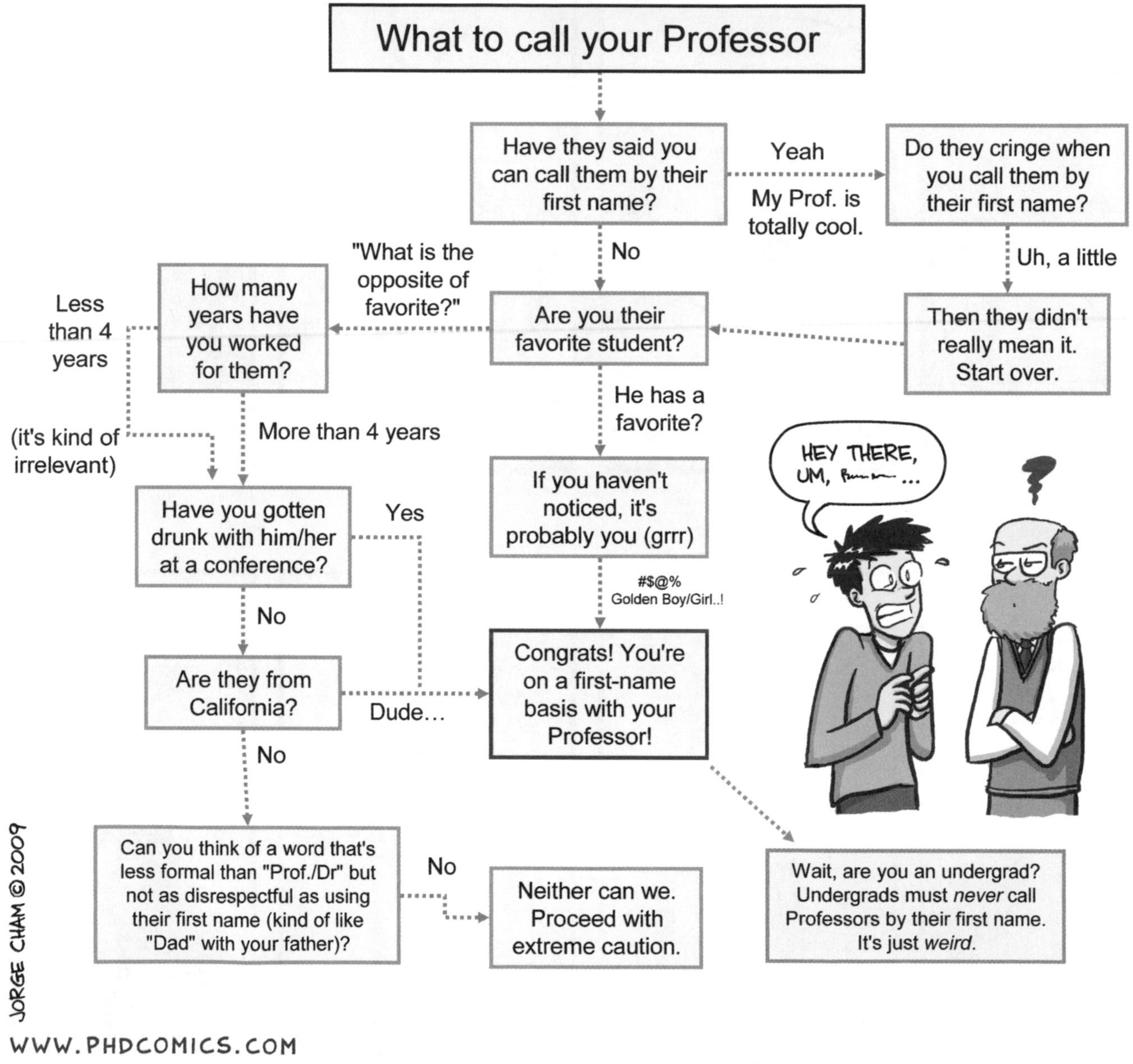
What to call your Professor
Have they said you can call them by their first name?
Yeah
My Prof. is totally cool.
Do they cringe when you call them by their first name?
Uh, a little
Then they didn't really mean it. Start over.
No
Are you their favorite student?
"What is the opposite of favorite?"
How many years have you worked for them?
Less than 4 years
(it's kind of irrelevant)
More than 4 years
He has a favorite?
If you haven't noticed, it's probably you (grrr)
#$@% Golden Boy/Girl..!
Have you gotten drunk with him/her at a conference?
Yes
No
Are they from California?
Dude...
Congrats! You're on a first-name basis with your Professor!
No
Can you think of a word that's less formal than "Prof./Dr" but not as disrespectful as using their first name (kind of like "Dad" with your father)?
No
Neither can we. Proceed with extreme caution.
Wait, are you an undergrad? Undergrads must *never* call Professors by their first name. It's just *weird*.
HEY THERE, UM, ...
JORGE CHAM © 2009
WWW.PHDCOMICS.COM

THIS IS RIDICULOUS. I'VE WORKED FOR THIS MAN FOR YEARS!
WE'RE BOTH HUMAN BEINGS. THERE IS NO REASON WHY I CAN'T LOOK HIM IN THE EYE AND CALL HIM BY HIS FIRST NAME.
JORGE CHAM © 2009
OH, HI, THERE... UH... UM...
PROF. SMITH.
HMPH.
...EXCEPT FEAR.
MAYBE YOU SHOULD WORK UP TO ACKNOWLEDGE-YOUR-EXISTENCE BASIS FIRST.

GUYS, THE GROUP NEXT DOOR TO US CALLS THEIR PROFESSOR BY HER FIRST NAME...
...IT'S LIKE THEY'RE BEST BUDDIES!
WHY CAN'T WE HAVE THAT KIND OF CLOSE RELATIONSHIP?
LIKE WATSON AND CRICK! OR PLATO AND SOCRATES!
JORGE CHAM © 2009
2,400 YEARS AGO:
ΘH, UH... HI, PRΘF. SOCRATΣS.
HMPH.

IF TV SCIENCE WAS MORE LIKE REAL SCIENCE

WWW.PHDCOMICS.COM

OK, I WANT TO WRITE MY THESIS, BUT WHERE DO I START??
remember, cecilia... every thesis begins with a single keystroke...
LAO-TZE!
JORGE CHAM © 2009
WAIT, WHICH K-
good luuuck!!
EVERY THESIS BEGINS WITH A SINGLE KEYSTROKE...
JORGE CHAM © 2009
Ctrl-...
...-C
copy...
OK, MAYBE TWO KEYSTROKES.

I'LL JUST COPY AND PASTE ALL THE PAPERS I'VE WRITTEN AND MAKE IT MY THESIS!
ctrl-c
ctrl-v
ctrl-c
ctrl-v
ctrl-c
ctrl-v
...AND I'M DONE!
JORGE CHAM © 2009
NO, YOU'RE NOT.
ctrl-z?

Not a good sign:
E(Thesis) ∉ ℝ
JORGE CHAM © 2009
WHAT IS MY THESIS FOR?
WELL, IT'S COMPLEX.
OK, IMAGINARY.

HOW A POSTDOC (SORT OF) DECIDES WHAT TO WEAR:
DO I DRESS NICE?
CAN I STILL DRESS LIKE A GRAD STUDENT?
I'M SO CONFUSED!
JORGE CHAM © 2009
HOW PROFESSORS DECIDE WHAT TO WEAR:

HERE'S TO YOU, ADMINISTRATIVE ASSISTANTS!
PURVEYORS OF PROFESSOR WHEREABOUTS...
?
...LAST-MINUTE SIGNATURES...
...PETTY CASH...
receipts
...AND SMILES!
JORGE CHAM © 2009
WWW.PHDCOMICS.COM

CECILIA, YOU CAN'T JUST PASTE TOGETHER ALL YOUR PAPERS AND MAKE IT YOUR THESIS...
YOU NEED TO HAVE A THEME. A CENTRAL QUESTION THAT BINDS IT ALL TOGETHER...
THAT'S THE TRUE TEST OF A PH.D...
TO TAKE 5 YEARS OF MARGINALLY RELATED WORK AND PRETEND YOU KNEW WHAT YOU WERE DOING THE WHOLE TIME.
JORGE CHAM © 2009
I JUST ASSUMED YOU KNEW WHAT I WAS DOING.
EXACTLY. THAT'S WHY I HAVE A PH.D.

WAH WAH WAH WAH WAH WAH WAH WAH...
WAH WAH WAH WAH WAH WAH WAH WAH...
JORGE CHAM © 2009
WAH WAH WAH WAH WAH WAH WAH WAH...
GRAD SCHOOL: IT'S LIKE CHARLIE BROWN, BUT IN REVERSE.
GOOD GRIEF...

BIRTHDAY POEM

YES, CECILIA, YOUR THESIS NEEDS TO HAVE A CENTRAL THEME.
THINK, WHAT DO ALL THE PROJECTS YOU'VE WORKED ON HAVE IN COMMON?
WHAT HAS BEEN THE UNDERLYING QUESTION ALL THESE YEARS?
JORGE CHAM © 2009
"WHY DID I COME TO GRAD SCHOOL?"
TOO BROAD. ALSO: TOO LATE.

click
JORGE CHAM © 2009
DID YOU GET THE E-MAIL I SENT??
AAAHH!!
KEEPING THEM ON THEIR TOES IS SOMETIMES HALF THE FUN.

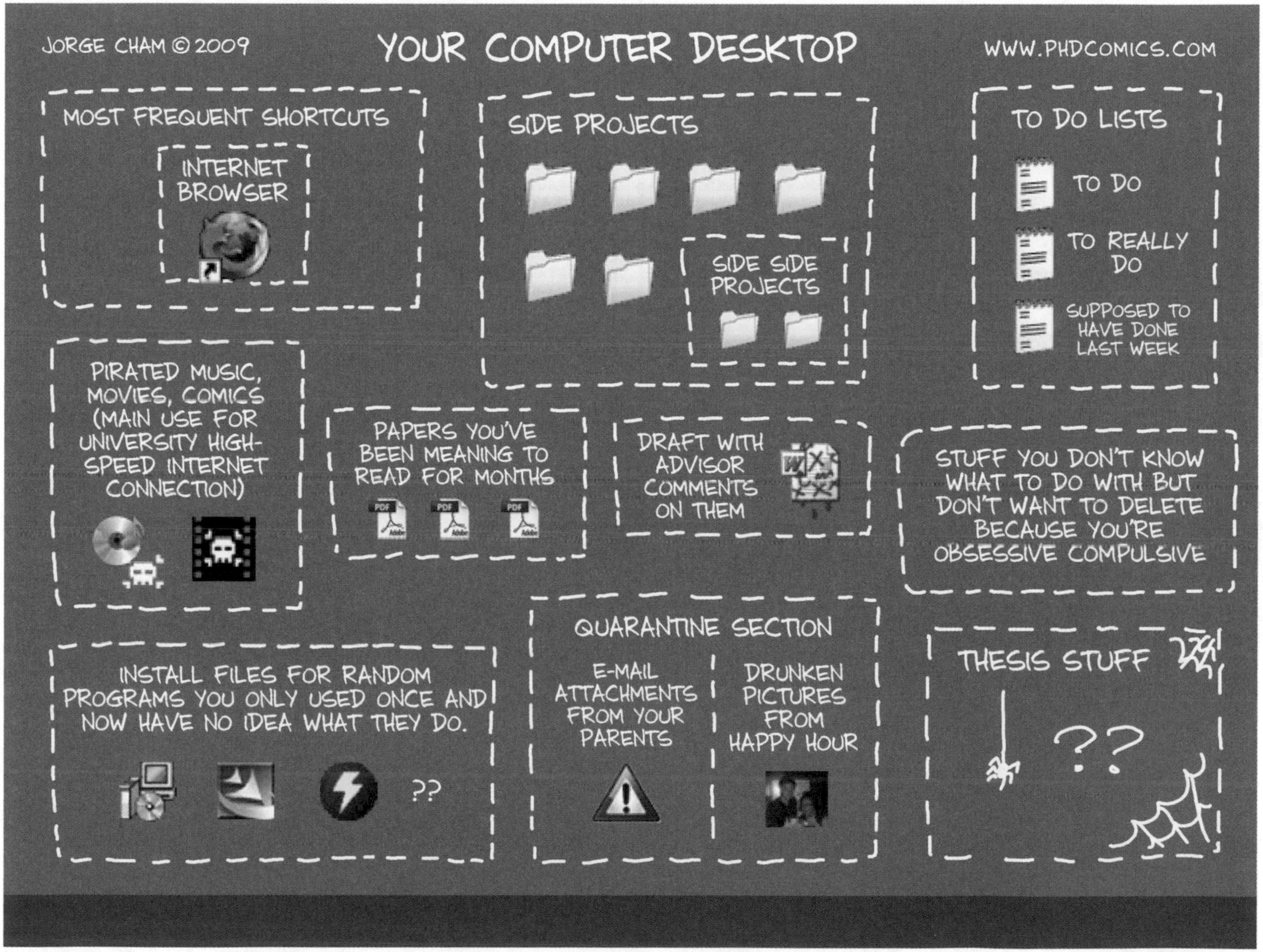
JORGE CHAM © 2009
YOUR COMPUTER DESKTOP
WWW.PHDCOMICS.COM
MOST FREQUENT SHORTCUTS
INTERNET BROWSER
SIDE PROJECTS
SIDE SIDE PROJECTS
TO DO LISTS
TO DO
TO REALLY DO
SUPPOSED TO HAVE DONE LAST WEEK
PIRATED MUSIC, MOVIES, COMICS (MAIN USE FOR UNIVERSITY HIGH-SPEED INTERNET CONNECTION)
PAPERS YOU'VE BEEN MEANING TO READ FOR MONTHS
DRAFT WITH ADVISOR COMMENTS ON THEM
STUFF YOU DON'T KNOW WHAT TO DO WITH BUT DON'T WANT TO DELETE BECAUSE YOU'RE OBSESSIVE COMPULSIVE
INSTALL FILES FOR RANDOM PROGRAMS YOU ONLY USED ONCE AND NOW HAVE NO IDEA WHAT THEY DO.
??
QUARANTINE SECTION
E-MAIL ATTACHMENTS FROM YOUR PARENTS
DRUNKEN PICTURES FROM HAPPY HOUR
THESIS STUFF
??

JORGE CHAM © 2009
Dear Gerard,
We regret to inform you that, due to the Economic Crisis, funding for all Humanities characters has been cut.
Please leave the comic at once, or switch to a more useful major.
Sincerely,
-PHD Comics
why do I have to go first??

AT THE PHD COMICS HUMANITIES FUNDING HEARING, DAY 1...
THANK YOU ALL FOR COMING.
WE ARE HERE TO DETERMINE WHETHER THIS COMIC SHOULD CONTINUE FUNDING A HUMANITIES CHARACTER, GIVEN THE CURRENT STATE OF THE ECONOMY.
JORGE CHAM © 2009
IN OTHER WORDS, HOW DO YOU JUSTIFY YOUR EXISTENCE?
ahem...
I SHALL BEGIN BY QUOTING THE 11th CENTURY SCANDINAVIAN SCHOLAR MUSSET, WHO SAID...
YEAH, THAT'S NOT HELPING.

ARE YOU AWARE THAT HUMANITIES ACCOUNT FOR ONLY 2.6% OF ALL GRAD DEGREES?
YES, BUT WE MAKE UP FOR IT IN VOLUME!
THESIS
GERARD, WE ASKED YOUR DEPARTMENT HEAD TO GIVE US JUSTIFICATION FOR THE HUMANITIES. THIS IS WHAT SHE SAID...
"YOU BOORISH BARBARIANS! JUST GIVE US THE MONEY AND LEAVE US ALONE!"
JORGE CHAM © 2009
HOW COME SHE STILL HAS A JOB?
TENURE. WE'RE WORKING ON IT.

IT'S HARD TO EXPLAIN MONETARILY, BUT HOW CAN YOU PUT A PRICE TAG ON THE HUMAN SOUL?
THE HUMANITIES HELP US APPRECIATE BEAUTY AND GROW AS INDIVIDUALS.
JORGE CHAM © 2009
WHAT GOOD ARE SCIENCE AND TECHNOLOGY IF WE DON'T ASK OURSELVES THE QUESTION, WHAT DOES IT MEAN TO BE A HUMAN BEING??
SO HOW'S THE ANSWER COMING ALONG?
OH NO, WE JUST ASK THE QUESTION, NOT ACTUALLY ANSWER IT.

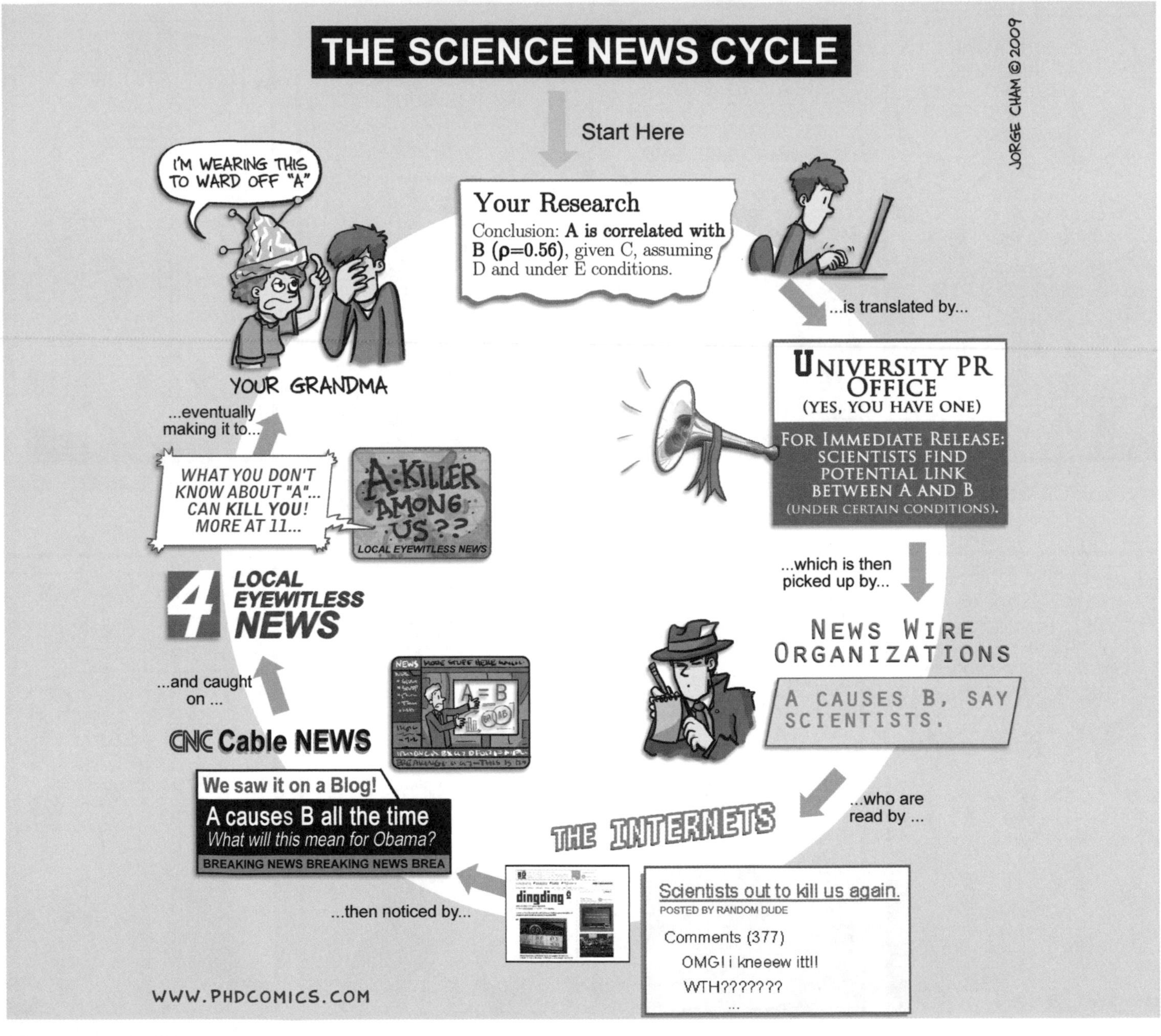
THE SCIENCE NEWS CYCLE
JORGE CHAM © 2009
Start Here
Your Research
Conclusion: A is correlated with B (ρ=0.56), given C, assuming D and under E conditions.
...is translated by...
UNIVERSITY PR OFFICE
(YES, YOU HAVE ONE)
FOR IMMEDIATE RELEASE: SCIENTISTS FIND POTENTIAL LINK BETWEEN A AND B (UNDER CERTAIN CONDITIONS).
...which is then picked up by...
NEWS WIRE ORGANIZATIONS
A CAUSES B, SAY SCIENTISTS.
...who are read by ...
THE INTERNETS
Scientists out to kill us again.
POSTED BY RANDOM DUDE
Comments (377)
OMG! i kneeew itt!!
WTH???????
...
dingding
...then noticed by...
We saw it on a Blog!
A causes B all the time
What will this mean for Obama?
BREAKING NEWS BREAKING NEWS BREA
CNC Cable NEWS
A = B
...and caught on ...
4 LOCAL EYEWITLESS NEWS
WHAT YOU DON'T KNOW ABOUT "A"... CAN KILL YOU! MORE AT 11...
A: KILLER AMONG US??
LOCAL EYEWITLESS NEWS
...eventually making it to...
YOUR GRANDMA
I'M WEARING THIS TO WARD OFF "A"
WWW.PHDCOMICS.COM

RESEARCH TOPICS GUARANTEED TO BE PICKED UP BY THE NEWS MEDIA
Chocolate! Anything that validates the public's wishful thinking that chocolate is secretly good for you is news gold.
A chocolate lover reacts to news that her chocolate addiction is making her smarter and saving the environment.
Unrealistic Sci-Fi Gadgets
Everyone is still waiting for their jet-packs, flying cars, and teleporters. Get on it, Science!
YOU CAN'T SEE ME
Engineers test latest invisibility cloak prototype.
ROBOTS!! Everyone loves robots. In fact, news outlets are required by law to feature a robot story every 7 days.
Roboticist demonstrates nose-picking robot, says will soon replace humans.
Experiments That Might Blow Up The World
Nothing gets the crazies riled up like recreating conditions of the Big Bang in the only planet you have. Hope your math is right!
"Oops," say scientis-
JORGE CHAM © 2009
WWW.PHDCOMICS.COM

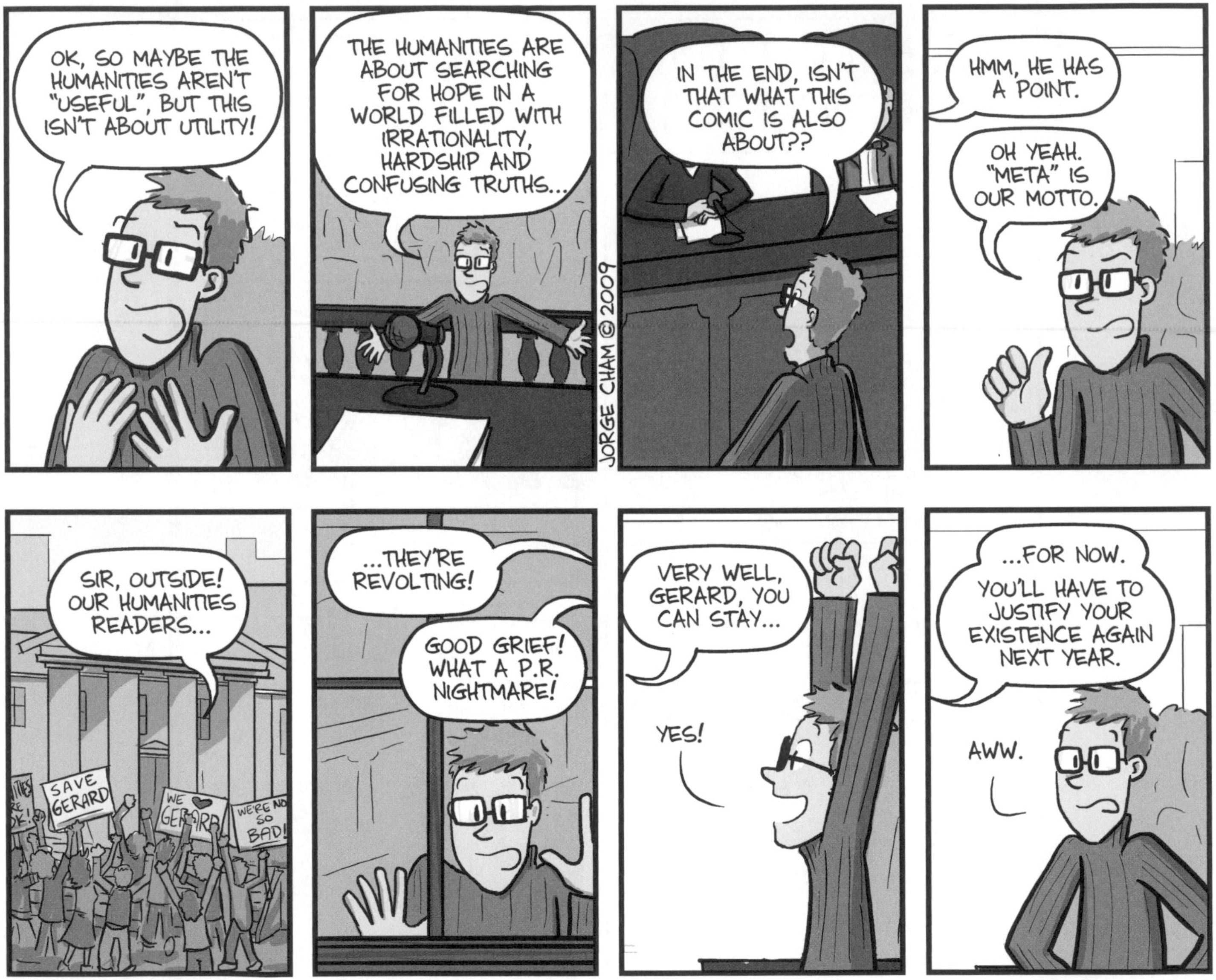

WWW.PHDCOMICS.COM

YOU KNOW, I HAVEN'T THOUGHT ABOUT WORK ONCE SINCE WE GOT HERE...
JORGE CHAM © 2009
TECHNICALLY, YOU JUST DID.
DOH.

SIGH... OUR VACATION IS ALMOST OVER.
IF ONLY WE COULD STAY HERE FOREVER, AND NEVER GO BACK TO OUR LIVES IN ACADEMIA...
JORGE CHAM © 2009
WE'D JUST BE REPLACING ONE UNREALISTIC FANTASY WITH ANOTHER.
BUT THIS ONE IS SO MUCH MORE PLEASANT...

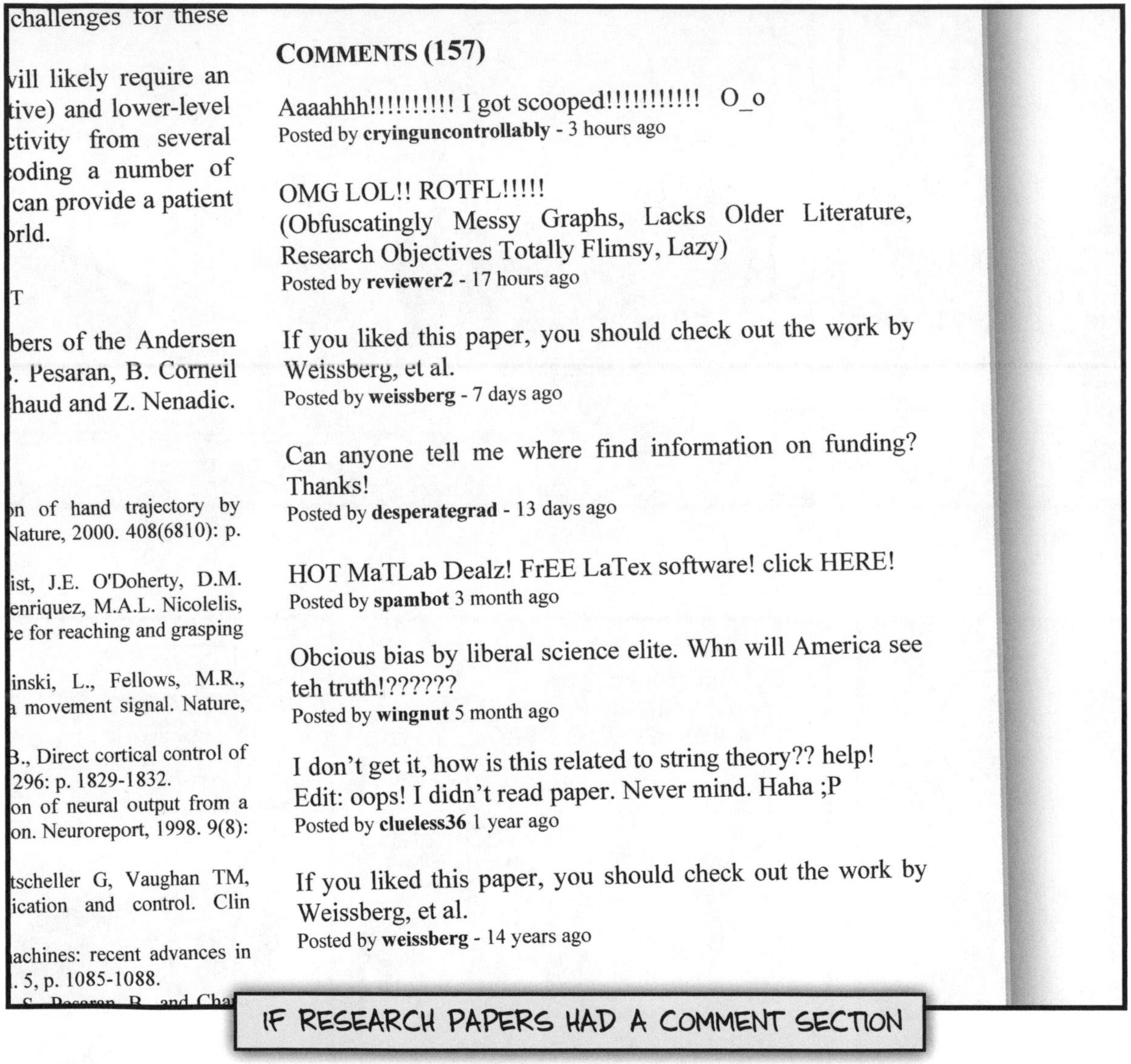
challenges for these
ill likely require an
ive) and lower-level
tivity from several
oding a number of
can provide a patient
rld.
T
bers of the Andersen
. Pesaran, B. Corneil
haud and Z. Nenadic.
n of hand trajectory by
ature, 2000. 408(6810): p.
ist, J.E. O'Doherty, D.M.
enriquez, M.A.L. Nicolelis,
e for reaching and grasping
inski, L., Fellows, M.R.,
movement signal. Nature,
., Direct cortical control of
296: p. 1829-1832.
on of neural output from a
on. Neuroreport, 1998. 9(8):
tscheller G, Vaughan TM,
ication and control. Clin
achines: recent advances in
. 5, p. 1085-1088.
COMMENTS (157)
Aaaahhh!!!!!!!!!! I got scooped!!!!!!!!!!! O_o
Posted by cryinguncontrollably - 3 hours ago
OMG LOL!! ROTFL!!!!!
(Obfuscatingly Messy Graphs, Lacks Older Literature, Research Objectives Totally Flimsy, Lazy)
Posted by reviewer2 - 17 hours ago
If you liked this paper, you should check out the work by Weissberg, et al.
Posted by weissberg - 7 days ago
Can anyone tell me where find information on funding? Thanks!
Posted by desperategrad - 13 days ago
HOT MaTLab Dealz! FrEE LaTex software! click HERE!
Posted by spambot 3 month ago
Obcious bias by liberal science elite. Whn will America see teh truth!??????
Posted by wingnut 5 month ago
I don't get it, how is this related to string theory?? help!
Edit: oops! I didn't read paper. Never mind. Haha ;P
Posted by clueless36 1 year ago
If you liked this paper, you should check out the work by Weissberg, et al.
Posted by weissberg - 14 years ago
IF RESEARCH PAPERS HAD A COMMENT SECTION

WHY?
WHY CAN'T WE LEAVE IT ALL BEHIND AND LIVE IN THIS PARADISE FOREVER?
UM, LET'S SEE... WE HAVE NO PRACTICAL SKILLS, NO BUSINESS SENSE, NO WEALTH AND WE'RE NOT REALLY FIT FOR PHYSICAL LABOR.
JORGE CHAM © 2009
BASICALLY, EVEN PARADISE WOULDN'T HIRE US.
I COULD TEACH ANTHROPOLOGY TO THESE COCONUTS!

SO, WHAT'S NEW?
UM... WELL, THIS WEEK WAS FINALS WEEK, SO...
JORGE CHAM © 2009
SO YOU DIDN'T DO ANY WORK FOR ME...
...BECAUSE YOU WERE TOO BUSY DOING WORK FOR OTHER PROFESSORS?
YES, BUT IT DIDN'T MEAN ANYTHING!

DON'T GET ME WRONG, I WANT YOU TO DO WELL ON YOUR FINAL EXAMS.
IT WOULD REFLECT BADLY ON ME IN FRONT OF THE OTHER PROFESSORS IF YOU FAILED.
JORGE CHAM © 2009
SO, I SUPPOSE IT'S NOT YOUR FAULT YOU DIDN'T DO ANY WORK THIS WEEK...
WOW, THANKS FOR UNDERSTA-
OBVIOUSLY, I SHOULD HAVE HIRED A POSTDOC INSTEAD OF YOU.

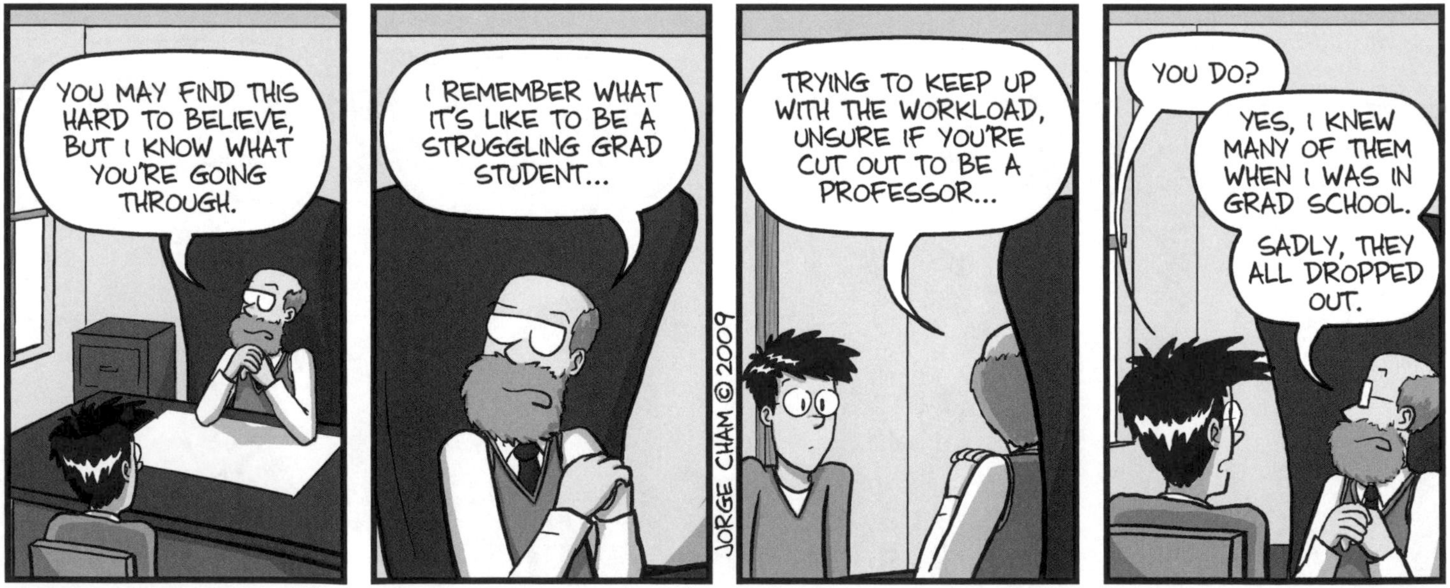
YOU MAY FIND THIS HARD TO BELIEVE, BUT I KNOW WHAT YOU'RE GOING THROUGH.
I REMEMBER WHAT IT'S LIKE TO BE A STRUGGLING GRAD STUDENT...
JORGE CHAM © 2009
TRYING TO KEEP UP WITH THE WORKLOAD, UNSURE IF YOU'RE CUT OUT TO BE A PROFESSOR...
YOU DO?
YES, I KNEW MANY OF THEM WHEN I WAS IN GRAD SCHOOL.
SADLY, THEY ALL DROPPED OUT.

CECILIA, CAN I BORROW YOUR COPY OF THE LIPPMAN BOOK?
YES, BUT ONLY IF YOU USE IT HERE WITHIN A FOUR FOOT RADIUS AND IF YOU GIVE IT BACK RIGHT AWAY.
JORGE CHAM © 2009
PEOPLE ARE ALWAYS "BORROWING" MY STUFF AND THEN I HAVE TO TRACK IT ALL OVER THE LAB BECAUSE THEY NEVER RETURN IT!
I HAVEN'T SEEN MY STAPLER IN FIVE YEARS!
THE RED ONE? I HAVE IT.

To: all group members
A film crew will be visiting the lab this week to do a feature on our research.
I realize this will be an enormous incon- venience on your busy work schedule...
JORGE CHAM © 2009
Still, I expect the utmost level of pro- fessionalism and seriousness on your part as we reach out to the ignorant masses. -Smith_
DUDE, WE'RE GONNA BE ON TV!!

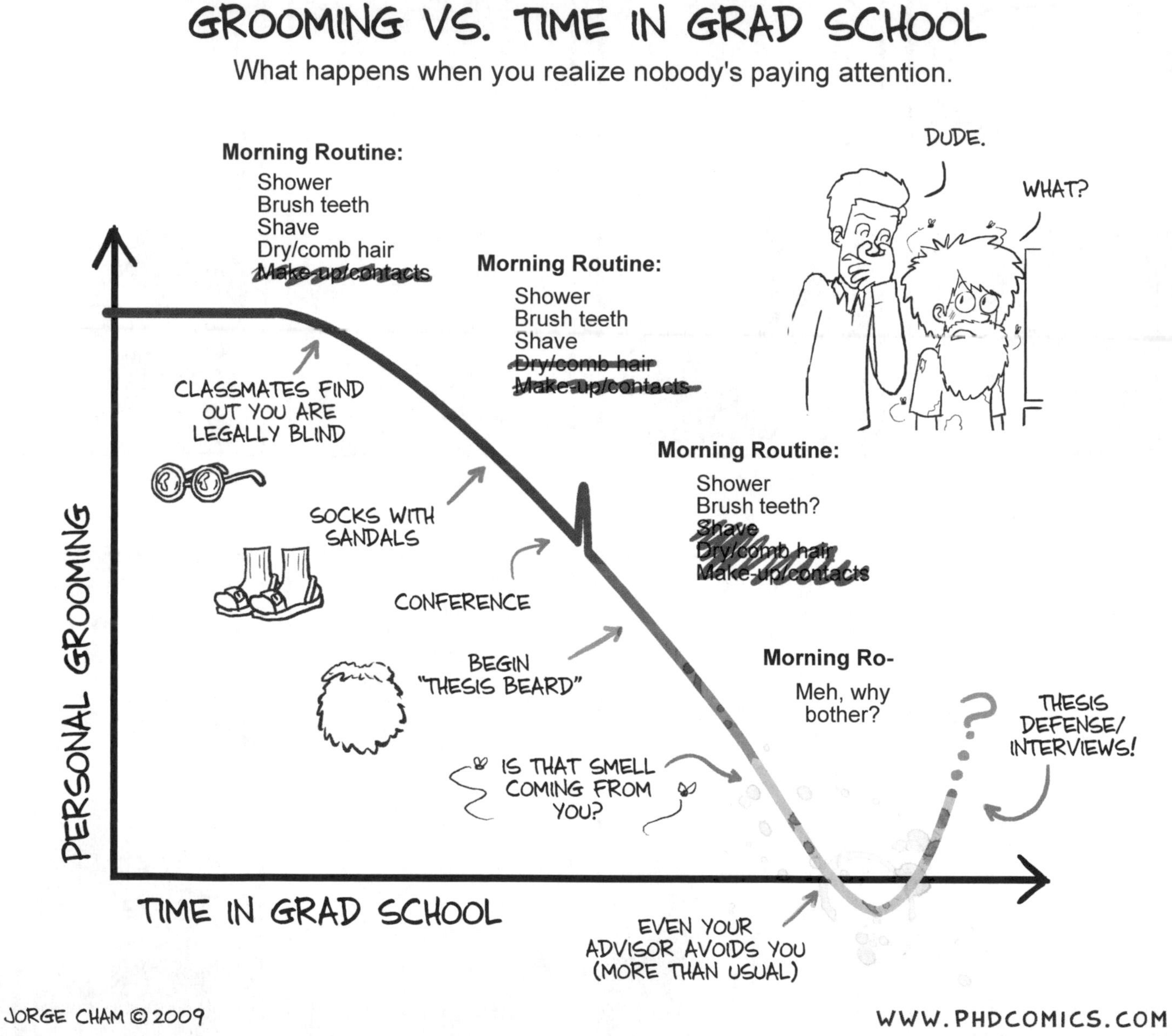
GROOMING VS. TIME IN GRAD SCHOOL
What happens when you realize nobody's paying attention.
Morning Routine:
Shower
Brush teeth
Shave
Dry/comb hair
~~Make-up/contacts~~
Morning Routine:
Shower
Brush teeth
Shave
~~Dry/comb hair~~
~~Make-up/contacts~~
DUDE.
WHAT?
Morning Routine:
Shower
Brush teeth?
~~Shave~~
~~Dry/comb hair~~
~~Make-up/contacts~~
CLASSMATES FIND OUT YOU ARE LEGALLY BLIND
SOCKS WITH SANDALS
CONFERENCE
BEGIN "THESIS BEARD"
Morning Ro-
Meh, why bother?
?
THESIS DEFENSE/ INTERVIEWS!
IS THAT SMELL COMING FROM YOU?
PERSONAL GROOMING
TIME IN GRAD SCHOOL
EVEN YOUR ADVISOR AVOIDS YOU (MORE THAN USUAL)
JORGE CHAM © 2009
WWW.PHDCOMICS.COM

WHOA...
OK, PEOPLE, LET'S GET SOME ESTABLISHING SHOTS. WHERE ARE THE GRAD STUDENTS?
UH, HERE.
JORGE CHAM © 2009
HMM, I GUESS YOU GOTTA TAKE WHAT YOU CAN GET.
OK, JUST ACT NORMAL. PRETEND THIS IS A REGULAR DAY WORKING IN THE LAB.
AND... ACTION!
ZZZ...
surf, surf...
CUT! CUT!

HMM, SOMETHING'S NOT RIGHT HERE. THIS PLACE DOESN'T QUITE LOOK SCIENCE-Y ENOUGH.
LIGHTING, LET'S GET SOME SPOTLIGHTS IN HERE...
JORGE CHAM © 2009
NOW DIM THE LIGHTS A LITTLE BIT...
THERE. PERFECT.
UH, I CAN'T SEE ANYTHING.

OK, LET'S GET SOME SHOTS OF PEOPLE LOOKING BUSY IN FRONT OF FANCY MACHINERY.
WHERE'S YOUR LAB COAT?
UH, WE DON'T NORMALLY-
YOU CAN'T DO SCIENCE WITHOUT A LABCOAT! WARDROBE!
JORGE CHAM © 2009
ALLRIGHT, JUST PRETEND YOU'RE WORKING ON SOMETHING REALLY COMPLICATED AND RESEARCH-Y.
THIS IS OUR MICROWAVE.
DOESN'T MATTER, JUST TWIDDLE SOME KNOBS. AND... ACTION!

LET'S DO SOME ONE-ON-ONES NOW.
TELL US ABOUT YOUR RESEARCH. AND REMEMBER, THIS IS FOR A LAY AUDIENCE.
WELL, OUR RESEARCH EXPLORES AUTOMATION TECHNIQUES FOR DETECTION OF MULTI-VARIABLE-
THAT'S TOO LONG.
JORGE CHAM © 2009
UM, WE AUTOMATE PROCEDURES FOR DESIGN TOOLS THAT-
TOO COMPLICATED.
UH...
AUTOMATE.
SO, ROBOTS THEN?

WELL, THAT'S A WRAP FOLKS!
LET'S PACK IT UP!
EXCUSE ME, SO WHEN IS THIS GOING TO AIR ON TV?
JORGE CHAM © 2009
WELL, WE'RE HOPING TO PUT IT IN FRONT OF AS MANY PEOPLE AS ARE HUNGRY TO LEARN ABOUT CUTTING EDGE SCIENTIFIC RESEARCH.
SO PROBABLY AN OBSCURE CABLE CHANNEL, LATE AT NIGHT, BETWEEN INFOMMERCIALS.
THAT'S STILL BIGGER THAN OUR USUAL AUDIENCE.
ONE YEAR LATER...
MA, I'M GONNA BE ON TV!
TONIGHT ON OUR PROGRAM...
THE EXCITING RESEARCH OF PROF. BRIAN SMITH!
PROF. SMITH
Works on Robots
JORGE CHAM © 2009
WORKING TIRELESSLY IN HIS LABORATORY, PROF. SMITH ANSWERS THE QUESTION: WILL ROBOTS ENSLAVE HUMANITY?
I SHOULD'VE JUST STAYED HOME THAT DAY.
DID YOU SEE? THAT WAS THE BACK OF MY HEAD!

I WANT YOU TO DO "X".
IS THAT POSSIBLE?
I'M SURE OF IT.
JORGE CHAM © 2009
I CAN'T GET IT TO WORK! WHAT'S WRONG WITH ME!??
A WEEK LATER...
IT'S IMPOSSIBLE.
REALLY? OH WELL.

ARE YOU SAYING THE TASK I ASSIGNED TO YOU IS IMPOSSIBLE?
YES.
ARE YOU SURE?
WELL...
TECHNICALLY, IT'S IMPOSSIBLE TO PROVE A NEGATIVE. THE ONLY WAY TO SHOW IT CAN'T BE DONE IS IF I SPENT AN INFINITE AMOUNT OF TIME TRYING TO DO IT.
JORGE CHAM © 2009
SO WHY ARE YOU STILL HERE?
I'M NOT SURE.

Is Your Research **IMPOSSIBLE?**

Take the Quiz!

Does it violate the Laws of Physics?

Yes

No

My research *is* to figure out the Laws of Physics

Why hasn't anyone done it before?

a) They were not as smart as me (I am the chosen one!)

b) No one's bothered to do it (Meh, it's not that useful)

c) Someone *has* done it, I just don't know about it. (Do I really want to know??)

Results: Realistically, it can't be done. Academically, it can still be published!

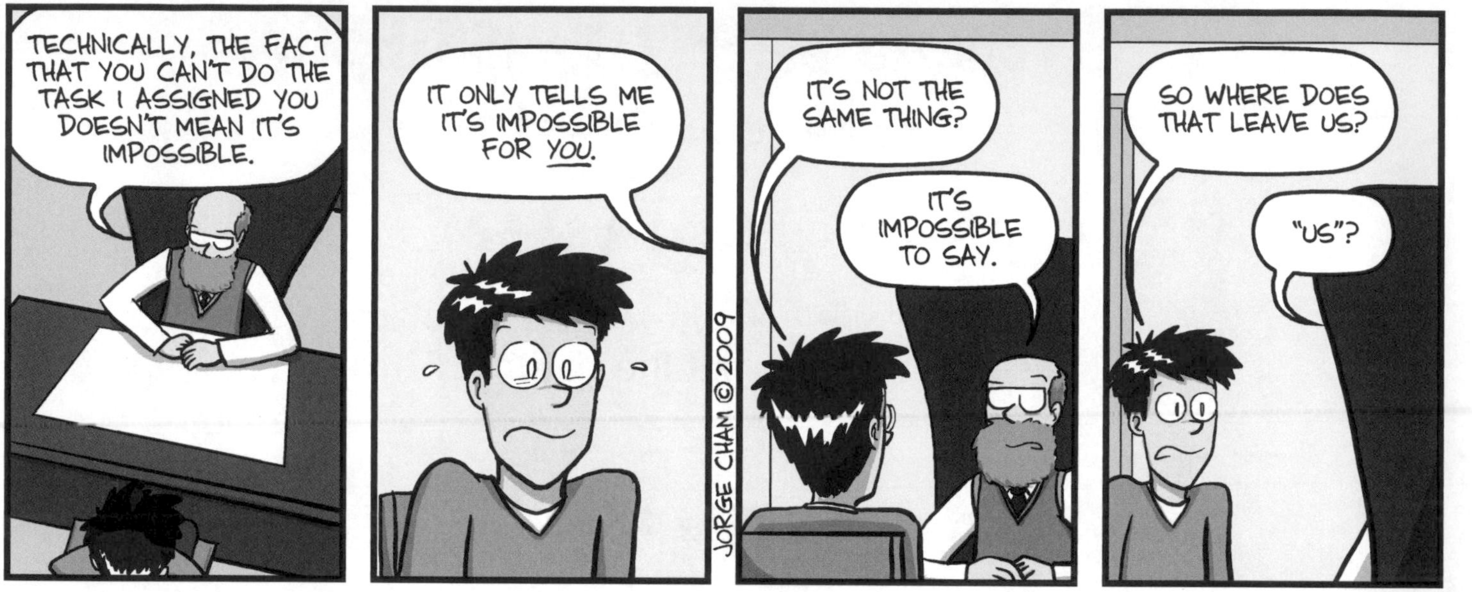
TECHNICALLY, THE FACT THAT YOU CAN'T DO THE TASK I ASSIGNED YOU DOESN'T MEAN IT'S IMPOSSIBLE.
IT ONLY TELLS ME IT'S IMPOSSIBLE FOR YOU.
JORGE CHAM © 2009
IT'S NOT THE SAME THING?
IT'S IMPOSSIBLE TO SAY.
SO WHERE DOES THAT LEAVE US?
"US"?

AAGH!
KHAAAAAANNNNN!!!
JORGE CHAM © 2009
YOU NAMED YOUR THESIS PROJECT "KHAN"?
IT'S EASIER TO VENT. NOW SET DEBUGGERS ON KILL.

Great Tweets of Science
newton chillin' in my garden, listening to- oww!!!
12:17 PM Oct 1666 from WoolsTwit.com
newton had apple for lunch.
12:18 PM Oct 1666 from WoolsTwit.com
Aristotle RT @Plato @Socrates "be as you wish to tweet"
8:50 AM 343 BC from AlexanTwit.com in reply to alex_da_great
watson @crick It's a double helix! sck it, @pauling !!!!!
5:15 PM Feb 28th 1953 from TweaglePub.com
chris_columbuz land ahead. anyone know a good Indian restaurant?
2:02 AM Oct 12th from santamariadeck.com
albert-e OH at the grocery store: "ever notice how the line to pay moves slower when you're in a hurry?" [hmmm...]
2:036 PM Sep 27th 1905 from mobile
nasa #followeveryday @armstrong @collins @aldrin
8:17 PM Jul 20th from HousTwit.com in reply to sputnik
darwin1 I'm on a boat! I'm on a boat! check out thz crazy turtles, yoooo http://twitpic.com/abfze
4:09 PM Sep 15th 1835 from TheTweagle.com in reply to GOD
copyright © 2009 @phdcomics Jorge Cham
www.phdcomics.com

	Nature	Science
FOUNDED:	1869	1880
Published by:	Nature Publishing Group (a division of MacMillan Publishers Ltd. of London, a subsidiary of Verlagsgruppe Georg Von Holtzbrinck, GmbH)	American Association for the Advancement of Science (AAAS)
Cost:	£10	$10
Impact Factor:	31.434	28.103
	(It is important to compute this to the third decimal. Units: inches)	
Sections:	News News Features Correspondence Perspectives Articles Letters Jobs To-*mah*-toe	News of the Week News Focus Letters Views Research Articles Reports Careers To*ma*to
Ads per issue:		
Full page ads:	16	9
Full page ads about itself:	6	5
Full page ads featuring people in white lab coats smiling and pipetting something:	5	4
Which one will you submit your paper to?	If only you had that problem.	

COMING BACK FROM VACATION, YEAR ONE:
I JUST GOT BACK, BUT I'M GONNA WORK HARD TO CATCH UP!
YOU WERE GONE?
JORGE CHAM © 2009
COMING BACK FROM VACATION, AFTER YEAR ONE:
I HAVEN'T HEARD FROM YOU IN A WHILE. HOW ARE THINGS?
OH, YOU KNOW... BUSY.

TAJEL, IT'S PERFECTLY OK FOR YOU TO GO ON VACATION.
I MEAN, YOU DID TAKE WORK WITH YOU, RIGHT?
EXCUSE ME?
JORGE CHAM © 2009
YOU SPENT THE WHOLE TIME THINKING AND OBSESSING ABOUT YOUR RESEARCH PROJECT, I ASSUME?
UH...
IN ACADEMIA, "VACATIONS" JUST MEAN YOU'RE DOING WORK SOMEWHERE ELSE.
I DON'T THINK WE'RE USING THE SAME DICTIONARY.

THE THING IS, THERE ARE NO OFFICIAL RULES OR GUIDELINES FOR GRAD STUDENTS TAKING VACATION.
YOU'RE NOT REALLY A STUDENT, SO YOU DON'T GET BREAKS.
JORGE CHAM © 2009
AND YOU'RE NOT REALLY AN EMPLOYEE, SO THERE'S NO PAID VACATION.
SO WHAT DO I GET THEN?
EXPLOITED, MOSTLY.

HEY, YOU'RE BACK! HOW WAS THE HONEYMOON VACATION?
OH, IT WAS GREAT! INSTEAD OF SITTING AROUND, WE DID VOLUNTEER WORK IN RURAL COMMUNITIES IN HONDURAS.
JORGE CHAM © 2009
WE WORKED WITH CHILDREN ON LITERACY, HELPED AID ORGANIZA-TIONS CONDUCT SURVEYS AND ASSISTED ENVIRONMENTAL CON-SERVATION PROGRAMS IN THE AREA.
GREAT. YOUR VACATION WAS MORE PRODUCTIVE THAN MY RESEARCH.
AND NOW, BACK TO WASTING MY TIME!

MAN, I WISH I COULD TAKE VACATION...
BUT I FEEL LIKE I DON'T DESERVE IT. I HAVEN'T DONE ANYTHING!
JORGE CHAM © 2009
THE ONLY TIME I'LL HAVE DONE SOMETHING IS WHEN I FINISH MY THESIS! UNTIL THEN, HOW CAN I JUSTIFY TAKING TIME OFF?
CAN'T YOU JUST LEAVE? IT'S NOT LIKE YOUR THESIS IS GOING ANYWHERE.
THAT'S THE PROBLEM!

WELL, I FINALLY DID THAT TASK YOU ASKED ME TO DO.
REALLY? IT WASN'T IMPOSSIBLE?
I GUESS NOT.
HUH.
JORGE CHAM © 2009
ARE YOU SURPRISED BY MY COMPETENCE?
I MUST BE LOSING MY TOUCH.

WHAT YOU WROTE IN YOUR E-MAIL:
Prof. Smith,
I finished the preliminary
analysis, but I'm having
problems with the statistics
software. The license has
expired and your approval is
needed to renew it. Can you
please call the support depart
ment at
423 and authorize th
purch
wise I can't co
WHAT YOUR PROFESSOR READ:
Prof. Smith,
I finished
JORGE CHAM © 2009
It's about time.
Send me a draft
tomorrow.
-Smith

EVEN IF I HAD TIME TO GO ON VACATION, WHERE WOULD I GO?
I HAVE NO MONEY...
NO FRIENDS TO GO WITH...
JORGE CHAM © 2009
NO HOBBIES OUTSIDE OF RESEARCH...
I NEED A LIFE BEFORE I NEED A VACATION!
THE OL' CHICKEN AND EGG PROBLEM.

Post hoc vs Post-Doc

The Post hoc Fallacy

To incorrectly assume "A" is the cause of "B" just because "A" preceded "B".

e.g. "All Professors have Ph.D.'s, therefore getting a Ph.D. means you'll get a Professor job (right?)"

The Post-Doc Fallacy

To incorrectly assume you'll have a job just because you have a PhD.

e.g. "Now what??"

mmm...
GOOD MORNING...
OR SHOULD I SAY GOOD AFTERNOON?
IT'S ALREADY NOON!
YOU KNOW, AT FIRST I WAS REALLY STRESSED OUT ABOUT GETTING LAID OFF, BUT NOW I'M ACTUALLY ENJOYING NOT HAVING ANYTHING TO DO.
IS THIS WHAT IT'S LIKE TO BE A GRAD STUDENT?
EXCEPT FOR THE ENJOYING PART.
JORGE CHAM © 2009

SO, WHAT ARE YOUR PLANS FOR TODAY?
I DUNNO...
RELAX...
HANG OUT...
MAYBE I'LL COOK!
GETTING LAID OFF HAS REALLY OPENED MY EYES. IT'S LIKE I'M FINALLY OUT OF THE CORPORATE RAT RACE I'D BEEN STUCK IN FOR YEARS!
DO YOU KNOW WHAT I MEAN?
ACADEMIA IS MORE OF A RAT MAZE.
JORGE CHAM © 2009

Conclusive proof it pays more to do nothing than it does to get a Ph.D.:

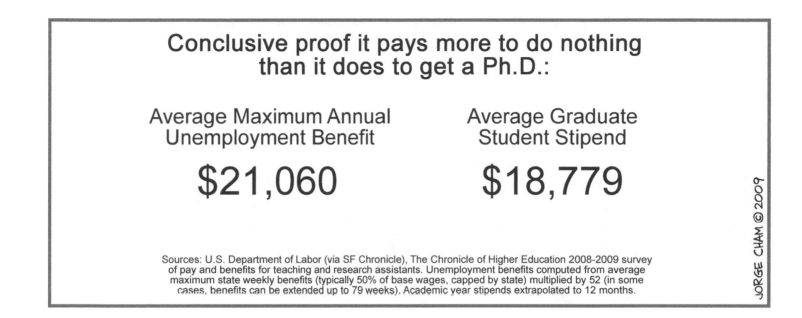

Average Maximum Annual Unemployment Benefit	Average Graduate Student Stipend
$21,060	$18,779

Sources: U.S. Department of Labor (via SF Chronicle), The Chronicle of Higher Education 2008-2009 survey of pay and benefits for teaching and research assistants. Unemployment benefits computed from average maximum state weekly benefits (typically 50% of base wages, capped by state) multiplied by 52 (in some cases, benefits can be extended up to 79 weeks). Academic year stipends extrapolated to 12 months.

THE PERILS OF SUMMER

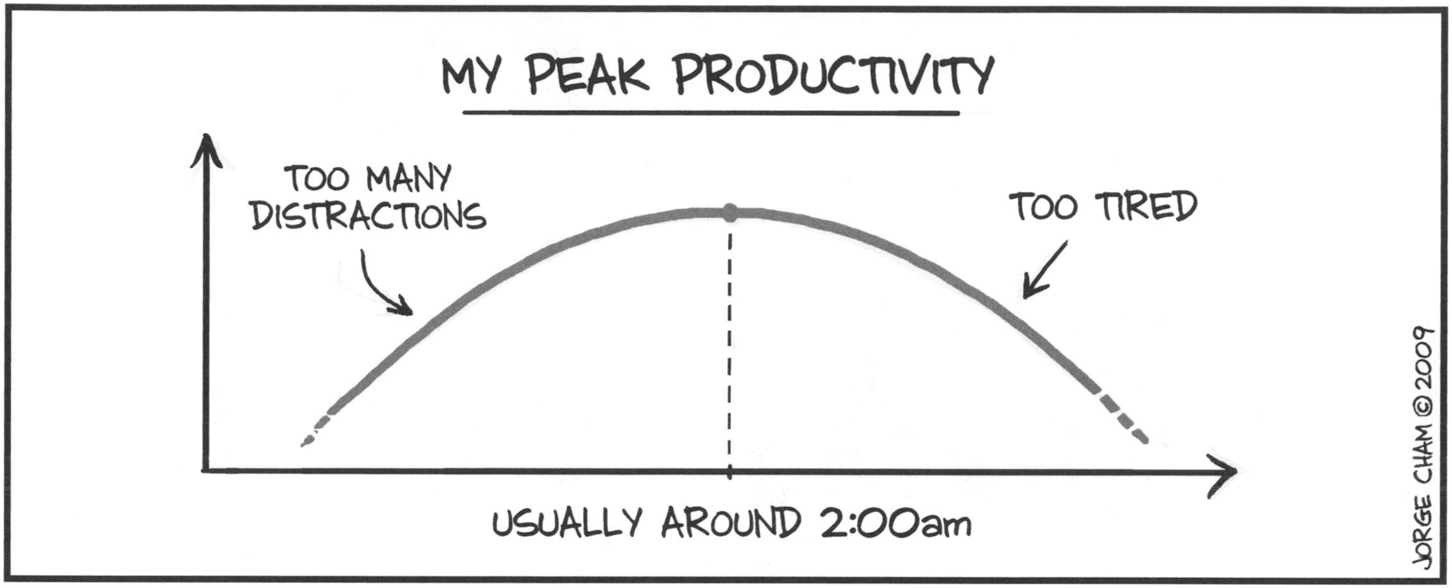
MY PEAK PRODUCTIVITY
TOO MANY DISTRACTIONS
TOO TIRED
USUALLY AROUND 2:00am
JORGE CHAM © 2009

PROF. JONES, THERE'S A CONFERENCE IN HAWAII COMING UP AND...
...YOU WANT TO GO? NO PROBLEM.
I'LL PAY FOR THE WHOLE THING. YOU CAN EVEN STAY LONGER AND ENJOY YOURSELF.
REALLY? WOW, THANKS!
JORGE CHAM © 2009
OH, INCIDENTALLY, I NEED YOU TO T.A. MY CLASS AGAIN THIS YEAR.
I CAN'T SAY "NO" NOW, CAN I?
I WOULDN'T SAY THAT.

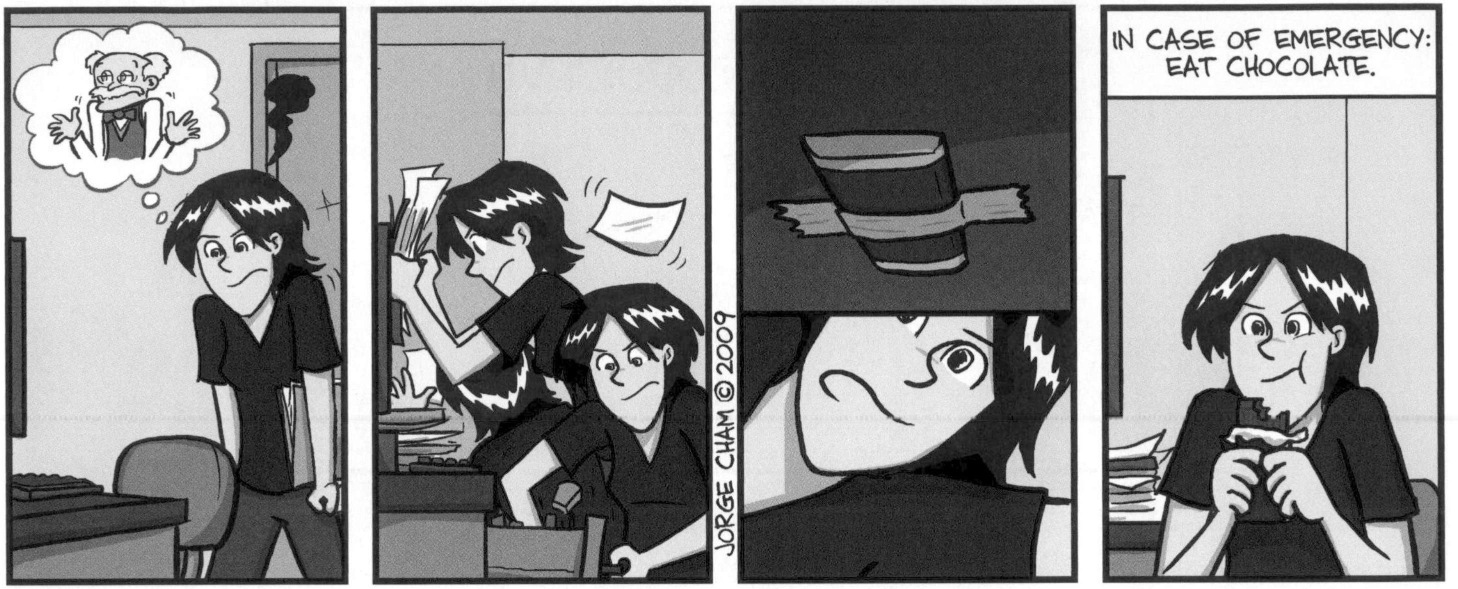
JORGE CHAM © 2009
IN CASE OF EMERGENCY: EAT CHOCOLATE.

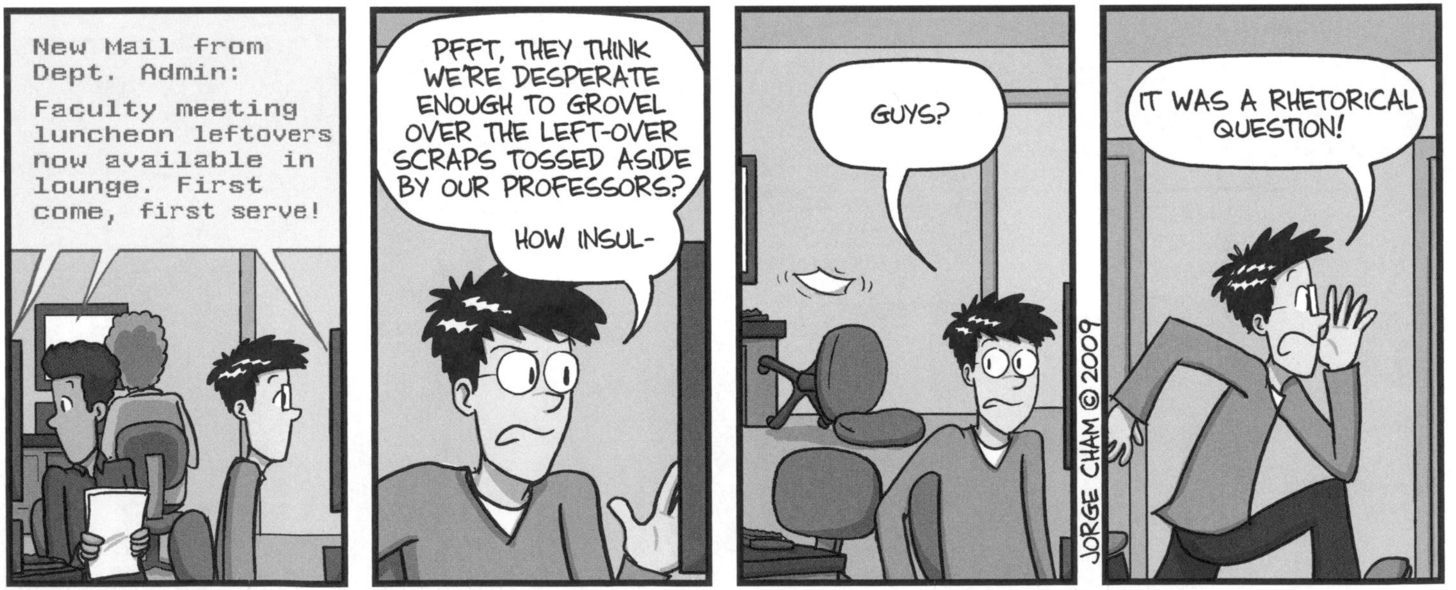
New Mail from Dept. Admin:
Faculty meeting luncheon leftovers now available in lounge. First come, first serve!
PFFT, THEY THINK WE'RE DESPERATE ENOUGH TO GROVEL OVER THE LEFT-OVER SCRAPS TOSSED ASIDE BY OUR PROFESSORS?
HOW INSUL-
GUYS?
JORGE CHAM © 2009
IT WAS A RHETORICAL QUESTION!

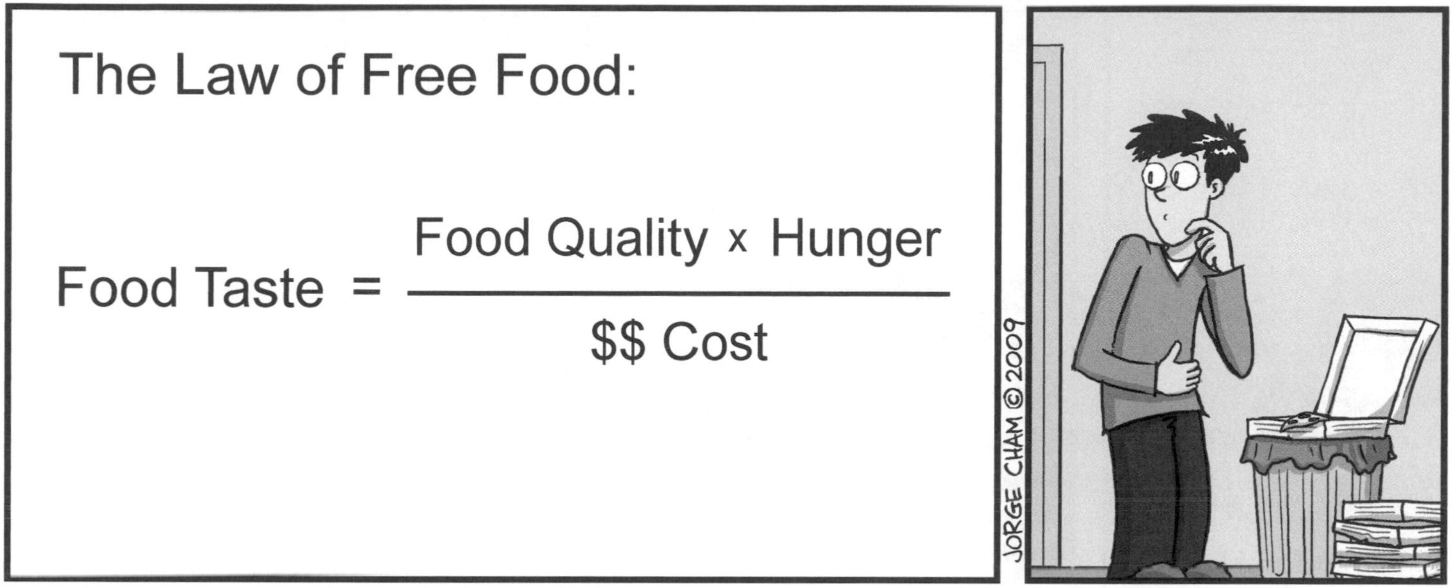
The Law of Free Food:
Food Taste = Food Quality x Hunger / $$ Cost
JORGE CHAM © 2009

LUNCH?
UH, NO THANKS, I BROUGHT MINE.
IS THAT THE FOOD FROM MONDAY'S FACULTY MEETING?
YEAH...
WE DIDN'T FINISH IT SO I TOOK SOME HOME FOR DINNER, BUT I DIDN'T EAT IT ALL SO I HAD SOME FOR BREAK-FAST AND BROUGHT THE REST FOR LUNCH.
JORGE CHAM © 2009
SO IT'S THE LEFT-OVERS OF LEFTOVERS OF LEFTOVERS OF LEFTOVERS OF...
IT HAS CHARACTER, YES.

WELCOME TO THE ANNUAL GRAD STUDENT/FACULTY SOFTBALL GAME!
BOB, WHAT ARE WE IN FOR THIS YEAR?
WELL, JIM, THIS YEAR THE GRADS HAVE A NEW MASTER'S STUDENT WHO PLAYED LITTLE LEAGUE WHEN HE WAS 10, SO AT LEAST ONE OF THEM WILL KNOW HOW TO PLAY THE GAME.
GRADS
VS
PROFS
JORGE CHAM © 2009
HOWEVER, IT APPEARS PROF. JOHNSON WILL NOT BE PLAYING DUE TO A PROPOSAL DEADLINE. THAT SHOULD GIVE THE PROFS AN ADVANTAGE.
HAHA, YES, THE MAN CAN'T EVEN CATCH A COLD.
OVERALL, I THINK WE'RE IN FOR ANOTHER AWKWARD DISPLAY OF ACADEMIC ATHLETICISM.
MY MONEY IS ON A Ø-Ø BLOW OUT.

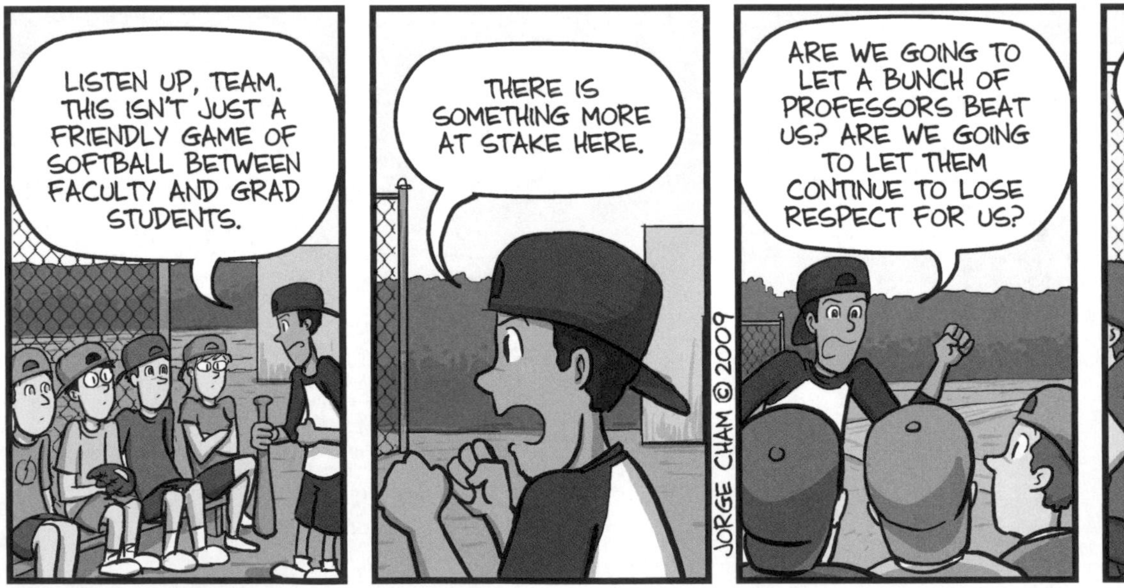
LISTEN UP, TEAM. THIS ISN'T JUST A FRIENDLY GAME OF SOFTBALL BETWEEN FACULTY AND GRAD STUDENTS.
THERE IS SOMETHING MORE AT STAKE HERE.
JORGE CHAM © 2009
ARE WE GOING TO LET A BUNCH OF PROFESSORS BEAT US? ARE WE GOING TO LET THEM CONTINUE TO LOSE RESPECT FOR US?
OF COURSE WE ARE! BECAUSE WE STILL WANT TO GRADUATE.
NOW GO OUT THERE AND MAKE IT LOOK GOOD!

PROFESSORS, I KNOW I SHARE THIS FEELING WITH ALL OF YOU WHEN I SAY THAT I HATE ATHLETIC ACTIVITY...
BUT I HATE LOSING EVEN MORE!
JORGE CHAM © 2009
OUR OPPONENTS MAY BE YOUNGER, FASTER AND LESS OUT OF SHAPE THAN WE ARE, BUT WE HAVE SOMETHING THEY'LL NEVER HAVE!
TENURE?
TENACITY!

STRIKE!
C'MON! IS THAT THE BEST YOU CAN DO? I'VE SEEN UNDERGRADS DERIVE EQUATIONS FASTER THAN THAT!
YOUR PITCH IS MAKING ME ROLL AND YAWN!
JORGE CHAM © 2009
HIS TRASH TALKING IS BAD, BUT AT LEAST IT'S THEORETICALLY SOUND.
WHICH SIDE ARE POSTDOCS SUPPOSED TO ROOT FOR?
your mom called, she wants her tuition back!

SAY, I'VE BEEN MEANING TO TALK TO YOU ABOUT THAT DATA YOU COLLECTED LAST TERM.
JORGE CHAM © 2009
OH, UH, WELL, IT'S... UM...
WHAP!
YOU'RE OUT!
WHO NEEDS TO RUN WHEN YOU CAN STUN?
AW, MAN...

FOUL BALL! MAN OUT!
CRACK!
OUT? THAT'S NOT RIGHT.
OH, ABSOLUTELY! YOU HAVE TWO STRIKES!
THAT'S NOT WHAT THE RULES SAY.
JORGE CHAM © 2009
WE'LL SETTLE THIS... ON WIKIPEDIA!
AS SOON AS WE FIND A SIGNAL...

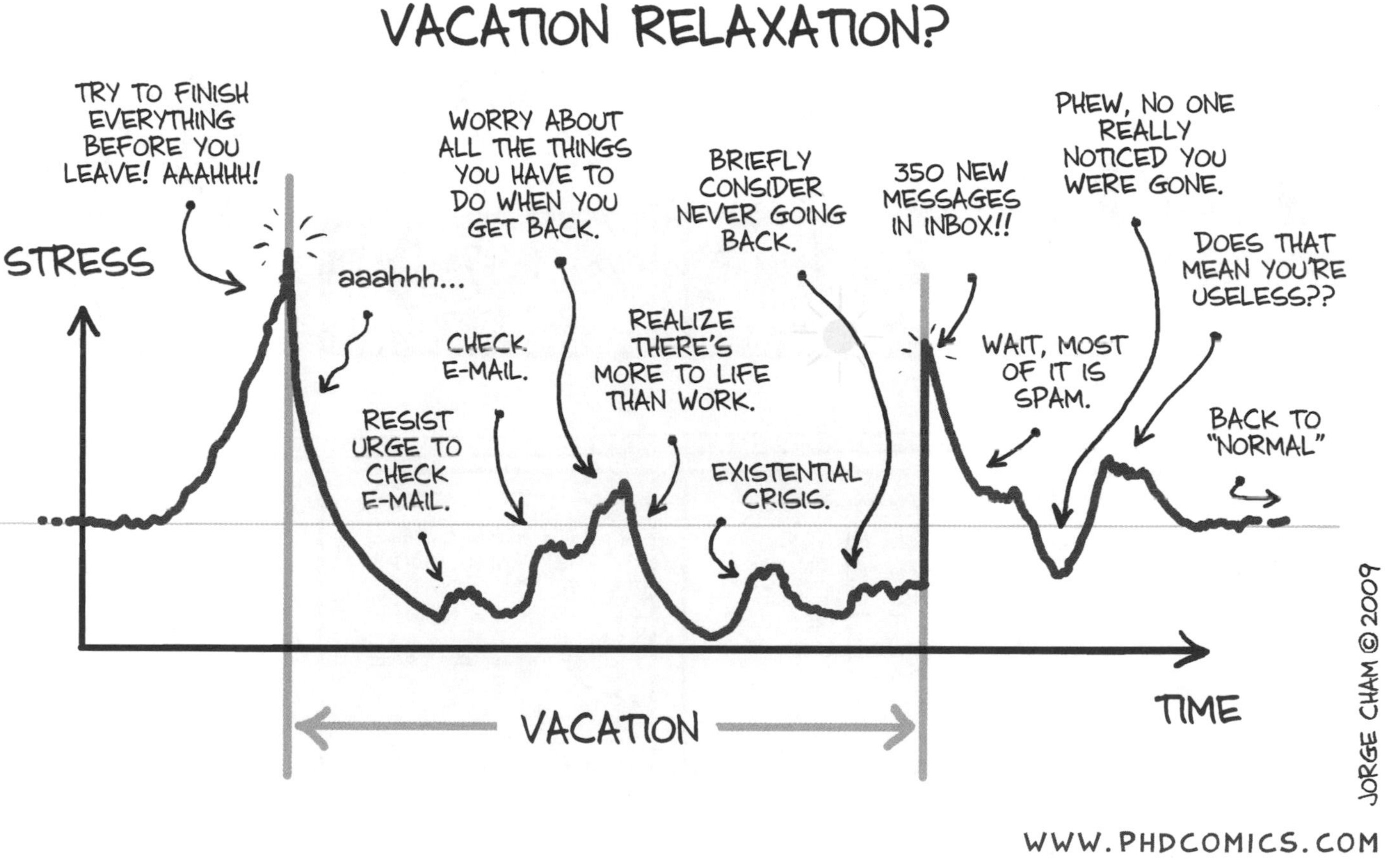
VACATION RELAXATION?
STRESS
TRY TO FINISH EVERYTHING BEFORE YOU LEAVE! AAAHHH!
aaahhh...
RESIST URGE TO CHECK E-MAIL.
CHECK E-MAIL.
WORRY ABOUT ALL THE THINGS YOU HAVE TO DO WHEN YOU GET BACK.
REALIZE THERE'S MORE TO LIFE THAN WORK.
EXISTENTIAL CRISIS.
BRIEFLY CONSIDER NEVER GOING BACK.
350 NEW MESSAGES IN INBOX!!
WAIT, MOST OF IT IS SPAM.
PHEW, NO ONE REALLY NOTICED YOU WERE GONE.
DOES THAT MEAN YOU'RE USELESS??
BACK TO "NORMAL"
VACATION
TIME
JORGE CHAM © 2009
WWW.PHDCOMICS.COM

MAN, BASEBALL IS BOR-
IF YOU WRITE IT, HE WILL SIGN IT.
JORGE CHAM © 2009
ISAAC NEWTON!
IF YOU WRITE YOUR THESIS, HE WILL SIGN IT...
THESIS
THE BALL HIT HIM ON THE HEAD. I THINK HE'S DREAMING.
HE'S FINE. PLAY BALL!
but will he like it?
JIM, IT DOESN'T GET LESS EXCITING THAN THIS: BOTTOM OF THE NINTH AND THE GAME IS TIED Ø-Ø!
hmm.
THE GRADS HAVE A MAN ON THIRD WITH ONE OUT TO GO...
JORGE CHAM © 2009
AND HERE COMES THE TEAM CAPTAIN TO TALK TO THE RUNNER NOW!
WHATEVER YOU DO, DO NOT SCORE!

CRACK!
UH OH, ALLISON HIT THE BALL! WHAT AM I SUPPOSED TO DO NOW??
JORGE CHAM © 2009
IS HE WAVING AT ME TO RUN OR STAY???
OH MAN, OH MAN, OH MAN...
JORGE CHAM © 2009

IS HE OUT?
IS HE SAFE??
HE'S SAFE.
JORGE CHAM © 2009
GRADS "WIN"!

VENI!
I CAME!
VIDI!
I SAW!
JORGE CHAM © 2009
VETERNI.
I TOOK A NAP.

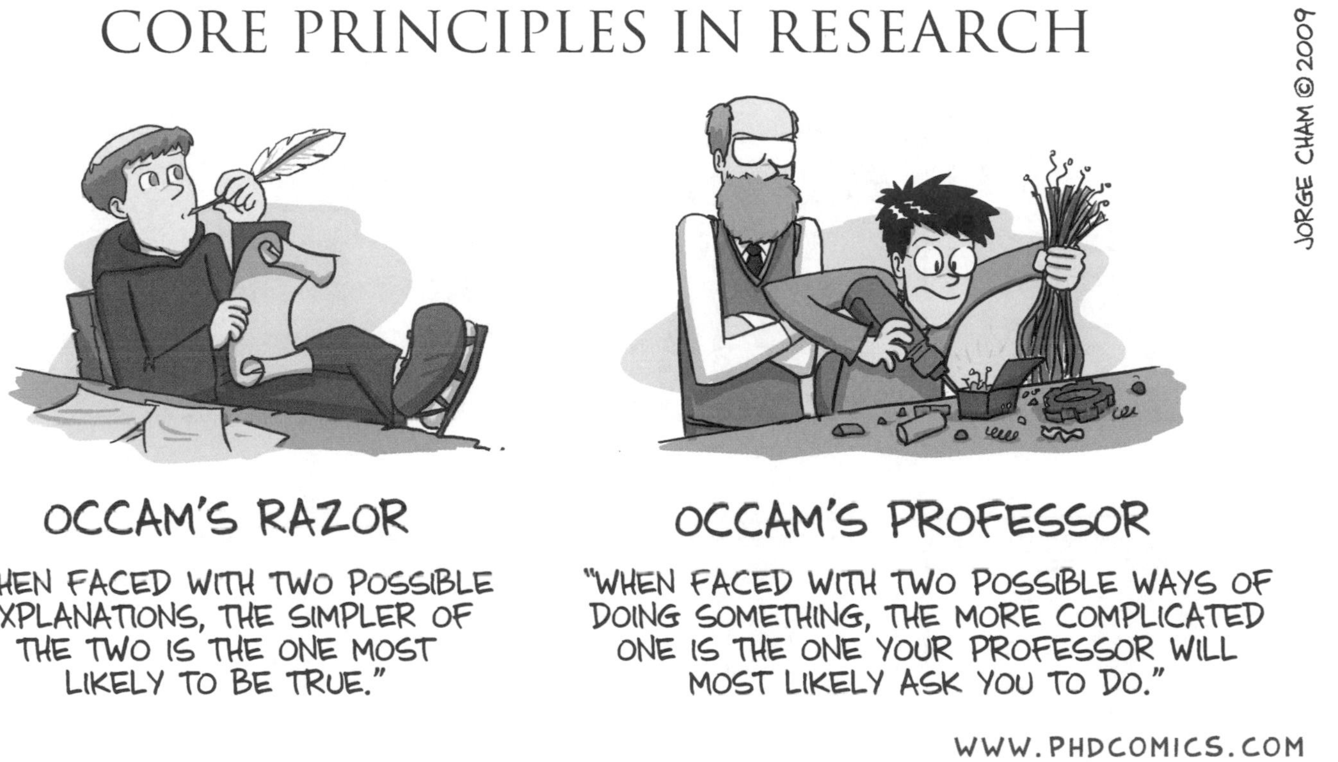
CORE PRINCIPLES IN RESEARCH
JORGE CHAM © 2009
OCCAM'S RAZOR
"WHEN FACED WITH TWO POSSIBLE EXPLANATIONS, THE SIMPLER OF THE TWO IS THE ONE MOST LIKELY TO BE TRUE."
OCCAM'S PROFESSOR
"WHEN FACED WITH TWO POSSIBLE WAYS OF DOING SOMETHING, THE MORE COMPLICATED ONE IS THE ONE YOUR PROFESSOR WILL MOST LIKELY ASK YOU TO DO."
WWW.PHDCOMICS.COM

ESPHD
POST-GAME WRAP-UP
YOU WON THE GAME FOR THE GRADS AND HUMILIATED YOUR PROFESSORS!
WHERE ARE YOU GOING NOW??
NOWHERE, PROBABLY.

RIIING
WHEN ARE YOU GOING TO GET MARRIED?
MOM, HOW DID YOU GET THIS NUMBER?
OK, OK, FORGET GETTING MARRIED...
...JUST HAVE BABIES. I WANT GRANDCHILDREN.
WHAT? YOU'RE BREAKING UP! I CAN'T HEAR YOU!
JORGE CHAM © 2009

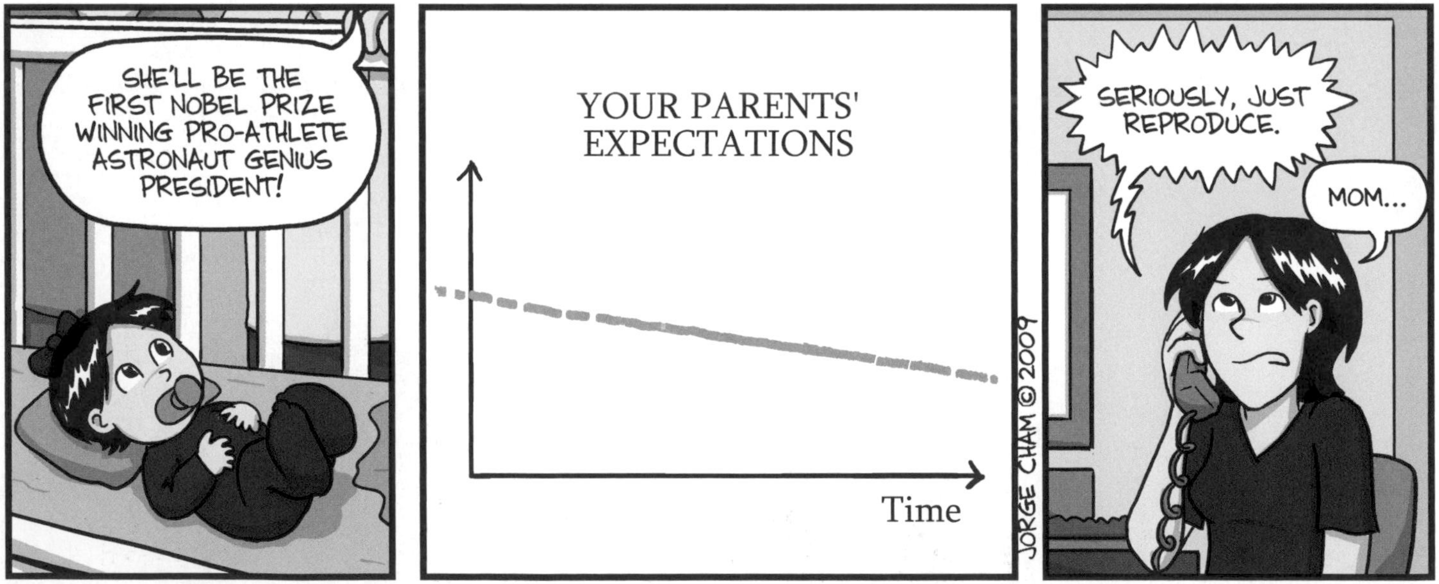
SHE'LL BE THE FIRST NOBEL PRIZE WINNING PRO-ATHLETE ASTRONAUT GENIUS PRESIDENT!
YOUR PARENTS' EXPECTATIONS
Time
JORGE CHAM © 2009
SERIOUSLY, JUST REPRODUCE.
MOM...

MOM, I'M TRYING TO FINISH MY PH.D. HAVING KIDS IS THE LAST THING ON MY MIND.
OK OK...
WHAT ABOUT AFTER?
WELL, I MIGHT DO A POSTDOC AFTER THIS.
JORGE CHAM © 2009
AND AFTER THAT?
I DON'T KNOW, ANOTHER POSTDOC? THEN TENURE TAKES AT LEAST SIX YEARS.
YOUR THESIS IS THE CLOSEST I'LL GET TO A GRANDCHILD, ISN'T IT?
YES, AND YOU'RE INTERRUPTING LABOR.

MOM, IS THAT REALLY ALL YOU CARE ABOUT? THAT I HAVE BABIES?
WELL...
I DON'T REALLY UNDERSTAND YOUR RESEARCH...
YOU DON'T SEEM TO BE MAKING ANY MONEY...
JORGE CHAM © 2009
AND IT DOESN'T LOOK LIKE YOU'RE GRADUATING ANY TIME SOON...
IF YOU CAN'T BE PRODUCTIVE, WHY NOT REPRODUCTIVE?
I NEED CALLER ID.

WHAT YOUR PARENTS SAY AND WHAT YOU HEAR IN YOUR HEAD:
HI, HOW ARE YOU?
WHY HAVEN'T YOU CALLED LATELY??
I'VE BEEN BUSY OK!!?
HOW'S IT GOING?
ARE YOU ACTUALLY DOING ANYTHING? WHEN ARE YOU GOING TO GRADUATE?
IT'S HARD, OK??!
SO, WHAT ELSE IS NEW?
WHAT ARE YOU DOING WITH YOUR LIFE?
I KNOW WHAT I'M DOING! SORT OF! SOB!
WHAT EVER HAPPENED TO THAT NICE BOY YOU WERE DATING?
WHAT'S THE MATTER WITH YOU?
WHOSE SIDE ARE YOU ON??
JORGE CHAM © 2009
WWW.PHDCOMICS.COM

MIKE, I WANT YOU TO TAKE OVER SUPERVISING SOME OF THE GRAD STUDENTS FOR ME.
THE GOAL IS TO CREATE A COMMAND STRUCTURE THAT REDUCES THE NUMBER OF PEOPLE I HAVE TO TALK TO.
THE LAB HIERARCHY
(golden boy)
me
research associate
postdocs
grad students
undergrads
JORGE CHAM © 2009
OR AT LEAST, REDUCE THE NUMBER OF PEOPLE I HAVE TO IGNORE.
WHAT ARE YOU GOING TO BE DOING THEN?
YOU KNOW, STUFF THAT DOESN'T WASTE MY TIME.

YOU WANT ME TO SUPERVISE SOME OF THE GRAD STUDENTS?
YES.
THE IDEA IS TO SEPARATE MYSELF FROM THE MUNDANE DETAILS OF THEIR DAY-TO-DAY RESEARCH.
IF THERE'S A PROBLEM, I DON'T WANT TO HEAR ABOUT IT.
JORGE CHAM © 2009
BUT YOU'RE SUPPOSED TO BE THEIR "ADVISOR."
WHAT DID I JUST SAY?

JORGE CHAM © 2009
DARN SCREEN-SAVER. I'M WORKING HERE!

IT'LL BE GOOD EXPERIENCE FOR YOU TO SUPERVISE STUDENTS, MIKE.
IT'S ONE OF THE MOST CHALLENGING ASPECTS OF BEING A PROFESSOR.
BY DOING IT NOW, YOU CAN AVOID SOME OF THE MISTAKES I MADE WHEN I FIRST STARTED.
JORGE CHAM © 2009
LIKE WHAT?
LIKE SUPERVISING STUDENTS.

THAT'S IT! I CAN'T LOOK AT THIS SCREEN ANYMORE!
I AM DONE FOR TODAY. I'M GOING HOME!
JORGE CHAM © 2009
...AND STARING AT THIS SCREEN FOR A WHILE.

FLUSH!
JORGE CHAM © 2009
HERE'S THE PRESENTATION YOU SENT ME WITH MY COMMENTS ON IT.

Buzzwords!

Number of papers published per year with the corresponding buzzword in the title.

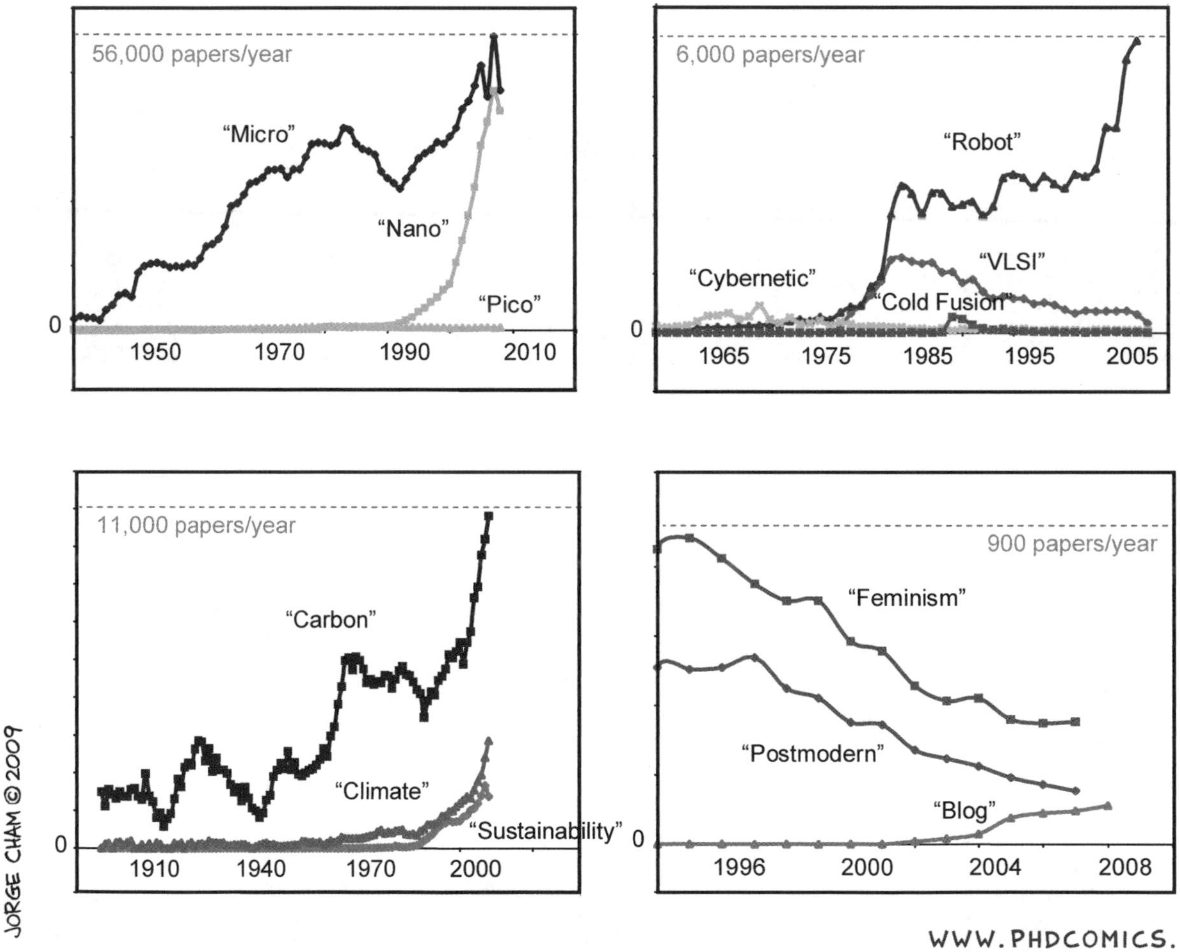

WWW.PHDCOMICS.COM

Scale: All figures normalized by number of journals in print each year.
Sources: ISI Web of Knowledge, Ulrich's Periodicals Directory.

I MADE ALL THE CHANGES PROF. SMITH WROTE ON MY DRAFT...
...EXCEPT FOR THESE MARKINGS. I CAN'T FIGURE OUT WHAT THEY MEAN!
JORGE CHAM © 2009
IS IT SOMETHING OBVIOUS I'M SUPPOSED TO KNOW? WHAT IF IT'S SOMETHING REALLY IMPORTANT??
EARLIER...
ME? PICK UP GROCERIES? BUT I'M A PROFE-! FINE. LET ME GRAB SOME PAPER.
...WE'LL DISCUSS THIS ON THURSDAY'S GROUP MEETING.
UM...
THURSDAY IS THANKSGIVING? PEOPLE DON'T REGULARLY WORK THAT DAY.
REALLY?
JORGE CHAM © 2009
WELL, THAT DOESN'T APPLY TO US.
WE'RE NOT REGULAR PEOPLE?
THANKFULLY, NO.

JUST BECAUSE THE FEDERAL GOVERNMENT MANDATES A HOLIDAY DOESN'T MEAN WE CAN'T WORK.
WE'RE ACADEMIA! NOBODY TELLS US WHAT TO DO!
JORGE CHAM © 2009
LIKE WEEKENDS. I MEAN, ON WHOSE AUTHORITY ARE WE SUPPOSED TO REST ON SUNDAY?
UH, A HIGHER POWER?
THE DEAN? DON'T MAKE ME LAUGH.

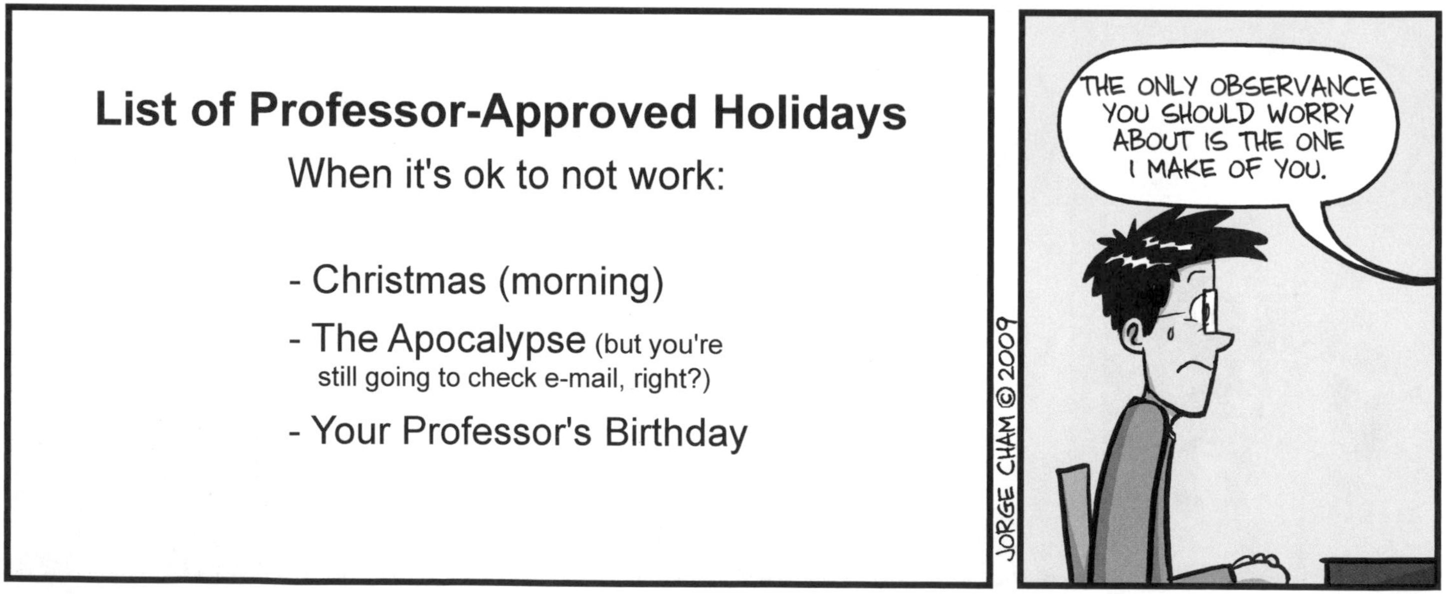
List of Professor-Approved Holidays
When it's ok to not work:
- Christmas (morning)
- The Apocalypse (but you're still going to check e-mail, right?)
- Your Professor's Birthday
JORGE CHAM © 2009
THE ONLY OBSERVANCE YOU SHOULD WORRY ABOUT IS THE ONE I MAKE OF YOU.

FINE, I WON'T SCHEDULE THE GROUP MEETING ON THURSDAY BECAUSE OF THE "HOLIDAY".
WE'LL DO IT ON SATURDAY.
JORGE CHAM © 2009
I'M JOKING, OF COURSE.
SUNDAY MORNING:
SO, WHAT DID YOU GET DONE YESTERDAY?

JORGE CHAM © 2009
sigh.

The Professor outside is frightful...
but your thesis ain't insightful...
and since you've no place to lurk...
Hope it works, hope it works, hope it works!
JORGE CHAM © 2009

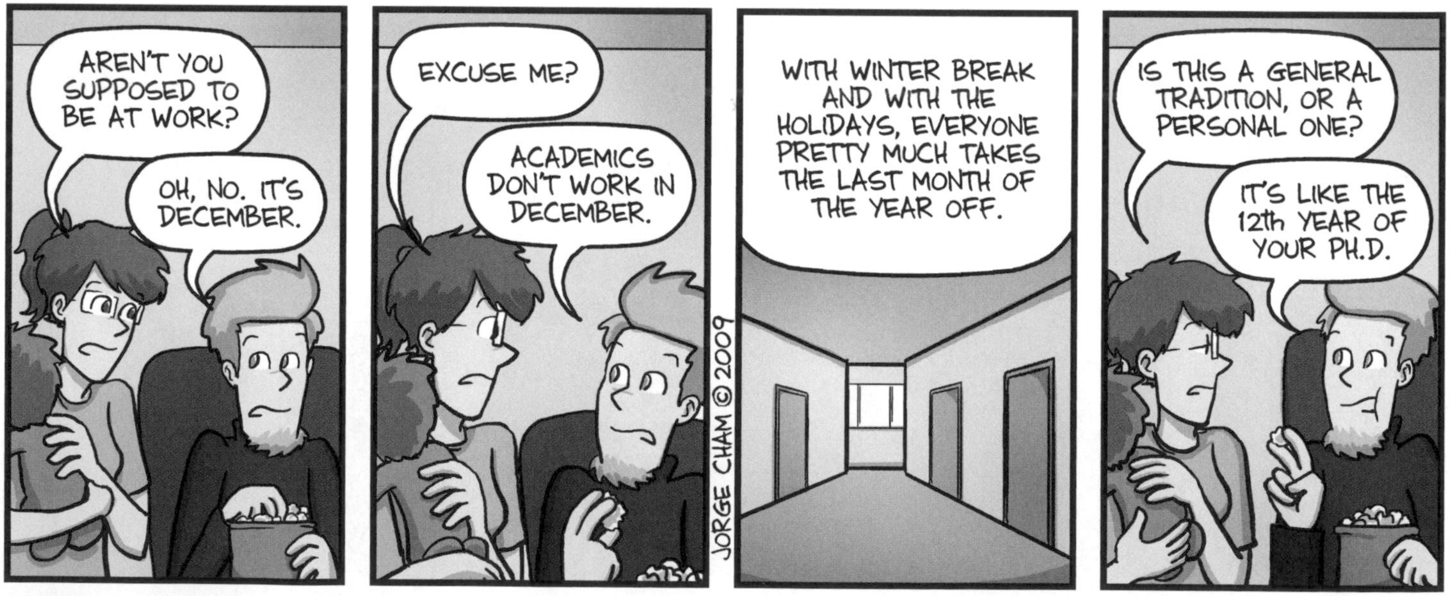

AREN'T YOU SUPPOSED TO BE AT WORK?
OH, NO. IT'S DECEMBER.
EXCUSE ME?
ACADEMICS DON'T WORK IN DECEMBER.
JORGE CHAM © 2009
WITH WINTER BREAK AND WITH THE HOLIDAYS, EVERYONE PRETTY MUCH TAKES THE LAST MONTH OF THE YEAR OFF.
IS THIS A GENERAL TRADITION, OR A PERSONAL ONE?
IT'S LIKE THE 12th YEAR OF YOUR PH.D.

A Christmas Reading List

Christmas disease: a condition previously mistaken for haemophilia. Biggs R, Douglas AS, MacFarlane RG, Dacie JV, Pitney WR, Merskey,
British Medical Journal, Vol. 2 (4799), Dec. 27 1952.
We have now found seven patients who by ordinary tests would be said to have haemophilia, but who from observations must be concluded to have a newly recognized condition which we propose to call "Christmas disease," after the name of the first patient examined in detail.

More Than a Labor of Love: Gender Roles and Christmas Gift Shopping. Fischer, E and Stephen JA
Journal of Consumer Research, Col 17, Dec. 1990.
Through a field study of 299 men and women, the effect of gender-related variables on Christmas-gift-shopping patterns was explored. Survey results suggest that women are more involved than men in the activity.

The Audubon Christmas Bird Counts. Butcher, GS
Biological report. U.S. Fish and Wildlife Service, vol. 90 (1), 1990.
The Christmas Bird Count (CBC) is the oldest and largest wildlife survey in the world. It began in 1900 when 26 individuals responded to an editorial in Bird-Lore magazine (Chapman 1900) by spending an hour or two counting birds in their neighborhood.

Looking at Christmas trees in the nucleolus. Scheer U, Xia B, Merkert H, Weisenberger D.
Chromosoma (1997) 105:470-480, June, 1997
We describe novel nucleolar structures of rDNA transcription units that resemble "Christmas trees," observed by thin section electron microscopy in oocyte nuclei of the grasshopper *Locusta migratoria*,

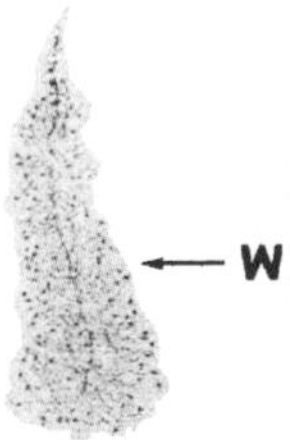

The Vela glitch of Christmas 1988. McCulloch PM, Hamilton PA, McConnell D, King EA
Nature 346, 822 - 824, 30 August 1990
In the past ten years, the Vela pulsar PSR 0833-45 has undergone several large, discontinuous changes—glitches—in its pulsation period. On 24 December 1988, we were making continuous radio measurements of the Vela pulsar with a 2-min time resolution when a glitch occurred.

Cardiac Mortality Is Higher Around Christmas and New Year's Than at Any Other Time: The Holidays as a Risk Factor for Death
Phillips DP, Jason R, Jarvinen, BA; Abramson IS, Phillips RR.
Circulation, vol. 110 3781-3788, December 13, 2004.
Cardiac mortality is highest during December and January.

Red Crabs in Rain Forest, Christmas Island: Biotic Resistance to Invasion by an Exotic Snail. Lake PS, O'Dowd DJ
Nordic Society Oikos, vol 62 25-29, 1991.
On Christmas Island, Indian Ocean, when introduced giant African snails (Achatina fulica) were transplanted and tethered, 97% were killed by the endemic red crab (Gecarcoidea natalis) in rain forest, but only 22% in disturbed habitat. These results suggest that an endemic omnivore may restrict the distribution of an invader.

C.H.R.I.S.T.M.A.S.: The Carvedilol Hibernation Reversible Ischaemia Trial, Marker of Success study. Pennell D
International Journal of Cardiology, vol. 72, (3) 265-274, February 2000
This paper describes the methodology and the rationale for the choice of the nuclear cardiology and echocardiography imaging techniques used in the C.H.R.I.S.T.M.A.S. study.

SIGH. I MISS MY FAMILY. I WISH WE COULD AFFORD TO FLY HOME FOR THE BREAK.
AWW, DON'T BE SAD, TAJEL.
REMEMBER, THE PEOPLE WE LOVE ARE NEVER TRULY FAR FROM US.
JORGE CHAM © 2009
YOU MEAN THEY'RE ALWAYS CLOSE TO MY HEART?
NO, I MEAN WE HAVE THE INTERNET.

AHH, DECEMBER. THE END OF ANOTHER YEAR.
PERHAPS I'LL WRITE A LIST OF MY ACCOMPLISHMENTS IN THE LAST 12 MONTHS.
JORGE CHAM © 2009
1) Received millions in funding.
2) Given numerous academic awards.
3) Inducted in various honorary societies.
4) Countless high-profile keynote lectures.
THE PROBLEM WITH BEING AT THE TOP IS THERE'S NO ONE AROUND TO PAT YOUR BACK.

I SUPPOSE IN THE SPIRIT OF THINGS, I SHOULD ALSO MAKE A LIST OF MY FAILURES, TO SEE WHAT I DID WRONG THIS YEAR.
1) My grad students should have written more papers.
2) My Postdocs should have written more grants.
JORGE CHAM © 2009
3) I should have hired better grad students and Postdocs.
EH, WHAT'S THIS?
JORGE CHAM © 2009
Prof. Smith,
We all chipped in and got you this. Happy Holidays!
- Your Grad Students
I SUPPOSE IT COULD HAVE BEEN A WORSE YEAR.

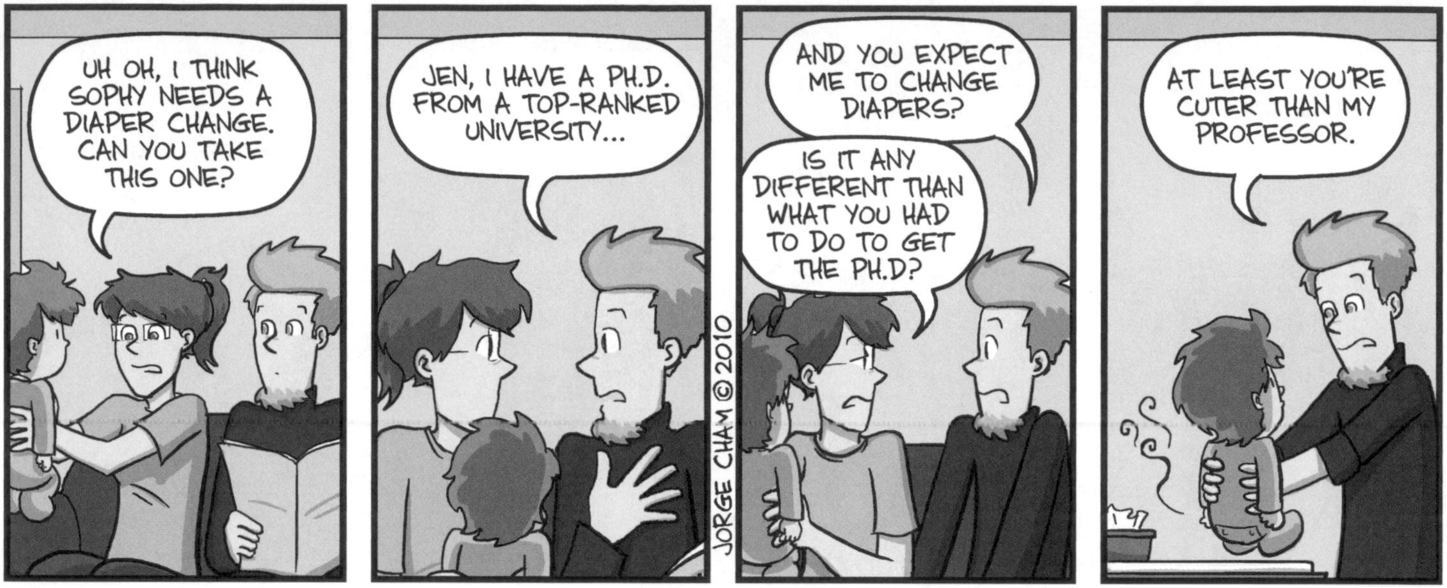
UH OH, I THINK SOPHY NEEDS A DIAPER CHANGE. CAN YOU TAKE THIS ONE?
JEN, I HAVE A PH.D. FROM A TOP-RANKED UNIVERSITY...
JORGE CHAM © 2010
AND YOU EXPECT ME TO CHANGE DIAPERS?
IS IT ANY DIFFERENT THAN WHAT YOU HAD TO DO TO GET THE PH.D?
AT LEAST YOU'RE CUTER THAN MY PROFESSOR.

SO, WHAT DID YOU DO THIS WEEK?
WELL, I CHANGED SEVERAL DOZEN DIAPERS.
I ALSO SPENT A LOT OF TIME COO'ING, SOOTHING, CALMING AND BURPING.
JORGE CHAM © 2010
I DIDN'T KNOW WE HAD UNDERGRADS IN THE LAB.
LESS WHINY, THOUGH.

YES, RAISING A CHILD IS A LOT OF WORK.
YOU FEED THEM, YOU CLOTHE THEM, YOU PAY FOR THEIR EDUCATION...
AND THEN ONE DAY, THEY GRADUATE.
JORGE CHAM © 2010
DID YOU SAY "GRADUATE"?
THEN THEY WON'T EVEN RETURN YOUR CITATIONS.

A.S.A.P. - THE GRAD STUDENT VERSION:
GET THIS DONE AS SOON AS POSSIBLE.
TRANSLATION: YOU SHOULD HAVE DONE THIS YESTERDAY.
JORGE CHAM © 2010
A.S.A.P. - THE PROFESSOR VERSION:
I WILL REVIEW YOUR PAPER AS SOON AS POSSIBLE.
TRANSLATION: I'LL GET IT DONE SOME TIME THIS CENTURY.

Dear News Media,
When reporting poll results, please keep in mind the following suggestions:
1. If two poll numbers differ by less than the margin of error, it's not a news story.
Candidate O's poll numbers are plummeting!
2. Scientific facts are not determined by public opinion polls.
Yes, Galileo, but what of the latest polls that show the earth is flat?
Medieval News Network
3. A poll taken of your viewers/internet users is not a scientific poll.
And now to fill air-time, a poll which shows people who think like me agree with me!
Am I right?
Of course 99%
ROTFL 67%
4. What if all polls included the option "Don't care"?
The election results are in!
Candidate A 30%
Candidate B 26%
"Whatever" 44%
Signed,
-Someone who took a basic statistics course.
JORGE CHAM © 2010
WWW.PHDCOMICS.COM

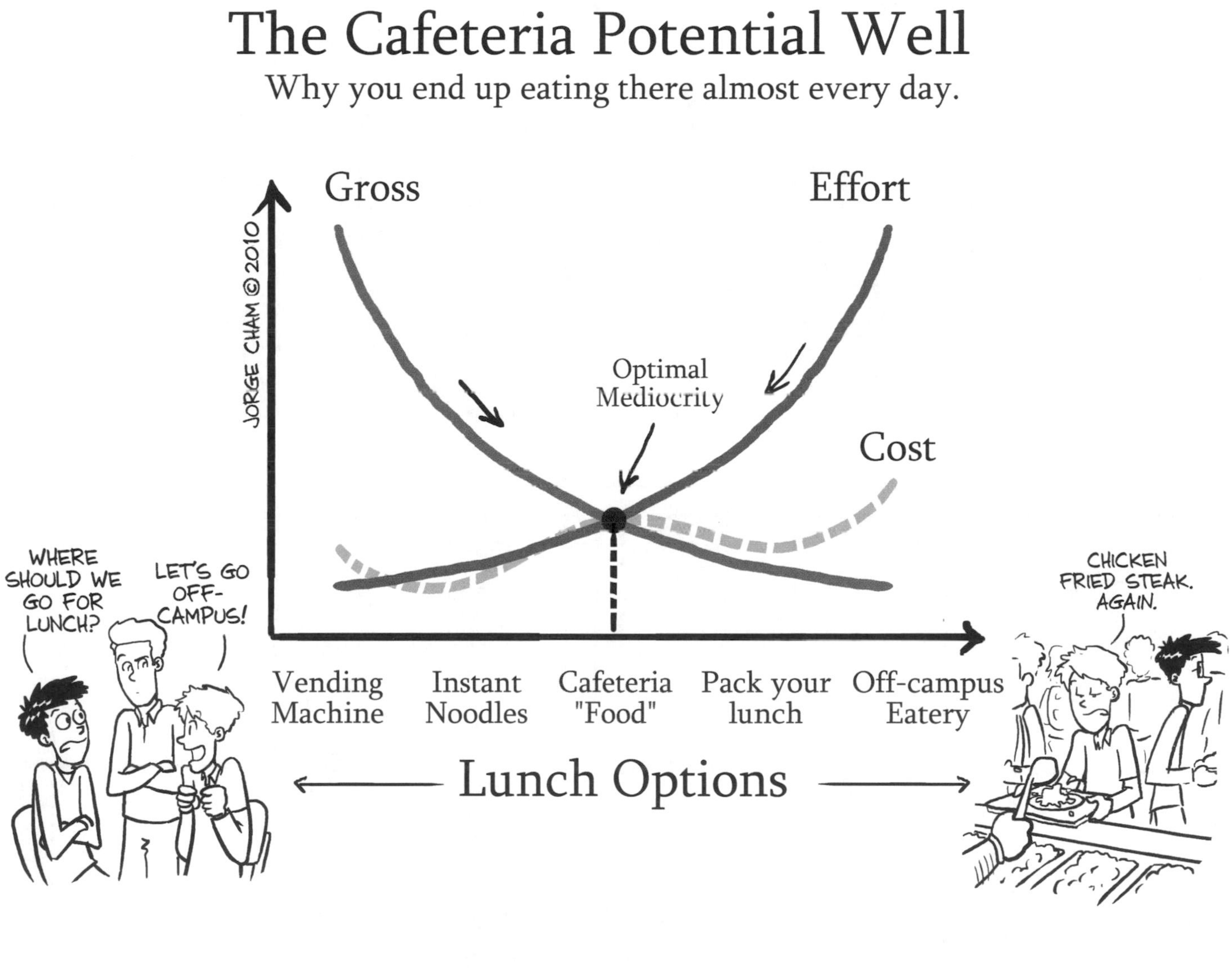
The Cafeteria Potential Well
Why you end up eating there almost every day.
Gross
Effort
JORGE CHAM © 2010
Optimal Mediocrity
Cost
WHERE SHOULD WE GO FOR LUNCH?
LET'S GO OFF-CAMPUS!
Vending Machine
Instant Noodles
Cafeteria "Food"
Pack your lunch
Off-campus Eatery
Lunch Options
CHICKEN FRIED STEAK. AGAIN.

dee
don't forget, next week is dad's birthday.
DOH, IT'S TOO LATE TO BUY HIM A GIFT. I'LL SEND HIM A CARD.
NEXT WEEK:
DOH, I FORGOT TO GET A CARD. I BETTER CALL HIM TONIGHT.
JORGE CHAM © 2010
THAT NIGHT:
OOPS, HE'S PROBABLY ASLEEP BY NOW. I'LL JUST WRITE HIM AN E-MAIL.
FIVE MINUTES BEFORE MIDNIGHT:
HE'S IN A DIFFERENT TIME ZONE. IT'S ALREADY THE NEXT DAY FOR HIM! I'M A BAD SON!!!
HAPPY BIRTHDAY, DAD.

SIGH...
JORGE CHAM © 2010
EVER HAVE ONE OF THOSE DAYS?

MORE AND MORE CURIOUS!
OOF!
JORGE CHAM © 2010
WHAT ARE ALL THESE REFERENCES..?
READ ME -Prof. Jones
READ ME -Prof. Jones
UH OH.

SO MANY REFERENCES TO READ! MY HEAD IS GOING TO EXPLODE!
I KNOW! I'LL THINK ABOUT HOW MANY PEOPLE WILL ACTUALLY READ MY THESIS...
CITE ME
JORGE CHAM © 2010
THERE. BACK TO BEING SMALL AND INSIGNIFICANT!

OH MAN, OH MAN, I'M LATE! I'M LATE!
EXCUSE M-
I'M LATE FOR MY MEETING WITH PROF. SMITH!
JORGE CHAM © 2010
I THOUGHT YOU WERE LATE.
HE'S NOT IN HIS OFFICE.

PROFESSORS!
FORGOT TO GET YOUR GRAD STUDENTS A GIFT FOR VALENTINE'S DAY? IT'S NOT TOO LATE! HERE ARE SOME LAST-MINUTE GIFT IDEAS:
Get them some perfume.
seriously, when was the last time you showered?
AIR-O-FRESH
Buy them some chocolates.
they have espresso beans injected with extra caffeine inside. you're not sleeping this week.
JORGE CHAM © 2010
Write them some poetry.
Roses are red, Violets are blue... Here is a list of the things you must do...
Let them know how you really feel.
words failed me. as did you.

WWW.PHDCOMICS.COM

WHAT A CURIOUS FEELING, BEING THOROUGHLY CONFUSED! I-
ACK!
JORGE CHAM © 2010
WHAT-?
UNDERGRADS?
CAN I GET AN EXTENSION?
IS THIS GONNA BE ON THE TEST?
DO WE HAVE TO MEMORIZE THIS?
ARE YOU GRADING ON A CURVE?
ARE YOU KIDDING ME??
DID YOU EVEN READ THE BOOK??
DUDES, I THINK WE GOT THE WRONG FAIRY TALE.
OOOOPS.
CAN WE STILL GET CREDIT FOR TRYING?
NO, YOU CAN'T GET CREDIT FOR TRYING!!
WWW.PHDCOMICS.COM

I DON'T KNOW. WHEN I FIRST STARTED, EVERYTHING SEEMED CURIOUS AND FULL OF WONDER...
BUT NOW EVERYTHING'S CHANGED.
OR MAYBE I'VE CHANGED.
DID YOU KNOW "LEWIS CARROLL" WAS ACTUALLY THE PEN NAME FOR A MATHEMATICIAN CALLED CHARLES DODGSON?
JORGE CHAM © 2010
BEFORE "ALICE'S ADVENTURES IN WONDERLAND," HE WROTE SHORT STORIES AND POEMS WHILE STILL IN GRAD SCHOOL, DESPITE BEING IN LINE FOR A LECTURESHIP AT OXFORD.
HE WENT ON TO WRITE SEVERAL BOOKS ON LOGIC, ALGEBRA AND GEOMETRY...
...BUT OF COURSE, PEOPLE ONLY REMEMBER HIM FOR HIS NON-ACADEMIC WORK.
ARE YOU SAYING MY THESIS DOESN'T MATTER?
I'M SAYING YOU NEED A HOBBY.
WWW.PHDCOMICS.COM

WHOA...
WELCOME TO HAPPY HOUR!
IT'S HAPPY HOUR ALREADY?
EVERY HOUR IS HAPPY HOUR!
ARE YOU MAD??
OH, WE'RE ALL MAD HERE...
WWW.PHDCOMICS.COM
WHY ELSE WOULD YOU COME TO GRAD SCHOOL?
IT'S BETTER THAN A REAL JOB?
WHO NEEDS A JOB THAT MAKES SENSE? JUST LOOK AT ALL THIS FREE FOOD!

COMMON SLEEP DISORDERS IN ACADEMIA

WHAT DO THESE RESULTS MEAN?
EXPLAIN YOURSELF!!
I CAN'T!
IT DOESN'T MAKE ANY SENSE!
NOTHING MAKES ANY...
...SENSE.
JORGE CHAM © 2010
WWW.PHDCOMICS.COM
...ISN'T THAT WONDERFUL!?
IT MEANS MY THESIS ADDRESSES A PROBLEM NO ONE'S FIGURED OUT YET!
IF EVERYTHING ALREADY MADE SENSE, IT WOULDN'T BE CALLED RESEARCH!

F! "F" WITH HER AD HOC CONCLUSION!!
Esc
F1
Backspace
Del
Enter

"I almost wish I hadn't
gone down that rabbit-hole
—and yet—and yet—
it's rather curious, you know,
this sort of life!"

– Alice

HOW GRAD SCHOOL IS JUST LIKE KINDERGARTEN
ALL DAY NAPPING IS ACCEPTABLE
THERE IS CONSTANT ADULT SUPERVISION
YOU GET COOKIES FOR LUNCH
MOST COMMON ACTIVITY: CUTTING AND PASTING
THERE ARE NO GRADES
(YOU JUST HAVE TO PLAY WELL WITH OTHERS)
CRYING FOR YOUR MOMMY IS NORMAL
JORGE CHAM © 2010
WWW.PHDCOMICS.COM

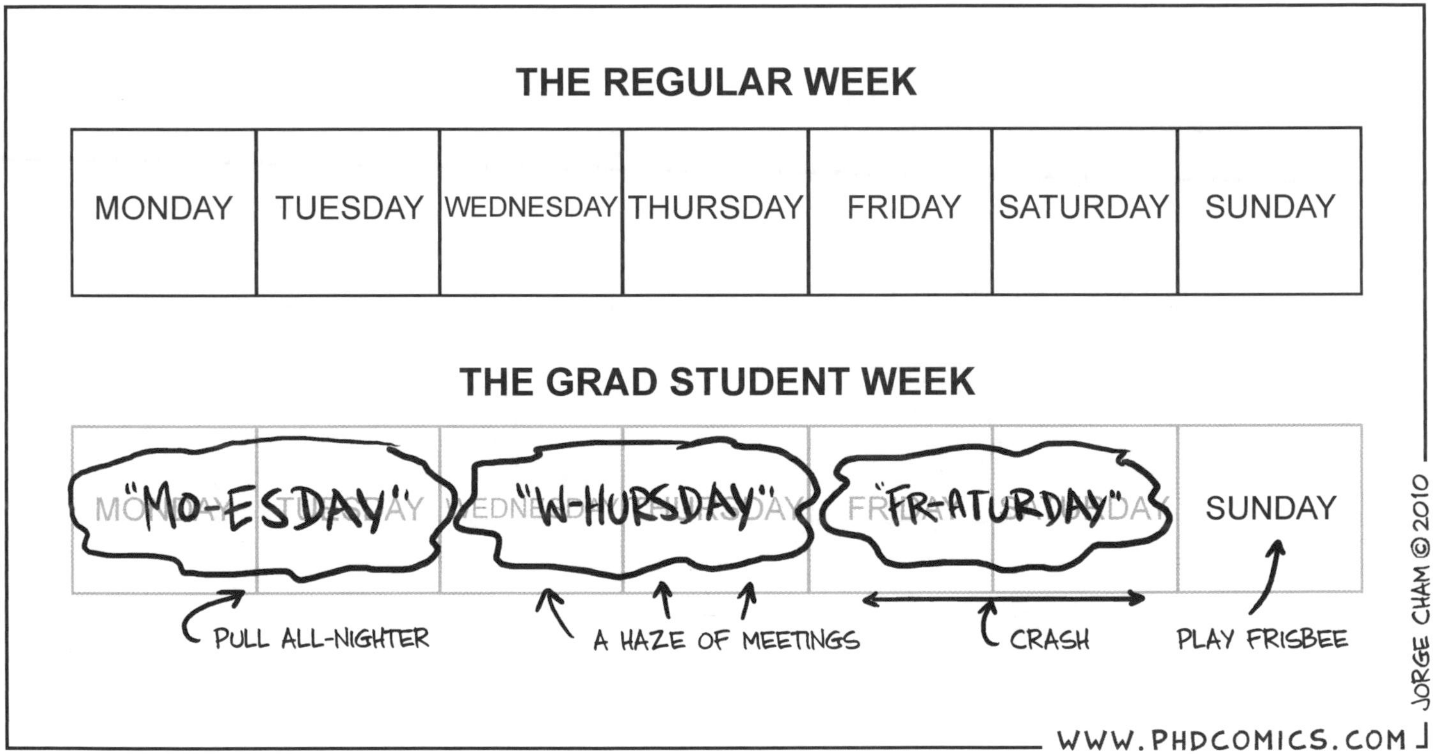
THE REGULAR WEEK
MONDAY
TUESDAY
WEDNESDAY
THURSDAY
FRIDAY
SATURDAY
SUNDAY
THE GRAD STUDENT WEEK
"MO-ESDAY"
"W-HURSDAY"
"FR-ATURDAY"
SUNDAY
PULL ALL-NIGHTER
A HAZE OF MEETINGS
CRASH
PLAY FRISBEE
JORGE CHAM © 2010
WWW.PHDCOMICS.COM

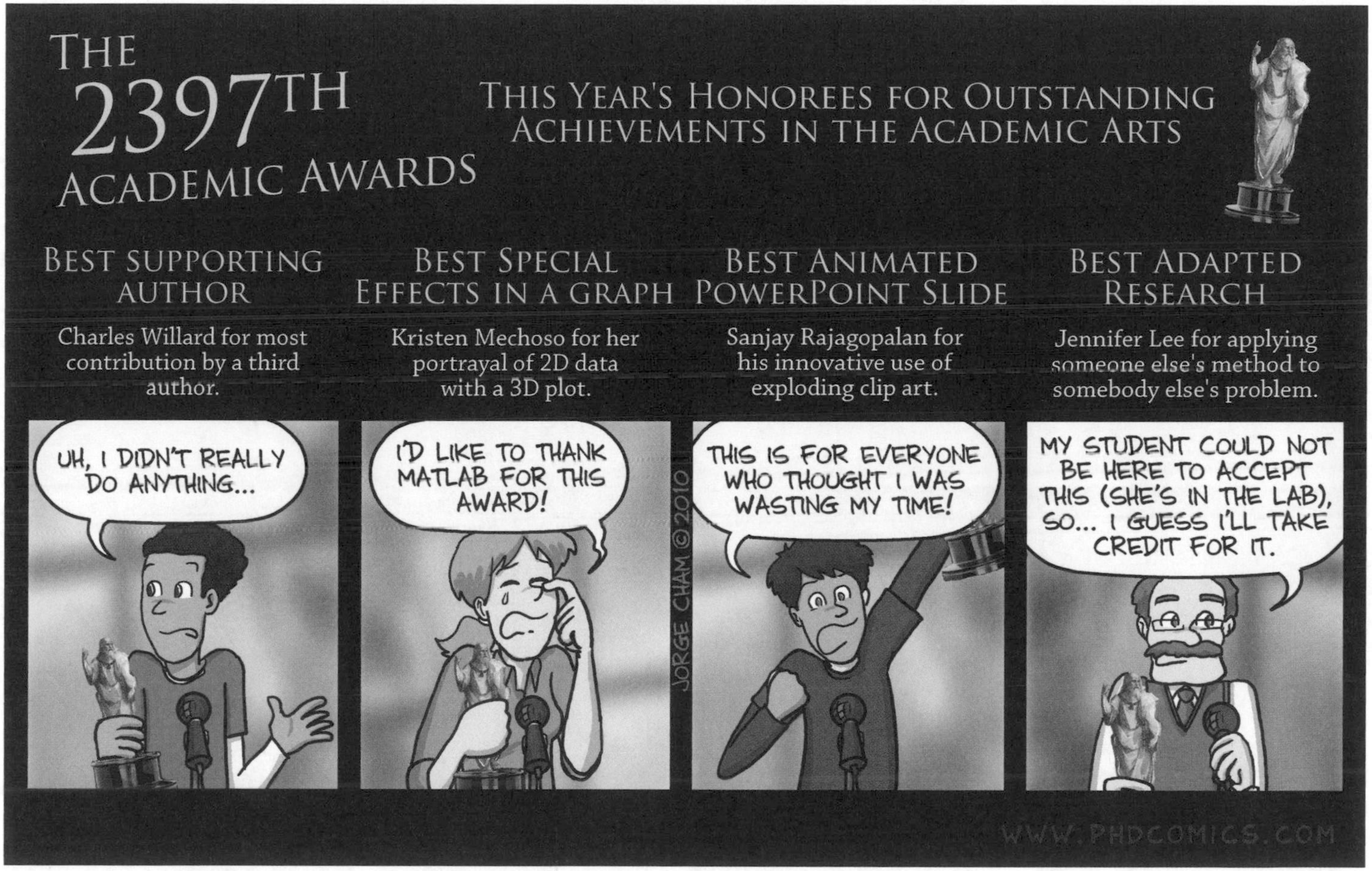
THE 2397TH ACADEMIC AWARDS
THIS YEAR'S HONOREES FOR OUTSTANDING ACHIEVEMENTS IN THE ACADEMIC ARTS
BEST SUPPORTING AUTHOR
Charles Willard for most contribution by a third author.
BEST SPECIAL EFFECTS IN A GRAPH
Kristen Mechoso for her portrayal of 2D data with a 3D plot.
BEST ANIMATED POWERPOINT SLIDE
Sanjay Rajagopalan for his innovative use of exploding clip art.
BEST ADAPTED RESEARCH
Jennifer Lee for applying someone else's method to somebody else's problem.
UH, I DIDN'T REALLY DO ANYTHING...
I'D LIKE TO THANK MATLAB FOR THIS AWARD!
JORGE CHAM © 2010
THIS IS FOR EVERYONE WHO THOUGHT I WAS WASTING MY TIME!
MY STUDENT COULD NOT BE HERE TO ACCEPT THIS (SHE'S IN THE LAB), SO... I GUESS I'LL TAKE CREDIT FOR IT.
WWW.PHDCOMICS.COM

TAJEL, ARE YOU READY?
I'M COMING!
WE'RE ALREADY LATE, YOU KNOW.
I JUST HAVE TO PUT ON MY MAKE-UP!
JORGE CHAM © 2010
OK, LET'S GO.
WHY

I CAN'T FIGURE OUT THIS PROBLEM, PROF. SMITH!
HMM, PERHAPS YOU NEED TO THINK OUTSIDE THE BOX.
JORGE CHAM © 2010
WHAT DO YOU MEAN?
I MEAN AWAY FROM MY OFFICE.
WHAT IF YOU DON'T LIKE MY SOLUTION?
BE CREATIVE.

THE RISING COST OF PUBLIC HIGHER EDUCATION

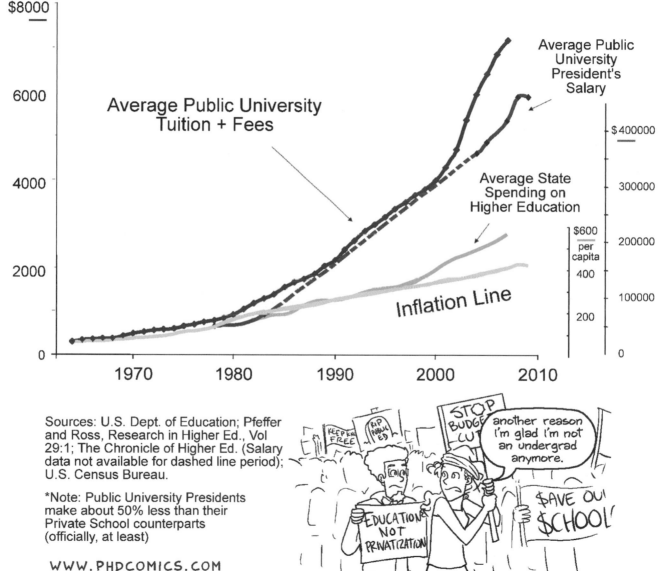

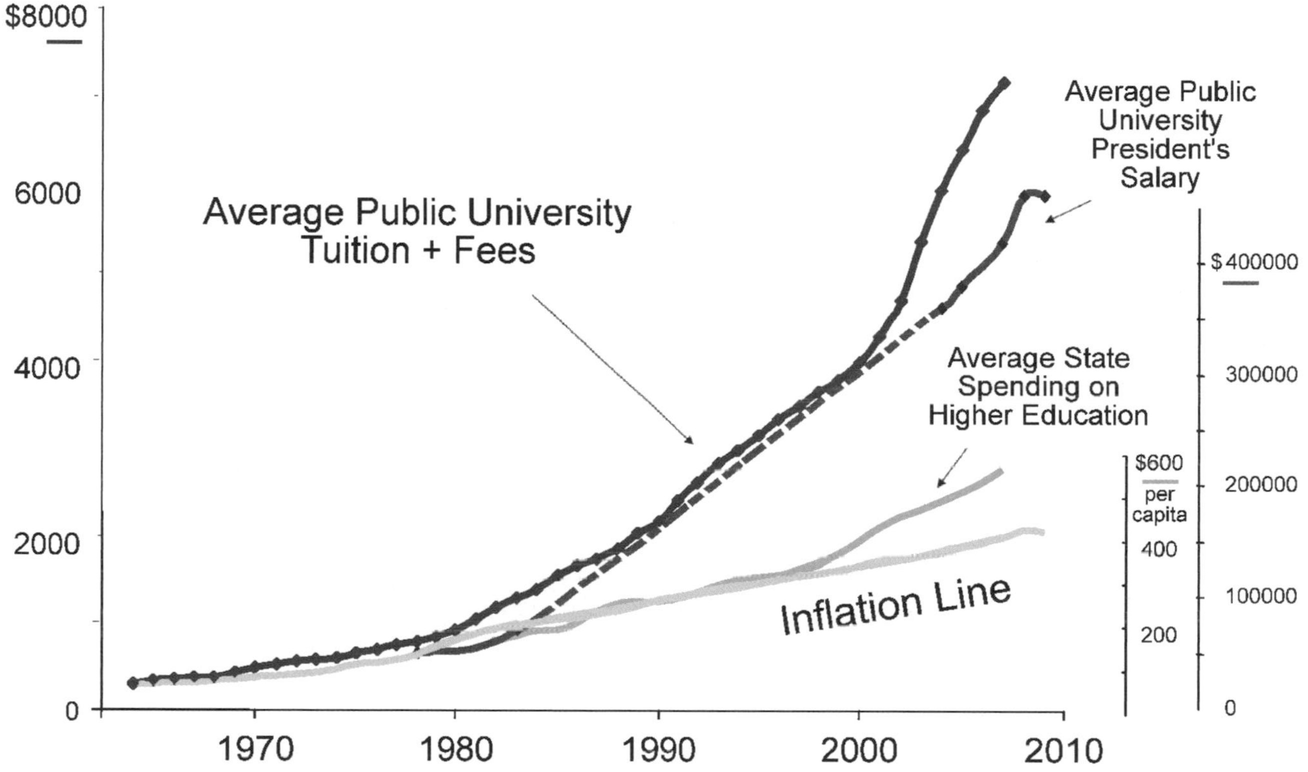

Sources: U.S. Dept. of Education; Pfeffer and Ross, Research in Higher Ed., Vol 29:1; The Chronicle of Higher Ed. (Salary data not available for dashed line period); U.S. Census Bureau.

*Note: Public University Presidents make about 50% less than their Private School counterparts (officially, at least)

WWW.PHDCOMICS.COM

RIP PUBLIC ED
STOP
another reason i'm glad i'm not an undergrad anymore.
EDUCATION NOT PRIVATIZATION

Interdisciplinary Madness!

I work in ________ (Lab)

but get paid by ________ (Program)

My Advisor is in ________ (Department)

...but my *real* Advisor is in ________ (another Department)

Officially, I'm part of ________ (Research Center)

...even though my office is in ________ (Basement of another building)

Most of my classes are on ________ (Stuff I haven't seen since High School)

yet technically, my degree is in ________ (Major other than my undergrad's)

Basically, I belong ________ (Nowhere)

MARRIAGE vs. The Ph.D.

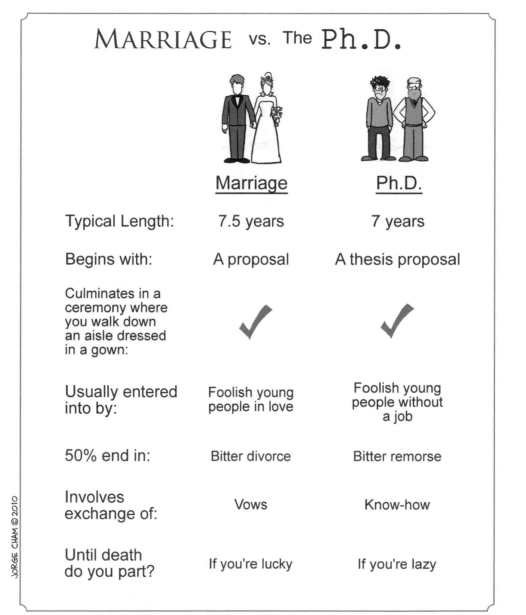

	Marriage	Ph.D.
Typical Length:	7.5 years	7 years
Begins with:	A proposal	A thesis proposal
Culminates in a ceremony where you walk down an aisle dressed in a gown:	✓	✓
Usually entered into by:	Foolish young people in love	Foolish young people without a job
50% end in:	Bitter divorce	Bitter remorse
Involves exchange of:	Vows	Know-how
Until death do you part?	If you're lucky	If you're lazy

Professor Emoticon

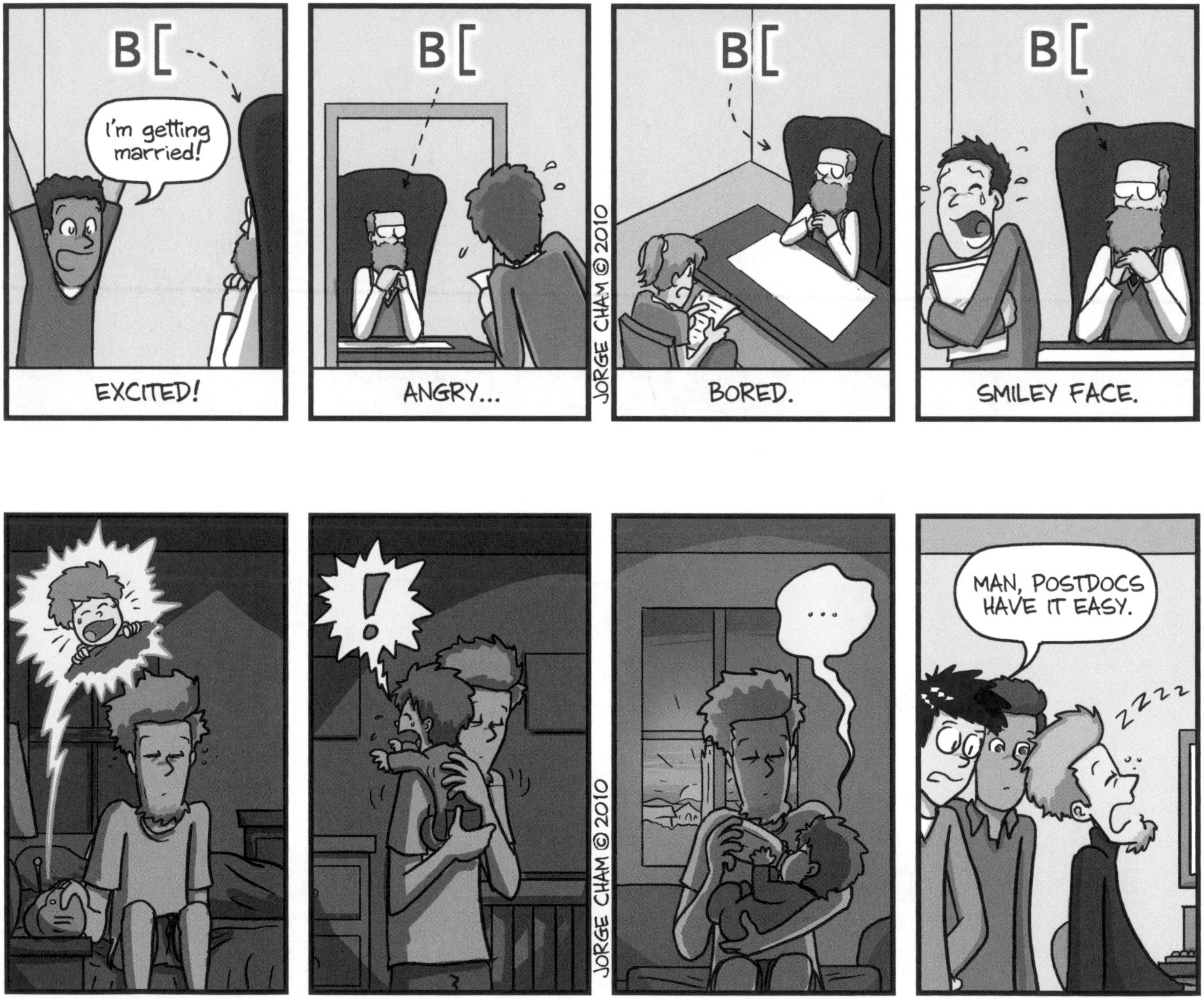

SPRING IS HERE!
WHEEE-
AHCHOO!
AHCHOO!
AHCHOO!
AHCHOO!
AHCHOO!
AHCHOO!
JORGE CHAM © 2010
IF ONLY I WAS THIS ALLERGIC TO WORK.

ACK! POLLEN!
ACK! DUST!
JORGE CHAM © 2010
ACK! MORE DUST!
AHHH...

I SNEEZE EVEN INSIDE THE CLEAN ROOM, DOCTOR... I DON'T KNOW WHAT TO DO!
HMM...
ALLERGIES USUALLY OCCUR WHEN YOU'VE BEEN OVER-EXPOSED TO SOMETHING IRRITATING OR UPSETTING.
YOU MEAN-
JORGE CHAM © 2010
YOU'RE ALLERGIC TO YOUR THESIS.
I KNEW IT!
LET'S TRY IT: WHAT ARE THE MAJOR CONTRIBUTIONS OF YOUR WORK?
I- ACHOO!
ACHOO!
ACHOO!

YES, THESIS ALLERGIES ARE VERY COMMON AMONG GRAD STUDENTS.
ESPECIALLY IN THE SPRING.
THE POLLEN MAKES IT WORSE?
EVERYONE ELSE GRADUATING MAKES IT WORSE.
JORGE CHAM © 2010
WE SEE ALL KINDS OF REACTIONS: HIVES, NAUSEA, VOMITING...
IT'S LIKE YOU'RE HYPERSENSITIVE TO THE MERE QUESTION OF FINISHING.
I'M ALMOST DONE, OK!!?
ACHOO!
ACHOO!

I TRY NOT TO THINK ABOUT WHERE OUR FUNDING COMES FROM.
TAXPAYERS, CHARITABLE FOUNDATIONS, INDUSTRY...
JORGE CHAM © 2010
IN ACADEMIA, IT ALL GETS CHOPPED UP AND GROUND UP AND IN THE END, OUT COMES RESEARCH.
LIKE A SAUSAGE.
A RESEARCH SAUSAGE, YES.

ARE TAXPAYERS GETTING THEIR MONEY'S WORTH WITH OUR RESEARCH?
THAT'S A DANGEROUS QUESTION TO ASK.
IT'S CALLED RESEARCH FOR A REASON.
JORGE CHAM © 2010
WE'RE AT THE CUTTING EDGE! WE CAN'T GUARANTEE RESULTS!
I DON'T HAVE TO GUARANTEE RESULTS?
ONLY TO ME.

BUT I'VE NEVER BEEN ALLERGIC, DOCTOR. WHAT HAPPENED?
IT'S CALLED THE HYGIENE HYPOTHESIS.
YOUR THESIS ALLERGY
YOU'VE BEEN INSIDE THE BUBBLE OF ACADEMIA FOR SO LONG, YOUR EGO'S IMMUNE SYSTEM HAS BECOME EXTREMELY SENSITIVE TO REALITY.
REALITY
MY WORK MATTERS!
"THE BUBBLE" (A.K.A. GRAD SCHOOL)
JORGE CHAM © 2010
ARE THERE ANY DRUGS FOR IT?
WELL, THERE'S DENIAL, BUT IT'S ADDICTIVE.
YOU MEAN I CAN'T STAY IN ACADEMIA FOREVER?
AS A REAL DOCTOR, I WOULDN'T RECOMMEND IT.

HEY, IS YOUR GRANT FUNDED BY THE GOVERNMENT?
YEAH. YOU?
MY FELLOWSHIP IS. DID YOU GET A LOT OF WORK DONE TODAY?
SOME, NOT MUCH. WHY?
JORGE CHAM © 2010
I JUST REALIZED, WHEN PEOPLE PAY THEIR TAXES THIS YEAR, THEY'RE ESSENTIALLY PAYING FOR OUR STIPENDS.
YOUR TAX DOLLARS AT WORK.

TECHNICALLY, WE'RE NOT PAID TO DO RESEARCH.
WE'RE GIVEN GRANTS.
THERE'S A DIFFERENCE?
OF COURSE!
JORGE CHAM © 2010
IF YOU'RE "PAID", IT MEANS YOU WORK FOR SOMEONE.
A GRANT IS A GIFT. YOU CAN'T TAKE IT BACK.
WHAT IF YOU'RE PAID VERY LITTLE?
I'LL GRANT YOU THAT.

JORGE CHAM © 2010
I SHOULD'VE GOTTEN ONE OF THESE SOONER!

The U.S. Federal Budget
($3,518 billion)

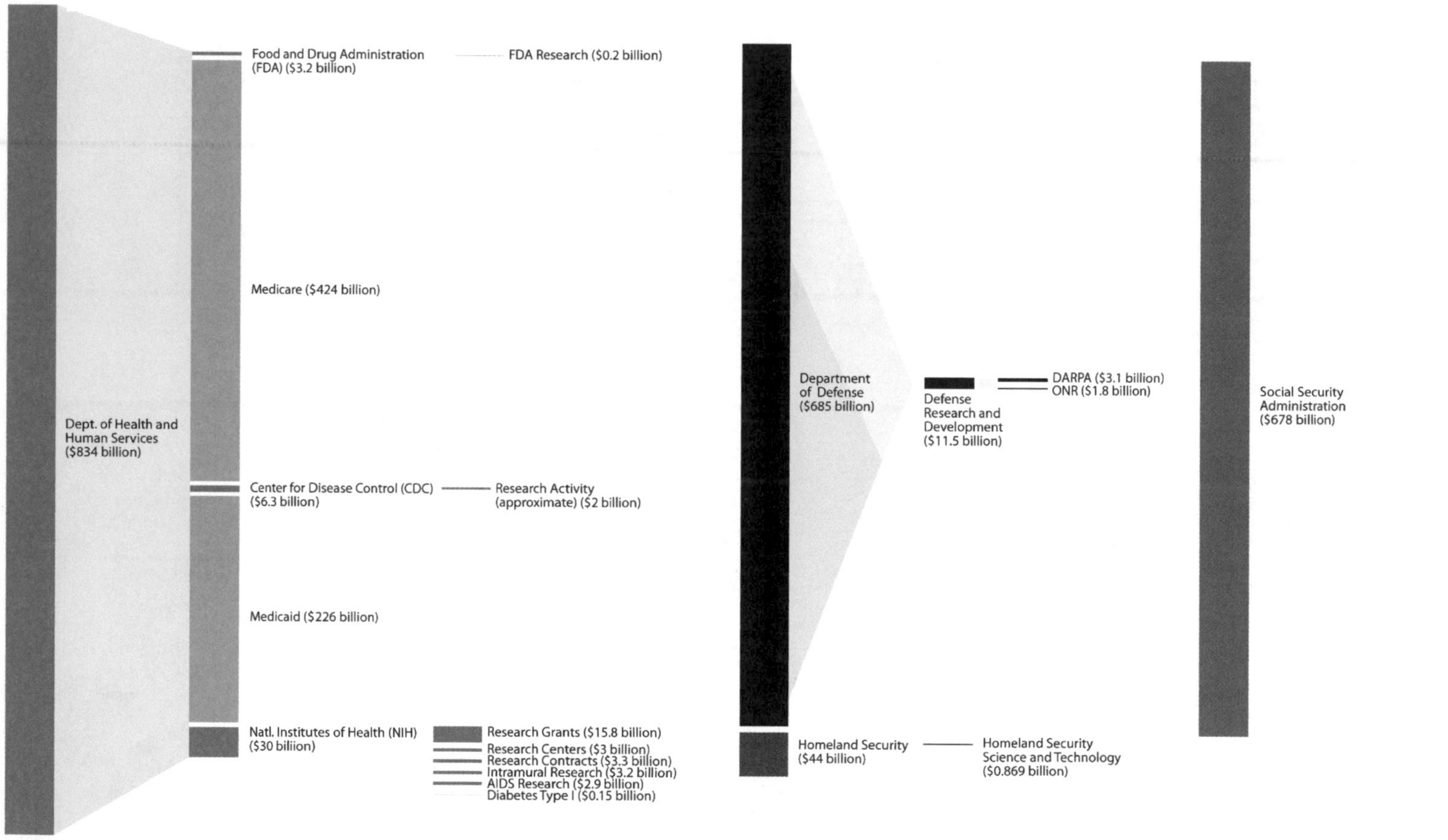

Food and Drug Administration (FDA) ($3.2 billion)
FDA Research ($0.2 billion)
Medicare ($424 billion)
Dept. of Health and Human Services ($834 billion)
Center for Disease Control (CDC) ($6.3 billion)
Research Activity (approximate) ($2 billion)
Medicaid ($226 billion)
Natl. Institutes of Health (NIH) ($30 billion)
Research Grants ($15.8 billion)
Research Centers ($3 billion)
Research Contracts ($3.3 billion)
Intramural Research ($3.2 billion)
AIDS Research ($2.9 billion)
Diabetes Type I ($0.15 billion)
Department of Defense ($685 billion)
Defense Research and Development ($11.5 billion)
DARPA ($3.1 billion)
ONR ($1.8 billion)
Homeland Security ($44 billion)
Homeland Security Science and Technology ($0.869 billion)
Social Security Administration ($678 billion)

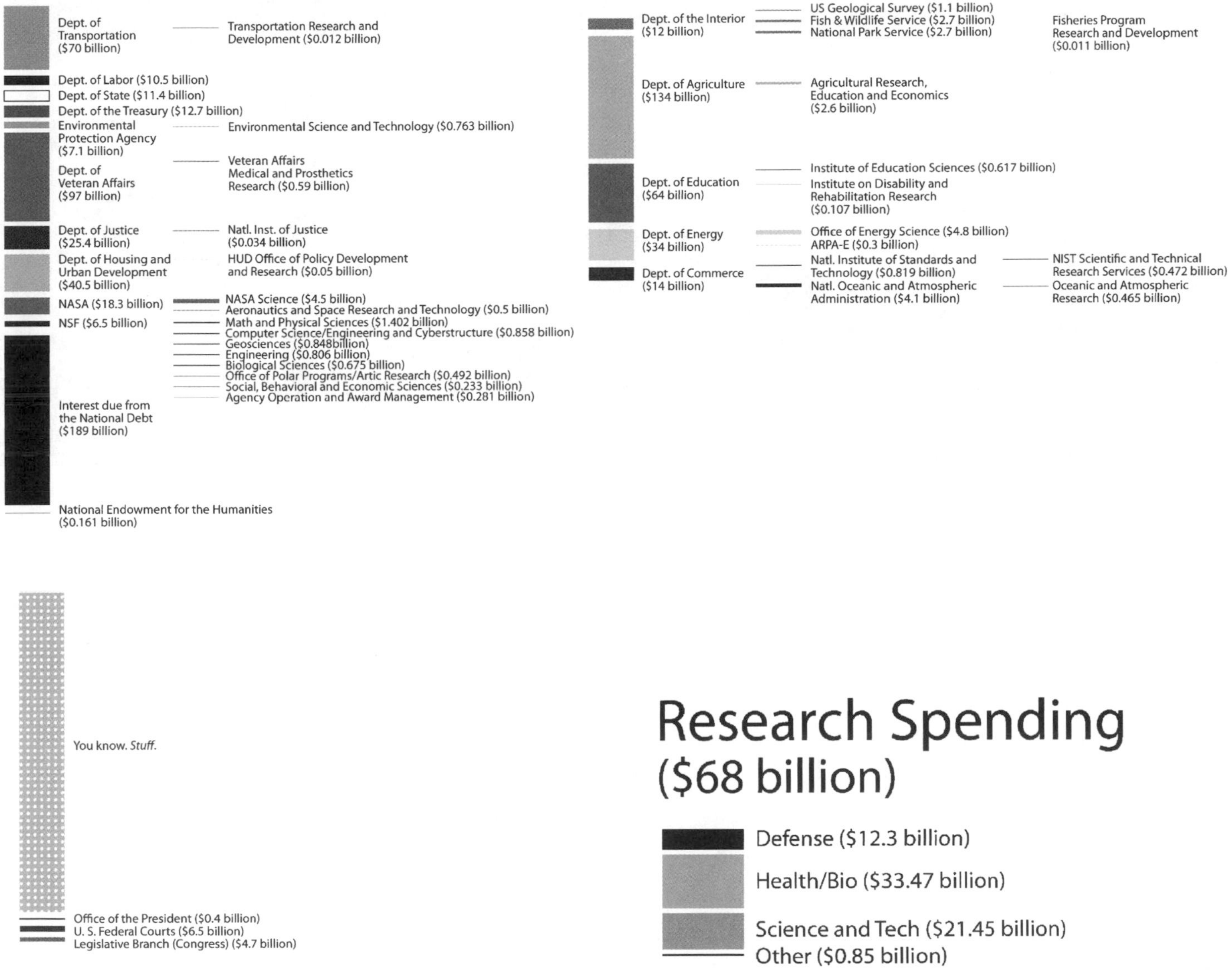
Dept. of Transportation ($70 billion)
Transportation Research and Development ($0.012 billion)
Dept. of Labor ($10.5 billion)
Dept. of State ($11.4 billion)
Dept. of the Treasury ($12.7 billion)
Environmental Protection Agency ($7.1 billion)
Environmental Science and Technology ($0.763 billion)
Dept. of Veteran Affairs ($97 billion)
Veteran Affairs Medical and Prosthetics Research ($0.59 billion)
Dept. of Justice ($25.4 billion)
Natl. Inst. of Justice ($0.034 billion)
Dept. of Housing and Urban Development ($40.5 billion)
HUD Office of Policy Development and Research ($0.05 billion)
NASA ($18.3 billion)
NASA Science ($4.5 billion)
Aeronautics and Space Research and Technology ($0.5 billion)
NSF ($6.5 billion)
Math and Physical Sciences ($1.402 billion)
Computer Science/Engineering and Cyberstructure ($0.858 billion)
Geosciences ($0.848billion)
Engineering ($0.806 billion)
Biological Sciences ($0.675 billion)
Office of Polar Programs/Artic Research ($0.492 billion)
Social, Behavioral and Economic Sciences ($0.233 billion)
Agency Operation and Award Management ($0.281 billion)
Interest due from the National Debt ($189 billion)
National Endowment for the Humanities ($0.161 billion)
Dept. of the Interior ($12 billion)
US Geological Survey ($1.1 billion)
Fish & Wildlife Service ($2.7 billion)
National Park Service ($2.7 billion)
Fisheries Program Research and Development ($0.011 billion)
Dept. of Agriculture ($134 billion)
Agricultural Research, Education and Economics ($2.6 billion)
Dept. of Education ($64 billion)
Institute of Education Sciences ($0.617 billion)
Institute on Disability and Rehabilitation Research ($0.107 billion)
Dept. of Energy ($34 billion)
Office of Energy Science ($4.8 billion)
ARPA-E ($0.3 billion)
Dept. of Commerce ($14 billion)
Natl. Institute of Standards and Technology ($0.819 billion)
NIST Scientific and Technical Research Services ($0.472 billion)
Natl. Oceanic and Atmospheric Administration ($4.1 billion)
Oceanic and Atmospheric Research ($0.465 billion)
You know. *Stuff.*
Office of the President ($0.4 billion)
U. S. Federal Courts ($6.5 billion)
Legislative Branch (Congress) ($4.7 billion)
Research Spending ($68 billion)
Defense ($12.3 billion)
Health/Bio ($33.47 billion)
Science and Tech ($21.45 billion)
Other ($0.85 billion)

LOST
NO MORE?
I BROUGHT YOU HERE TO BE... CANDIDATES.
Ph.D. Candidates.
SECRETS REVEALED!
ALTERNATE TIMELINES!
WHAT IF I HAD STAYED IN ACADEMIA?
THE UNTHINKABLE MUST BE PREVENTED!
HE MUST NOT LEAVE THIS DEPARTMENT!
IS THIS REALLY... THE END??
I'M GETTING OUT OF THIS PLACE!

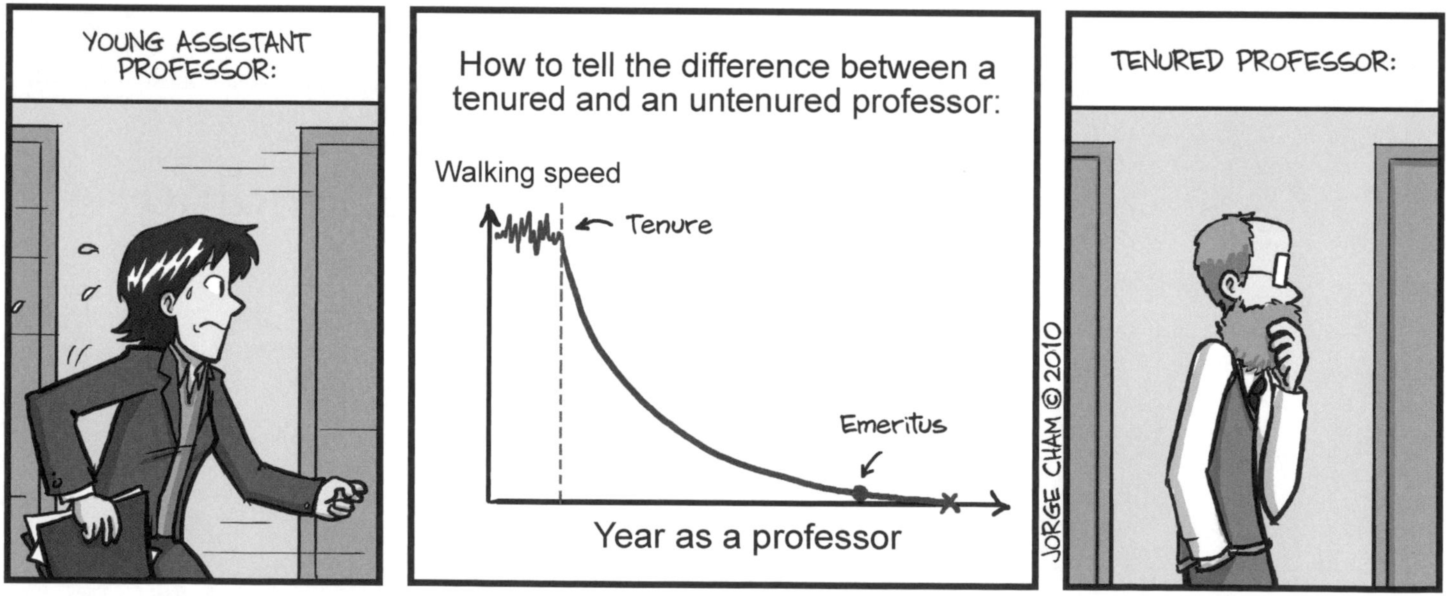
YOUNG ASSISTANT PROFESSOR:
How to tell the difference between a tenured and an untenured professor:
Walking speed
Tenure
Emeritus
Year as a professor
JORGE CHAM © 2010
TENURED PROFESSOR:

Sentences you will probably never read in a published paper:

"We were totally surprised it worked!"

"We just thought it'd be a neat thing to do."

"I'm only doing this to get tenure."

"Oops."

"Previous work by XXX et al. is actually pretty good!"

"To be honest, we came up with the hypothesis *after* doing the experiment."

"The results are just 'OK'."

"Future work will... ah, who are we kidding? We won't get more funding to do this."

I TRIED THE ALTERNATE METHOD, BUT IT DIDN'T WORK.
WHAT? WHO TOLD YOU TO DO THAT?
UH, YOU DID.
JORGE CHAM © 2010
HMPH.
WELL, YOU SHOULD KNOW BETTER.
THAN TO DO WHAT YOU TELL ME?
THAN TO TELL ME YOU FAILED.

I NEED YOU TO GRADE THESE PAPERS FOR ME, CECILIA.
DON'T WORRY, THEY'RE NOT DUE UNTIL THE 17th.
THAT'S NEXT MONDAY.
JORGE CHAM © 2010
IS IT?
WELL, YOU DON'T HAVE TO HAVE THEM READY UNTIL FRIDAY.
TODAY IS FRIDAY.
WHAT HAPPENED TO TUESDAY?
GONE, SIR. LIKE MY YOUTH.

ODE TO THE LASER

The laser turns fifty this week,
An important event in history!
But who developed this amazing technique?
That's still kind of a mystery...

Was it Ted Maiman
who built the first laser?
Or was it Townes and Schawlow
who wrote the seminal paper?

Was it Basov and Prokhorov
who toiled in academic obscurity?
or was it Gordon Gould
who won the patents (eventually)?

Perhaps we should credit Einstein
who had the key precognition
"A splendid light has dawned on me" he wrote
when he discovered stimulated emission.

Beautiful beams of light
coherent in frequency and phase.
The public expected your biggest impact
to be Star Wars-like Death Rays.

Instead you're in our everyday lives
from bar codes to pointers to DVD drives
They say in Science is your biggest contribution
shining a light on stars and molecular distributions.

But as all things cyber
connect through optical fibers
Let us not forget:
Without the laser, there'd be no Internet!

FOR CREDIBLE LASERS SEE INSIDE

WWW.PHDCOMICS.COM

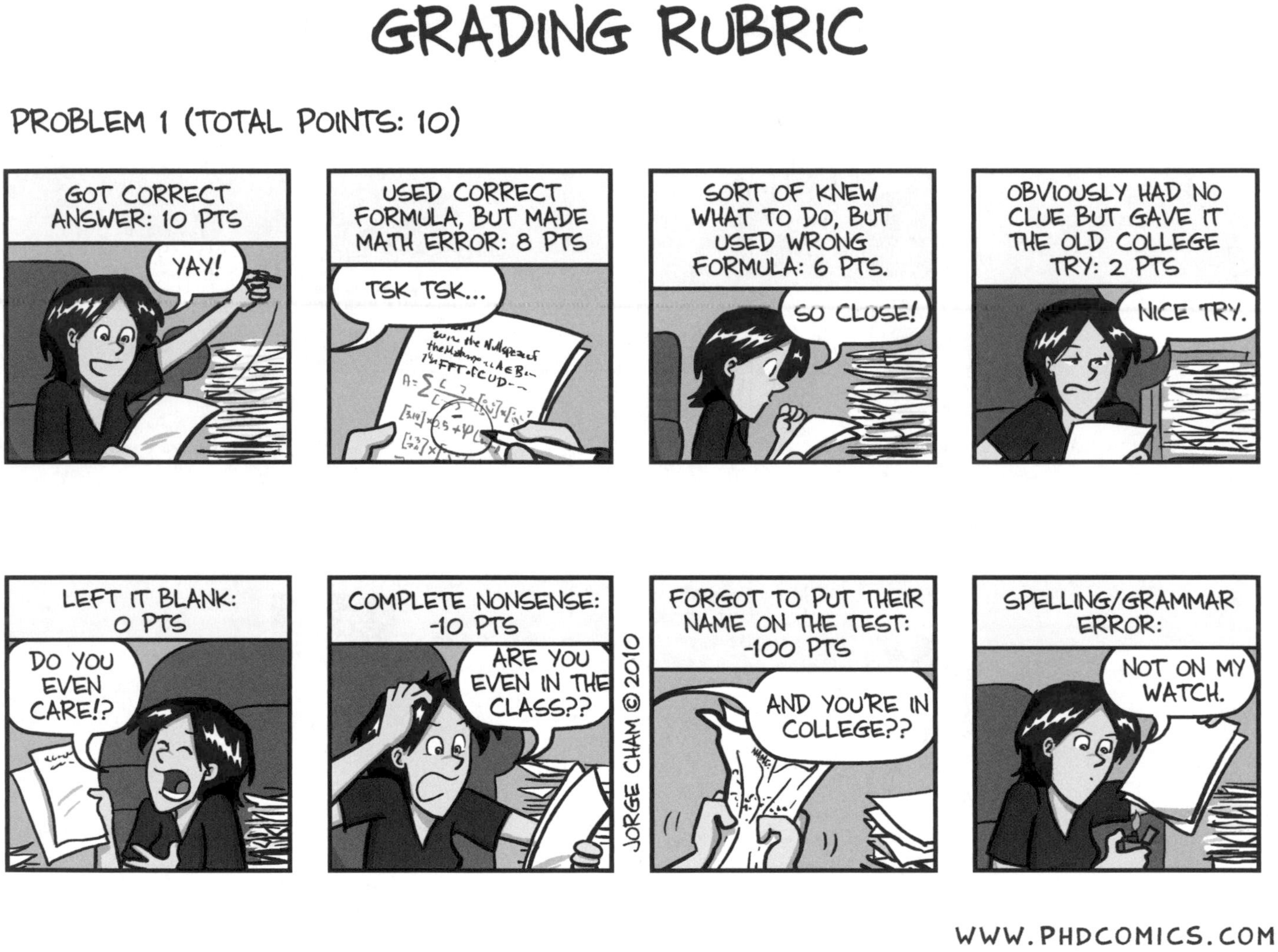
GRADING RUBRIC
PROBLEM 1 (TOTAL POINTS: 10)
GOT CORRECT ANSWER: 10 PTS
YAY!
USED CORRECT FORMULA, BUT MADE MATH ERROR: 8 PTS
TSK TSK...
SORT OF KNEW WHAT TO DO, BUT USED WRONG FORMULA: 6 PTS.
SO CLOSE!
OBVIOUSLY HAD NO CLUE BUT GAVE IT THE OLD COLLEGE TRY: 2 PTS
NICE TRY.
LEFT IT BLANK: 0 PTS
DO YOU EVEN CARE!?
COMPLETE NONSENSE: -10 PTS
ARE YOU EVEN IN THE CLASS??
JORGE CHAM © 2010
FORGOT TO PUT THEIR NAME ON THE TEST: -100 PTS
AND YOU'RE IN COLLEGE??
SPELLING/GRAMMAR ERROR:
NOT ON MY WATCH.
WWW.PHDCOMICS.COM

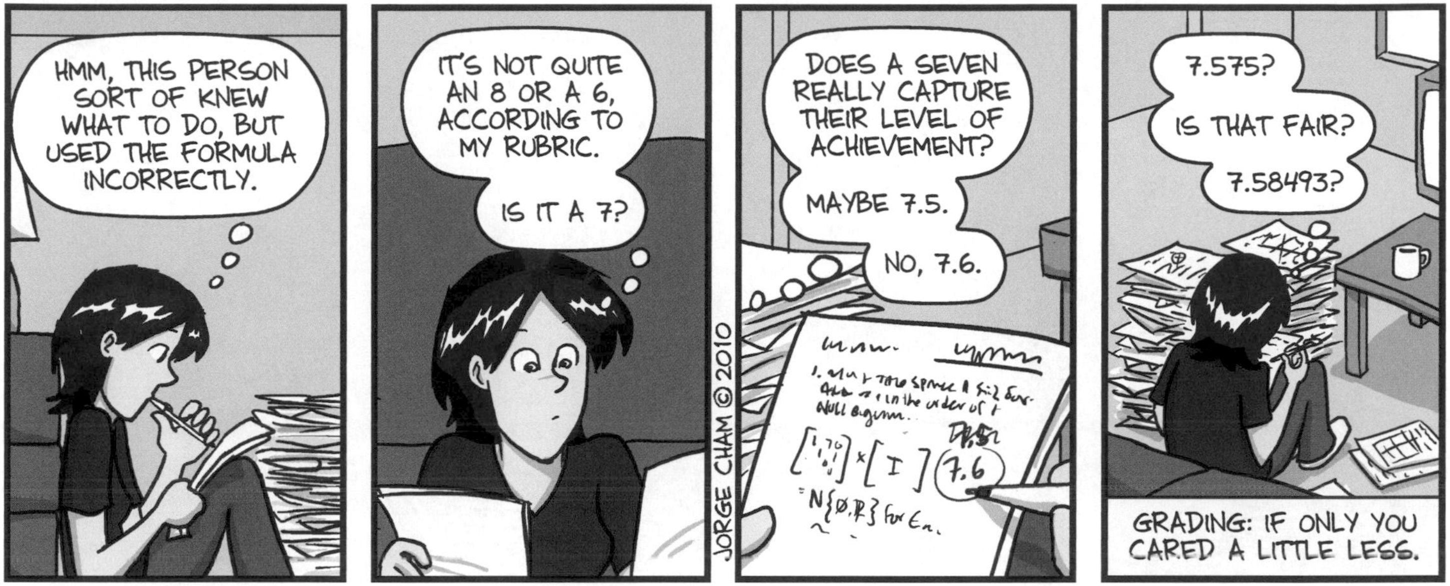
HMM, THIS PERSON SORT OF KNEW WHAT TO DO, BUT USED THE FORMULA INCORRECTLY.
IT'S NOT QUITE AN 8 OR A 6, ACCORDING TO MY RUBRIC.
IS IT A 7?
JORGE CHAM © 2010
DOES A SEVEN REALLY CAPTURE THEIR LEVEL OF ACHIEVEMENT?
MAYBE 7.5.
NO, 7.6.
7.6
7.575?
IS THAT FAIR?
7.58493?
GRADING: IF ONLY YOU CARED A LITTLE LESS.

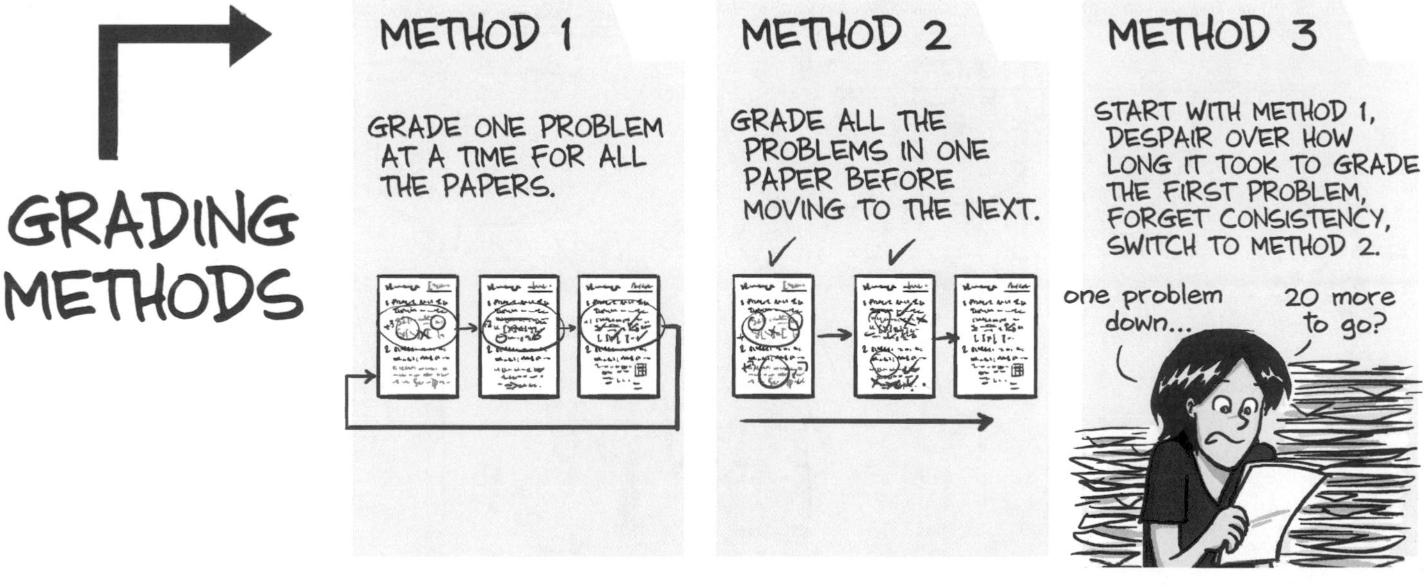
GRADING METHODS
METHOD 1
GRADE ONE PROBLEM AT A TIME FOR ALL THE PAPERS.
METHOD 2
GRADE ALL THE PROBLEMS IN ONE PAPER BEFORE MOVING TO THE NEXT.
METHOD 3
START WITH METHOD 1, DESPAIR OVER HOW LONG IT TOOK TO GRADE THE FIRST PROBLEM, FORGET CONSISTENCY, SWITCH TO METHOD 2.
one problem down...
20 more to go?

I FINALLY FINISHED GRADING ALL THE PAPERS, PROF. JO-
OH. BEFORE YOU GIVE THOSE TO ME...
HERE ARE SOME MORE THAT WERE TURNED IN LATE.
CAN YOU GRADE THESE TOO?
JORGE CHAM © 2010
WHAT? BUT... I... IT'S...
CAN'T WE JUST BURY THEM??
NOPE. JUST YOUR FEELINGS.

WORKING ON A HOLIDAY, EH? THAT'S EXACTLY THE KIND OF DEDICATION I EXPECT FROM MY STUDENTS.
JORGE CHAM © 2010
KEEP IT UP.
I EXPECT A FULL REPORT TOMORROW.
TODAY IS A HOLIDAY???

A STORY TOLD IN FILE NAMES:

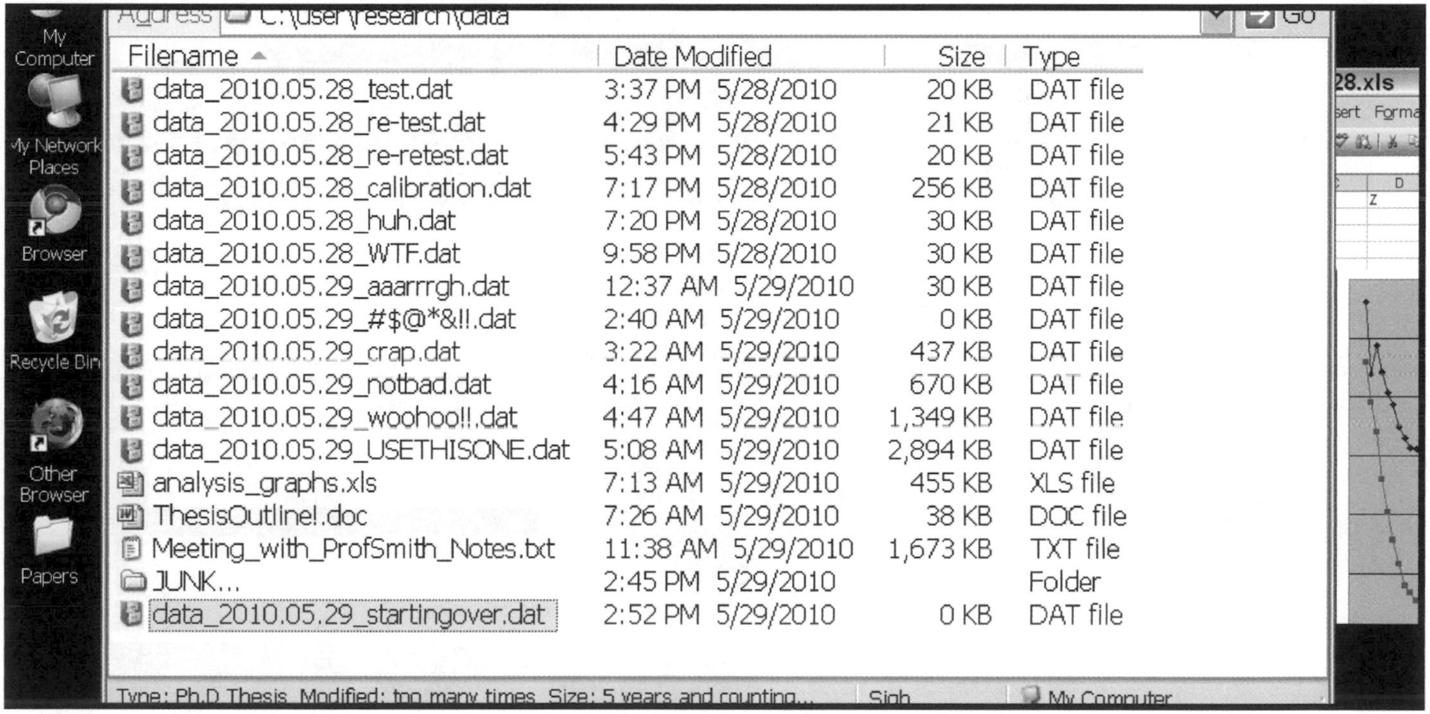

C:\user\research\data
Go
My Computer
Places
Browser
Other Browser
Papers
Filename
Date Modified
Size
Type
data_2010.05.28_test.dat 3:37 PM 5/28/2010 20 KB DAT file
data_2010.05.28_re-test.dat 4:29 PM 5/28/2010 21 KB DAT file
data_2010.05.28_re-retest.dat 5:43 PM 5/28/2010 20 KB DAT file
data_2010.05.28_calibration.dat 7:17 PM 5/28/2010 256 KB DAT file
data_2010.05.28_huh.dat 7:20 PM 5/28/2010 30 KB DAT file
data_2010.05.28_WTF.dat 9:58 PM 5/28/2010 30 KB DAT file
data_2010.05.29_aaarrrgh.dat 12:37 AM 5/29/2010 30 KB DAT file
data_2010.05.29_#$@*&!!.dat 2:40 AM 5/29/2010 0 KB DAT file
data_2010.05.29_crap.dat 3:22 AM 5/29/2010 437 KB DAT file
data_2010.05.29_notbad.dat 4:16 AM 5/29/2010 670 KB DAT file
data_2010.05.29_woohoo!!.dat 4:47 AM 5/29/2010 1,349 KB DAT file
data_2010.05.29_USETHISONE.dat 5:08 AM 5/29/2010 2,894 KB DAT file
analysis_graphs.xls 7:13 AM 5/29/2010 455 KB XLS file
ThesisOutline!.doc 7:26 AM 5/29/2010 38 KB DOC file
Meeting_with_ProfSmith_Notes.txt 11:38 AM 5/29/2010 1,673 KB TXT file
JUNK... 2:45 PM 5/29/2010 Folder
data_2010.05.29_startingover.dat 2:52 PM 5/29/2010 0 KB DAT file
Type: Ph.D Thesis Modified: too many times Size: 5 years and counting...
Sigh
My Computer

WWW.PHDCOMICS.COM

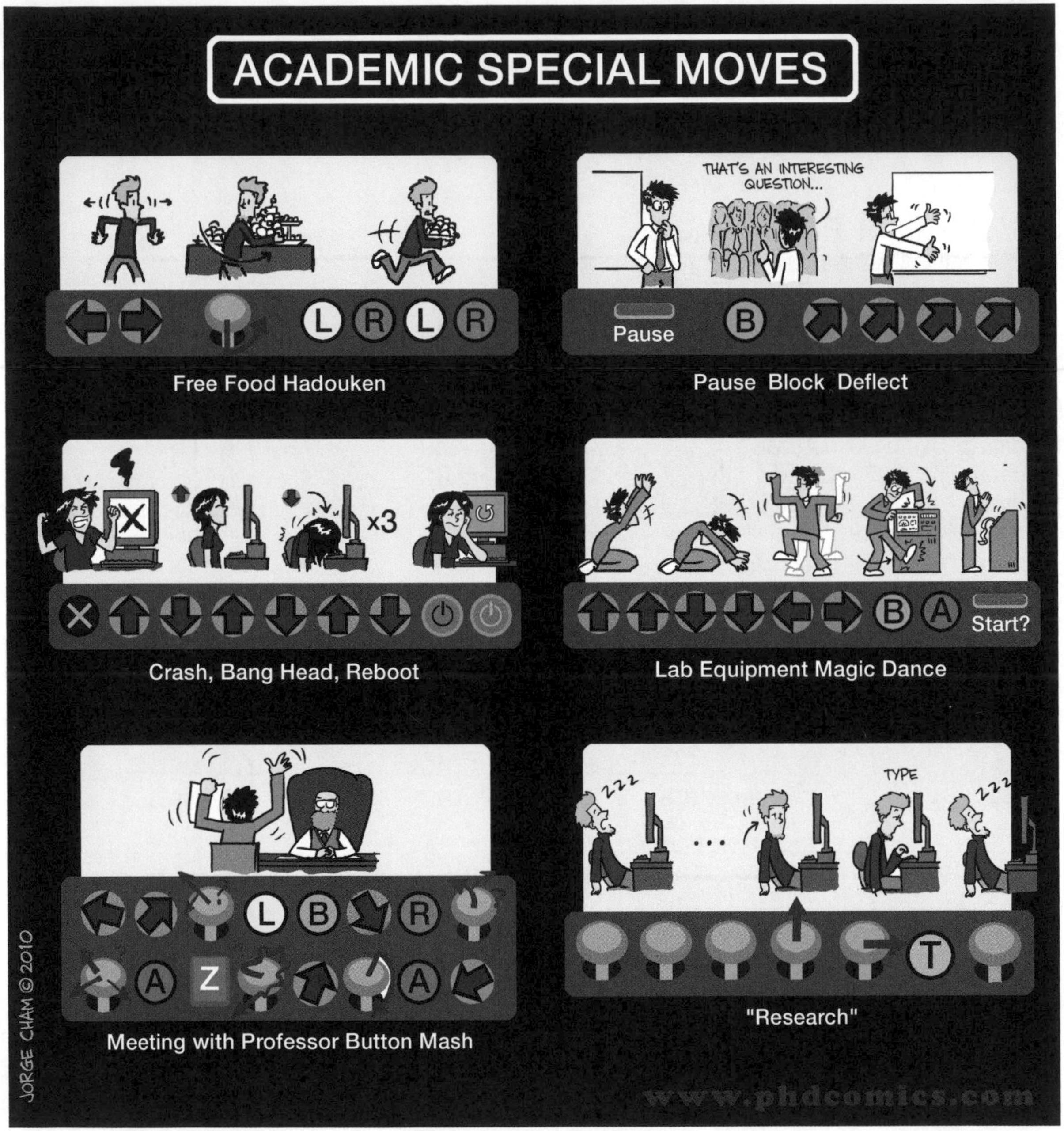
ACADEMIC SPECIAL MOVES
L R L R
Free Food Hadouken
THAT'S AN INTERESTING QUESTION...
Pause
B
Pause Block Deflect
x3
Crash, Bang Head, Reboot
B A
Start?
Lab Equipment Magic Dance
L B R
A Z A
Meeting with Professor Button Mash
ZZZ
...
TYPE
ZZZ
T
"Research"
JORGE CHAM © 2010
www.phdcomics.com

HOW DID IT GO?
UGH, NOT GOOD.
NOBODY IS HIRING IN FINANCE.
IF I DON'T FIND A JOB SOON, I DON'T KNOW WHAT WE'RE GOING TO DO.
JORGE CHAM © 2010
HAVE NO FEAR, JEN. SOPHY AND I HAVE THE PERFECT SOLUTION FOR THESE TRYING ECONOMIC TIMES.
SO... WHAT? WE'RE JUST GONNA WALK UP AND GRAB FOOD?
IT'S FREE!
IT'S NOT "FREE"
DO YOU SEE ANYONE PAYING FOR IT?
NO, BUT, IT'S BEEN LAID OUT FOR A REASON!
JORGE CHAM © 2010
TECHNICALLY, THAT WOULD NOT INTERFERE WITH THE DEFINITION OF FREE.
WHAT ARE WE TEACHING OUR DAUGHTER??
FREEDOM IS GOOD.

EVERYONE IS WEARING SUITS, MIKE. I DON'T KNOW IF I CAN DO THIS!
JACKPOT.
JEN, THE ONLY THING WE HAVE TO FEAR IS FEAR THEY'LL RUN OUT OF FOOD.
JORGE CHAM © 2010
FREE FOOD FAVORS THE BOLD!
WE HAVE NOTHING TO LOSE!
...(EXCEPT OUR DIGNITY).
TOO LATE.

PROCESS THE DATA USING METHOD X.
UH, THAT WON'T WORK. WE TRIED IT LAST YEAR.
REALLY?
YEAH, REMEMBER? I SPENT WEEKS ON IT BECAUSE YOU INSISTED IT SHOULD WORK.
JORGE CHAM © 2010
HMM.
SHOULD I TRY IT AGAIN?
NO, NO. THAT WOULD BE A WASTE OF EFFORT.
I'LL ASK ONE OF THE OTHER STUDENTS TO DO IT.
I'M... ACTUALLY OK WITH THAT.

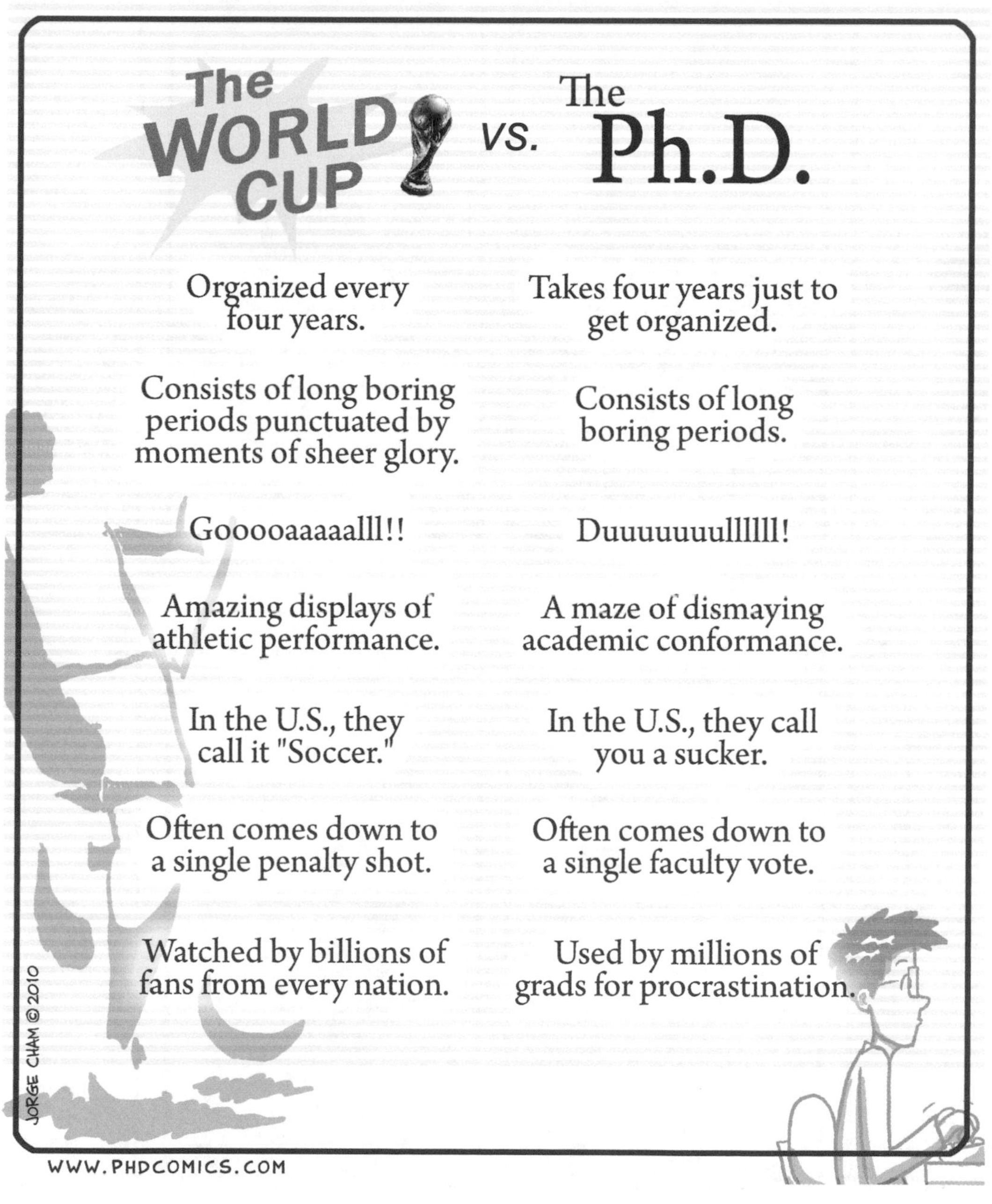
The WORLD CUP vs. The Ph.D.
Organized every four years.
Takes four years just to get organized.
Consists of long boring periods punctuated by moments of sheer glory.
Consists of long boring periods.
Goooooaaaaalll!!
Duuuuuuulllllll!
Amazing displays of athletic performance.
A maze of dismaying academic conformance.
In the U.S., they call it "Soccer."
In the U.S., they call you a sucker.
Often comes down to a single penalty shot.
Often comes down to a single faculty vote.
Watched by billions of fans from every nation.
Used by millions of grads for procrastination.
JORGE CHAM © 2010
WWW.PHDCOMICS.COM

SO, I WAS THINKING THAT THE DATA COULD-
UM...
JORGE CHAM © 2010
ZZZZ...
YOUR PROFESSOR FELL ASLEEP. DO YOU:
a) LEAVE QUIETLY
b) COUGH POLITELY
c) WONDER IF THIS IS THE MOST AWKWARD SITUATION YOU'VE EVER BEEN IN.
zzzz

zzzz
WHTRMM ZZZZ URMLKD
JORGE CHAM © 2010
zzzz
ZZZzzz

YAAAAWWWN..!
TIRED?
BORED.
JORGE CHAM © 2010
SHOULD I COME BACK..?
WHEN YOU HAVE MORE EXCITING RESULTS, YES.
REALLY? THESE KEPT ME UP ALL NIGHT.
ZZZZ.

HMM, FRIDAY AFTERNOON.
BETTER CHECK THIS WEEK'S TO-DO LIST.
TO DO:
☐ REVIEW JOURNAL PAPERS
☐ COORDINATE CONFERENCE WORKSHOP
☐ PREPARE SLIDES FOR SPONSOR VISIT
☐ WRITE GRANT EXPERIMENTAL SECTION
☐ PASS OFF TO-DO LIST TO GRAD STUDENTS
JORGE CHAM © 2010
THAT WAS EASY.

Call for Papers!

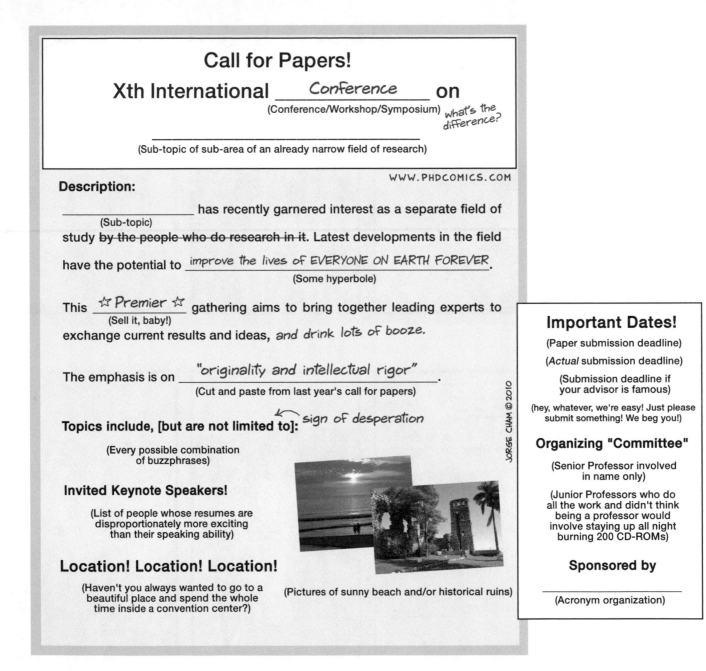

Xth International ___Conference___ on

(Conference/Workshop/Symposium) *what's the difference?*

____
(Sub-topic of sub-area of an already narrow field of research)

WWW.PHDCOMICS.COM

Description:

______________ has recently garnered interest as a separate field of
(Sub-topic)
study ~~by the people who do research in it~~. Latest developments in the field have the potential to *improve the lives of EVERYONE ON EARTH FOREVER*.
(Some hyperbole)

This *☆ Premier ☆* gathering aims to bring together leading experts to
(Sell it, baby!)
exchange current results and ideas, *and drink lots of booze.*

The emphasis is on *"originality and intellectual rigor"*.
(Cut and paste from last year's call for papers)

Topics include, [but are not limited to]: ← *sign of desperation*

(Every possible combination of buzzphrases)

Invited Keynote Speakers!

(List of people whose resumes are disproportionately more exciting than their speaking ability)

Location! Location! Location!

(Haven't you always wanted to go to a beautiful place and spend the whole time inside a convention center?)

(Pictures of sunny beach and/or historical ruins)

JORGE CHAM © 2010

Important Dates!

(Paper submission deadline)

(*Actual* submission deadline)

(Submission deadline if your advisor is famous)

(hey, whatever, we're easy! Just please submit something! We beg you!)

Organizing "Committee"

(Senior Professor involved in name only)

(Junior Professors who do all the work and didn't think being a professor would involve staying up all night burning 200 CD-ROMs)

Sponsored by

____
(Acronym organization)

HOLIDAY!

HOW A NORMAL PERSON CELEBRATES:
WOO HOO! NO WORK TODAY!
JORGE CHAM © 2010
HOW A GRAD STUDENT CELEBRATES:
WOO HOO! FREE PARKING TODAY!

Status Update:
Proposal accepted!! Woo hoo!!!
RIIIING!!
JORGE CHAM © 2010
HELLO?
NO, MOM. I MEANT MY THESIS PROPOSAL. I'M NOT GETTING MARR-
CLICK.
THE DANGERS OF SOCIAL NETWORKING.

WHY DON'T WE JUST ASK SOMEONE IF THE FOOD IS FREE?
NOOOO... THAT'S THE LAST THING YOU WANT TO DO!
WHY NOT?
PLAUSIBLE DENIABILITY.
JORGE CHAM © 2010
THAT WAY, IF SOMEONE ASKS, YOU CAN SAY YOU DIDN'T KNOW THE FOOD WASN'T FREE!
LIKE WHEN YOU SAID YOU DIDN'T KNOW THE PH.D. WOULD TAKE THAT LONG?
I HAD NO IDEA!

NO, NO, YOU WANT VEGGIES ON THE BOTTOM, PROTEINS ON TOP...
YOU CAN GET A MUCH HIGHER MEAT STRUCTURE THIS WAY...
JORGE CHAM © 2010
WHAT ABOUT CARBS?
THAT'S WHAT POCKETS ARE FOR!
AHEM.
THE HARD PART IS RUNNING WITH ALL THIS STUFF.

UH, MIKE?
STAND BACK!
JORGE CHAM © 2010
C'MON! NOT EVEN A SMILE!
those cold, cold eyes...

PANT PANT... DID WE LOSE HER??
who knew you could run that fast in heels?
OH MAN, THERE GOES DINNER!
WAIT, WHAT'S SOPHY HOLDING?
JORGE CHAM © 2010

I HAVE TO ADMIT, THAT WAS ACTUALLY KIND OF FUN..!
HEY, MAYBE I'LL GO BACK TO GRAD SCHOOL INSTEAD OF GETTING A JOB! I COULD GET AN M.B.A!
WHOA WHOA..!
JORGE CHAM © 2010
JEN, YOU KNOW I SUPPORT YOU IN EVERYTHING, BUT IN THIS CASE I HAVE TO DRAW THE LINE...
IS AN M.B.A. REALLY "GRAD SCHOOL"?
i mean, "business administration"?

SO, HOW'S THE THESIS GOING, CECILIA?
IT'S NOT GOING, PROF. JONES!
I'VE BEEN SWAMPED WITH ALL THE THINGS YOU'VE ASKED ME TO DO!
GRADE PAPERS, ORGANIZE SEMINARS, PREPARE SLIDES...
JORGE CHAM © 2010
IT'S LIKE YOU DON'T THINK I HAVE ANYTHING BETTER TO DO!
DO YOU?
YES!
BETTER... FOR ME?

YOU'RE RIGHT, CECILIA. I SHOULD LET YOU FOCUS ON YOUR THESIS.
IF YOU KEEP DOING ALL THESE MENIAL TASKS FOR ME, YOU'RE NEVER GOING TO GRADUATE.
JORGE CHAM © 2010
ALTHOUGH... IF YOU NEVER GRADUATE, YOU'LL BE AROUND LONGER TO DO ALL MY MENIAL TASKS.
I'M JUST SAYING, THE INCENTIVES ARE NOT IN YOUR FAVOR.
YOU DON'T SAY.
THAT'S AN IMPORTANT LESSON IN GETTING A PH.D., CECILIA: LEARNING TO SAY "NO".
AS AN ACADEMIC, YOU'LL BE FACED WITH ENDLESS REQUESTS FOR YOUR TIME AND ATTENTION.
JORGE CHAM © 2010
IF YOU DON'T SAY NO TO THE ONES THAT DON'T MATTER, YOU'LL NEVER GET ANYTHING DONE.
REALLY? USUALLY YOU JUST IGNORE MY REQUESTS.
THAT'S ANOTHER LESSON.

YOUR "TO DO" LIST

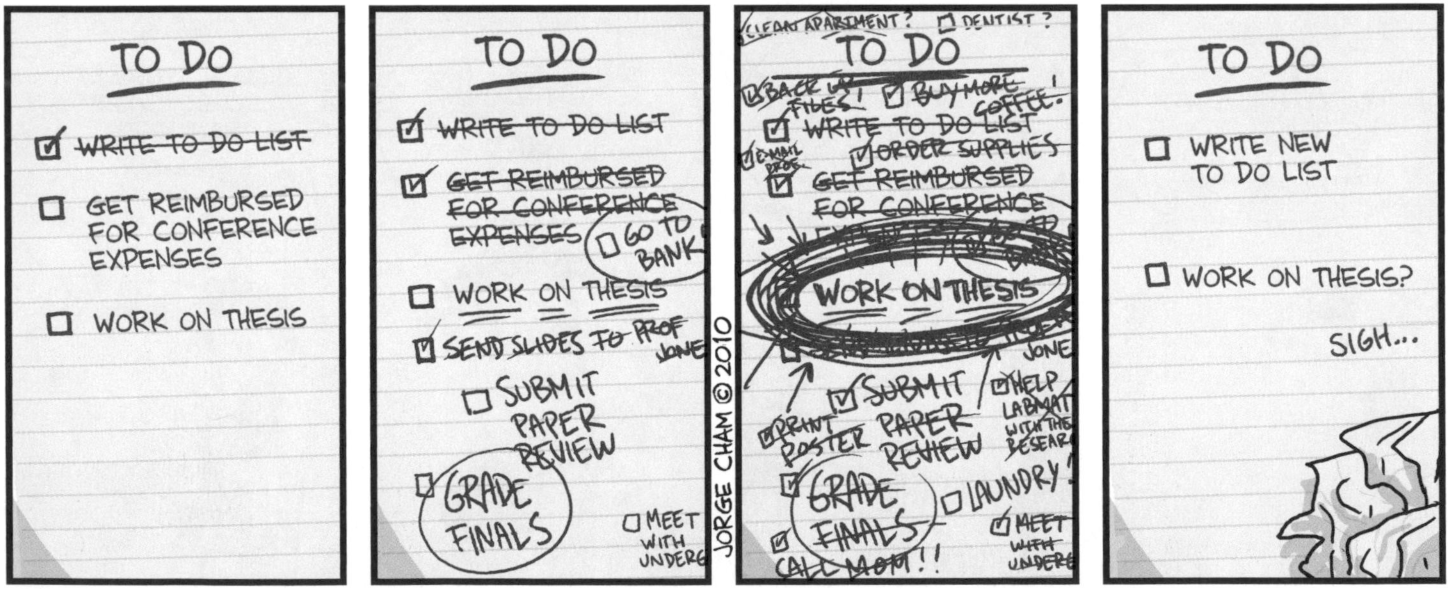

FROM NOW ON, I WILL NOT WORK ON ANYTHING ELSE EXCEPT MY THESIS..!
CECILIA, CAN YOU..?
NO.
WOULD YOU..?
NO.
JORGE CHAM © 2010
COULD YOU..?
NO.
WILL YOU..?
NO.
ANY PROGRESS?
NO...

ACTUALLY, IT HASN'T BEEN THAT BAD.
IT'S SLOW GOING, BUT...
...THAT'S OK.
CHAPTER 1
JORGE CHAM © 2010
I MEAN, ROME WASN'T BUILT IN A DAY! TOLSTOY DIDN'T WRITE "WAR AND PEACE" IN ONE SITTING..!
ACTUALLY, IT TOOK HIM SIX YEARS.
SIX-?
I'M ALREADY BEHIND!

THE PROBLEM IS THAT I WANT TO WORK ON MY THESIS...
...BUT WHEN I SIT DOWN TO WRITE, I CAN'T STAND BEING THERE!
JORGE CHAM © 2010
IF I MAP IT OUT AS A VECTOR FIELD, THERE'S A GENERAL ATTRACTOR POTENTIAL TOWARDS MY THESIS, BUT A STRONG LOCALIZED REPULSOR AT ITS CORE.
I HAVE A MATHEMATICAL MODEL OF WHY I HAVEN'T FINISHED MY THESIS.
I DON'T THINK MATH IS YOUR PROBLEM.

URGH... SO TIRED...
BUT I'M ALSO HUNGRY...
JORGE CHAM © 2010
SHOULD I EAT OR GO TO SLEEP?
EAT OR SLEEP?
EAT OR SLEEP?
THE 2am DILEMMA.
UURRRHHH...

THE THESIS REPULSOR FIELD

The Thesis Repulsor Field (TRF) is a generalized model of the forces experienced by an individual in the final stages of graduate space-time*.

It is characterized by an attractor vector field directed towards completion of the thesis but with an intense repulsive singularity at its origin.

Several trajectories are possible due to this vector field:

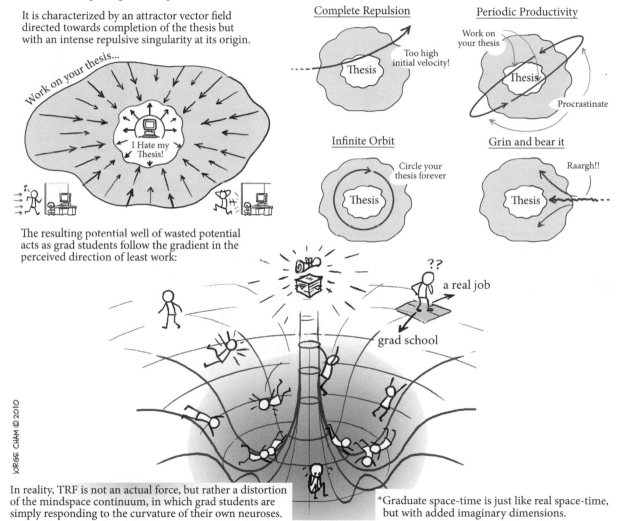

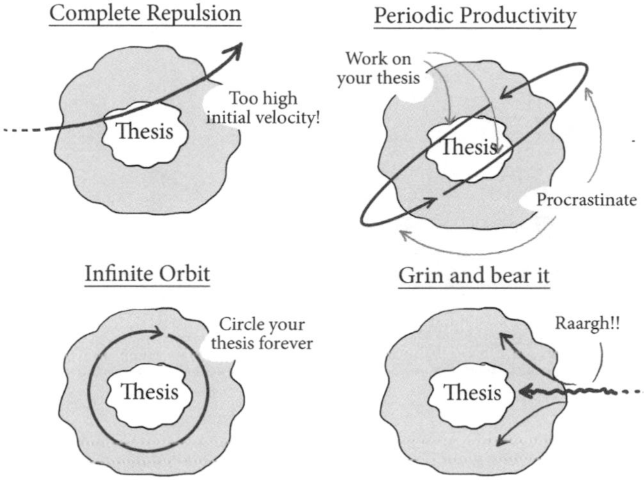

The resulting potential well of wasted potential acts as grad students follow the gradient in the perceived direction of least work:

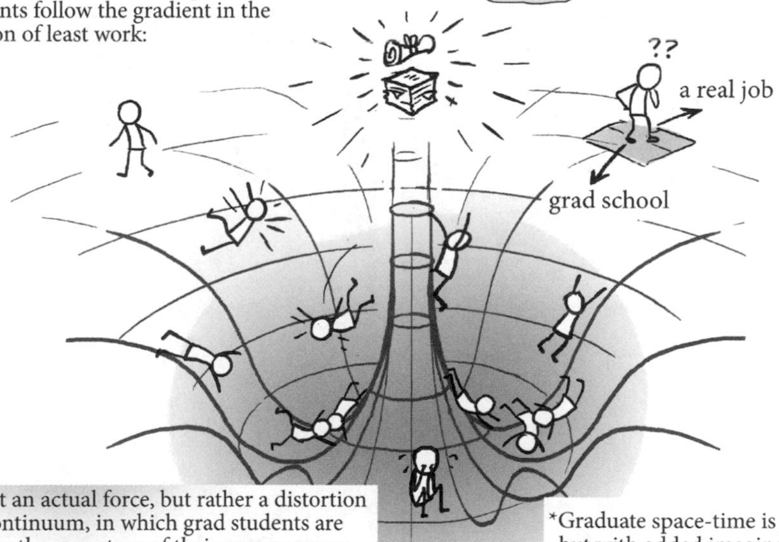

In reality, TRF is not an actual force, but rather a distortion of the mindspace continuum, in which grad students are simply responding to the curvature of their own neuroses.

*Graduate space-time is just like real space-time, but with added imaginary dimensions.

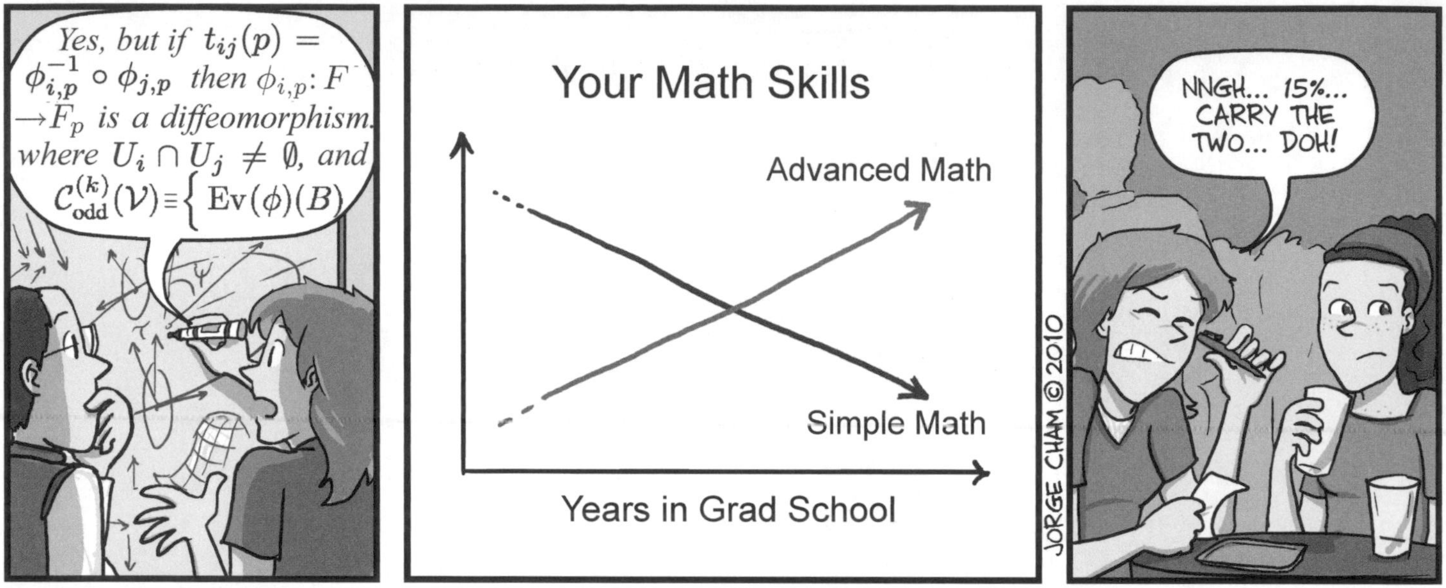
Yes, but if $t_{ij}(p) = \phi_{i,p}^{-1} \circ \phi_{j,p}$ then $\phi_{i,p}\colon F \to F_p$ is a diffeomorphism where $U_i \cap U_j \neq \emptyset$, and $\mathcal{C}^{(k)}_{\mathrm{odd}}(\mathcal{V}) \equiv \{ \mathrm{Ev}(\phi)(B)$
Your Math Skills
Advanced Math
Simple Math
Years in Grad School
JORGE CHAM © 2010
NNGH... 15%... CARRY THE TWO... DOH!

LOL Grads!
Pwned undrgrd n00bs!!!!
I'M IN UR OFFICE
WASTIN UR TIME.
JORGE CHAM © 2010
i can haz thesiz
plz??

HEY, MIKE IS A "POST"-DOC, RIGHT?
BECAUSE HE FINISHED HIS PH.D.?
YEAH.
WHAT DOES THAT MAKE US?
"PRE-DOCS"?
"SUB-DOCS"?
"ANTE-DOCS"?
??
"POST-DOC"
PhD.
t
JORGE CHAM © 2010
"UNDER-DOCS."
WE ARE FAVORED TO LOSE.

OK, SO IF YOU'RE A "PRE"-DOC BEFORE GETTING A PH.D.,
AND A "POST"-DOC AFTER THE PH.D...
"PRE" DOC
"POST" DOC
PhD
t
...THAT MEANS YOU'RE ONLY A "DOC" FOR AN INFINITESIMAL AMOUNT OF TIME!
PhD
WE'VE BEEN SPENDING YEARS ON WHAT IS ESSENTIALLY AN INSTANTANEOUS PROPERTY!
JORGE CHAM © 2010
IS IT WORTH IT, MIKE?
I DON'T KNOW. I MUST HAVE BLINKED.

OK, WHAT ABOUT STEVE OVER THERE?
HE ALREADY DEFENDED AND SUBMITTED HIS THESIS, HE'S JUST WAITING AROUND UNTIL THEY OFFICIALLY GIVE HIM THE DEGREE.
WHAT DO YOU CALL THAT?
HEEY. S'UP.
JORGE CHAM © 2010
A LAME DOC.
WHAT?

AH, THE FALL SEASON...
A TIME OF RENEWAL.
OLD LEAVES FADING AWAY, MAKING WAY FOR FRESH NEW ONES...
JORGE CHAM © 2010
ARE YOU SAYING I NEED TO GRADUATE?
JUST FALL OFF THE TREE.

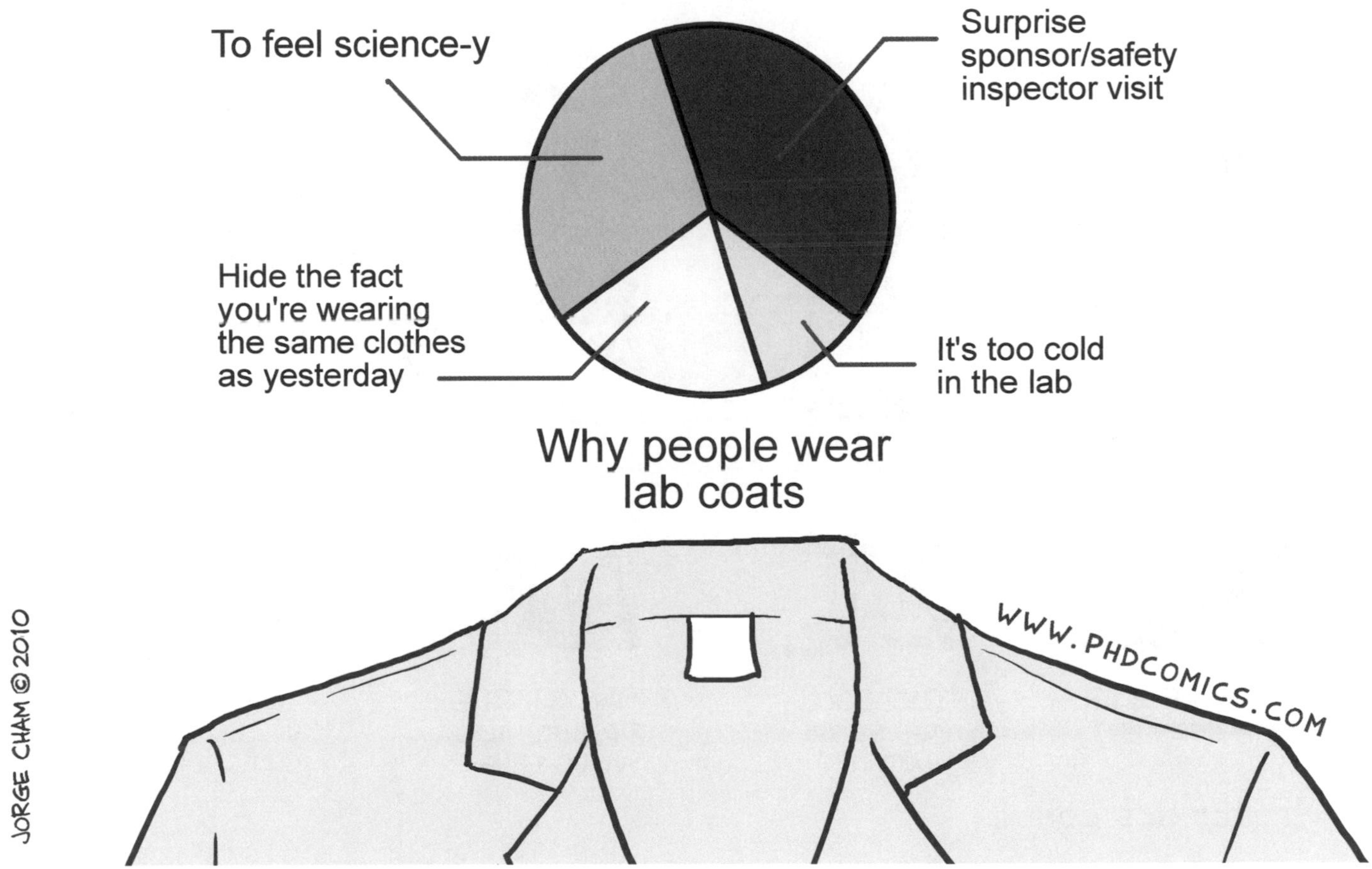
To feel science-y
Surprise sponsor/safety inspector visit
Hide the fact you're wearing the same clothes as yesterday
It's too cold in the lab
Why people wear lab coats
JORGE CHAM © 2010
WWW.PHDCOMICS.COM

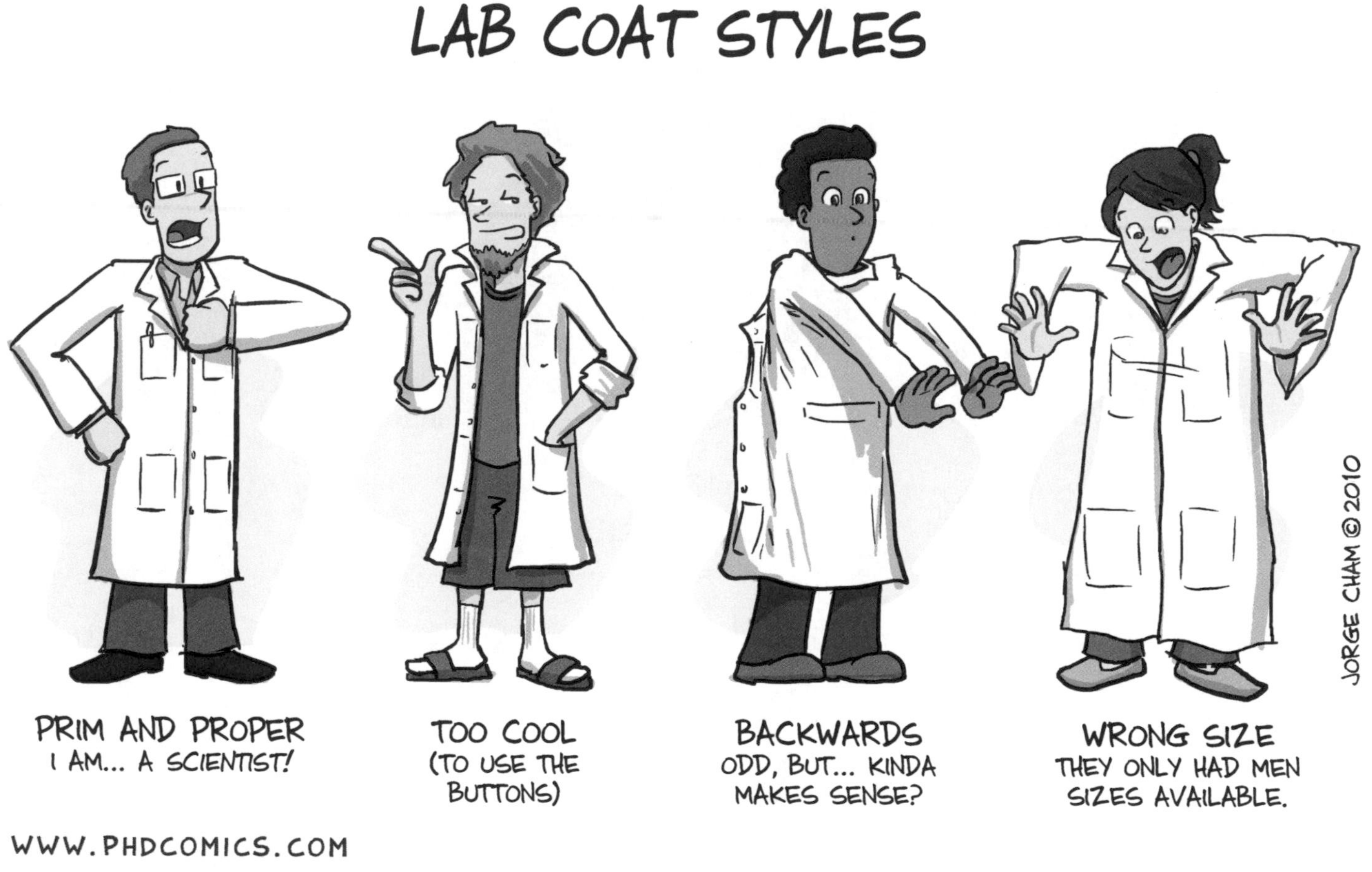
LAB COAT STYLES
JORGE CHAM © 2010
PRIM AND PROPER
I AM... A SCIENTIST!
TOO COOL
(TO USE THE BUTTONS)
BACKWARDS
ODD, BUT... KINDA MAKES SENSE?
WRONG SIZE
THEY ONLY HAD MEN SIZES AVAILABLE.
WWW.PHDCOMICS.COM

THE LAB COAT RACK

WHEREIN THE PURPOSE OF THE LAB COAT IS UTTERLY DEFEATED.

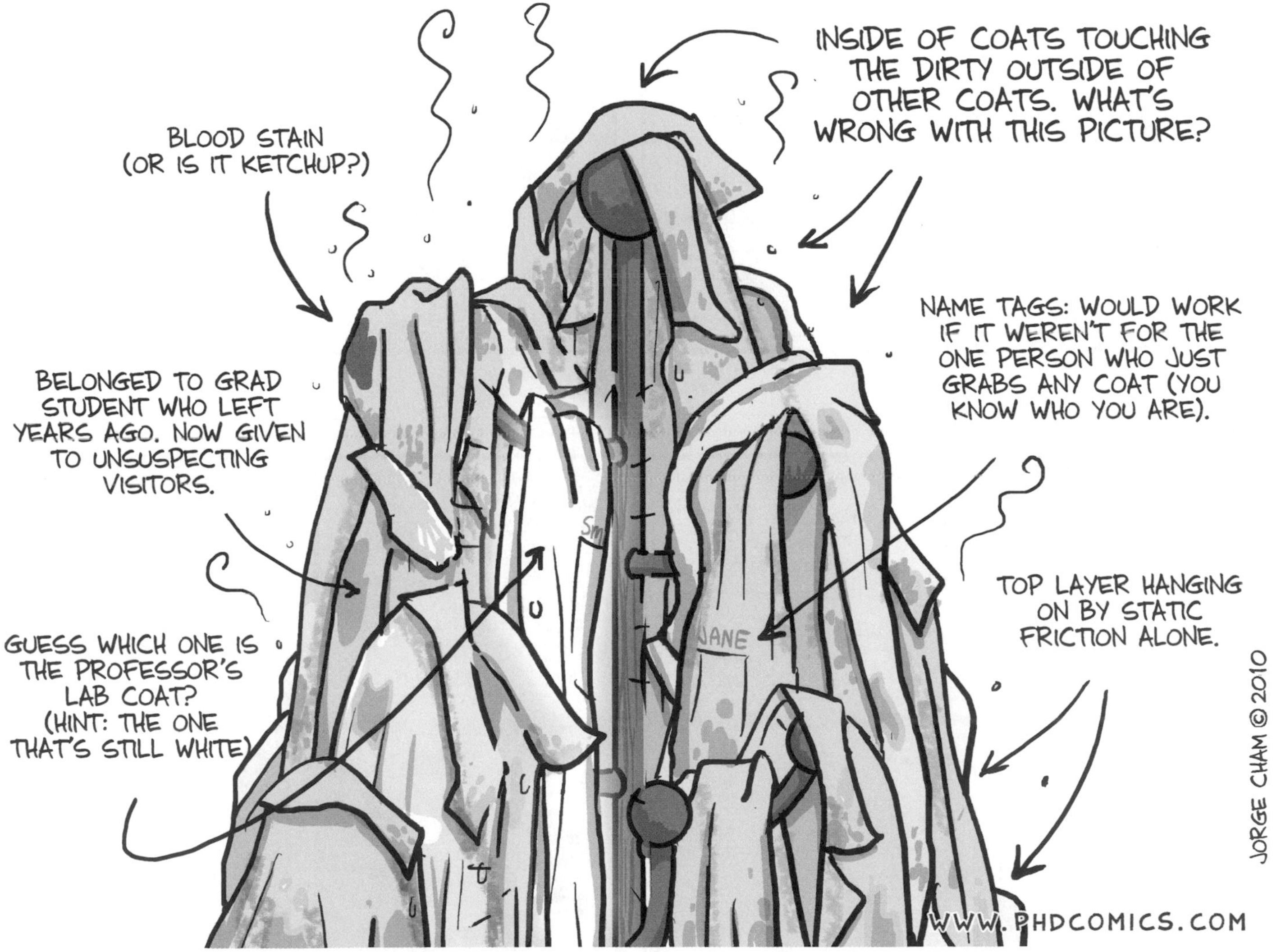

PERHAPS IT'S TIME WE CAME UP WITH A PLAN FOR HOW YOU'RE GOING TO FINISH YOUR THESIS.
ARE YOU READY? HERE IT IS.
I'M GOING TO TELL YOU THAT YOU NEED TO FINISH YOUR THESIS, AND YOU'RE GOING TO DO IT.
JORGE CHAM © 2010
THAT DOESN'T INVOLVE YOU VERY MUCH.
THAT'S THE PLAN.

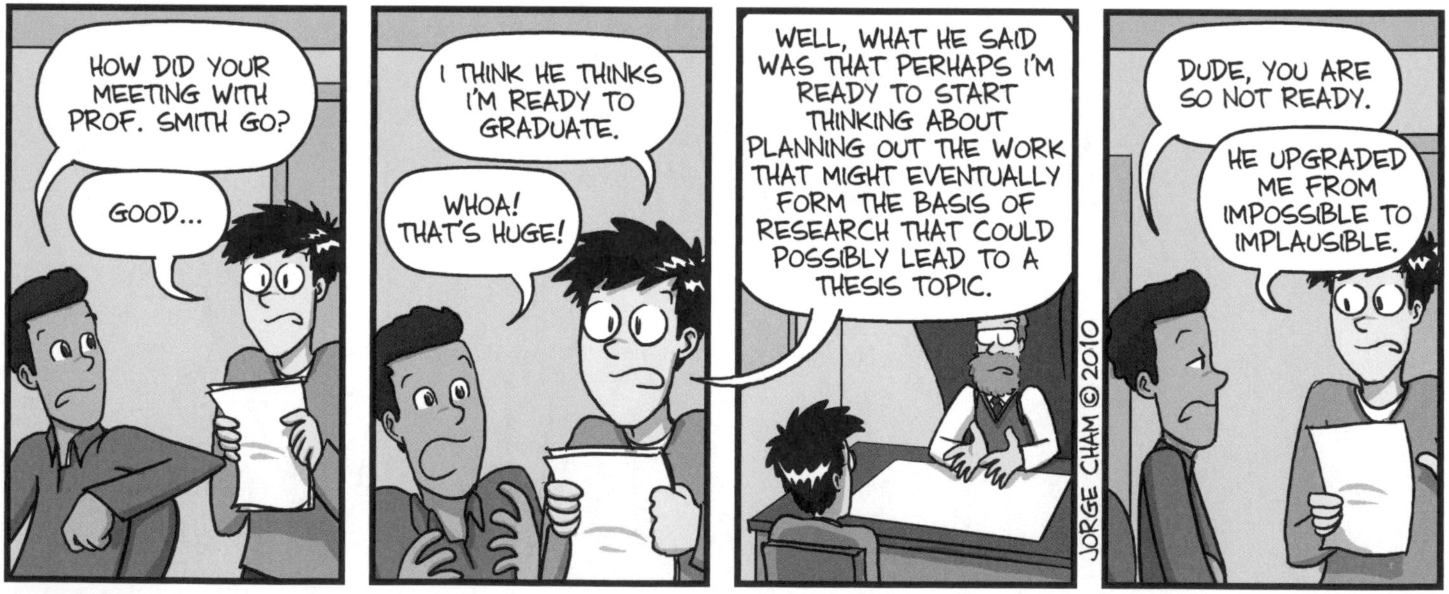
HOW DID YOUR MEETING WITH PROF. SMITH GO?
GOOD...
I THINK HE THINKS I'M READY TO GRADUATE.
WHOA! THAT'S HUGE!
WELL, WHAT HE SAID WAS THAT PERHAPS I'M READY TO START THINKING ABOUT PLANNING OUT THE WORK THAT MIGHT EVENTUALLY FORM THE BASIS OF RESEARCH THAT COULD POSSIBLY LEAD TO A THESIS TOPIC.
JORGE CHAM © 2010
DUDE, YOU ARE SO NOT READY.
HE UPGRADED ME FROM IMPOSSIBLE TO IMPLAUSIBLE.

AREN'T YOU BEING A LITTLE PARANOID?
ENTHUSIASM IS HIGHLY CONTAGIOUS!
JORGE CHAM © 2010

FALL TERM
BACK TO SCHOOL SALE!
To: All *returning* grad students...
SO, ARE YOU "BACK IN SCHOOL"?
I'VE BEEN HERE THE WHOLE TIME!
JORGE CHAM © 2010

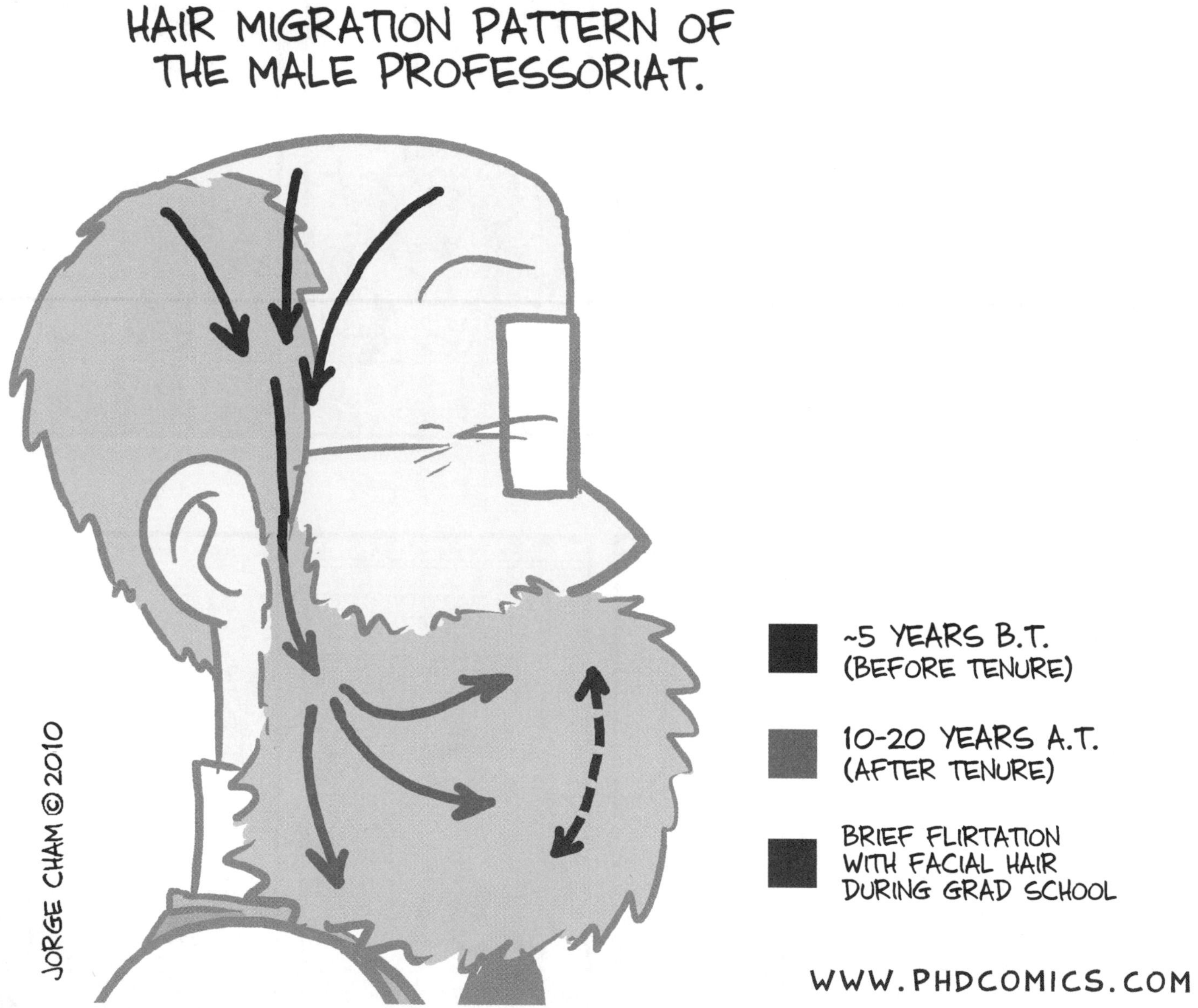
HAIR MIGRATION PATTERN OF THE MALE PROFESSORIAT.
~5 YEARS B.T. (BEFORE TENURE)
10-20 YEARS A.T. (AFTER TENURE)
BRIEF FLIRTATION WITH FACIAL HAIR DURING GRAD SCHOOL
JORGE CHAM © 2010
WWW.PHDCOMICS.COM

Prof. Rivera,
Is there a time we can meet to discuss my thesis?
Ping!
Reply from Prof. Rivera!
tajel,
i have about 20 minutes right now. after that i'll be out of the country for the next 5 months.
JORGE CHAM © 2010
20 MINUTES HERE I COME!!
I MUST ADMIT, TAJEL, I HAVEN'T READ THAT LAST DRAFT YOU SENT ME.
NOR HAVE I READ ANY OF THE MULTIPLE E-MAILS, NOTES, OR PAPERS YOU'VE LEFT ME.
IN OTHER WORDS, I HAVE NO IDEA WHAT'S GOING ON WITH YOU OR YOUR LIFE.
CAN YOU GIVE ME THE FIVE MINUTE VERSION?
JORGE CHAM © 2010
IT'LL TAKE ME LONGER THAN FIVE MINUTES TO TELL YOU WHAT I'M THINKING RIGHT NOW.
FOUR MINUTES NOW.

...AND SO, THAT'S WHAT I'VE BEEN STRUGGLING WITH FOR THE LAST FIVE MONTHS, PROF. RIVERA.
HMM, DID YOU TRY A TRANS-ETHNOCENTRIC COMPARATIVE APPROACH?
I-
HUH. I HADN'T THOUGHT OF THAT.
JORGE CHAM © 2010
YOU JUST SOLVED MY PROBLEM IN FIVE MINUTES.
GREAT. SEE YOU IN FIVE MONTHS.

MIKE, I KNOW I DON'T SAY THIS ENOUGH, BUT...
I REALLY APPRECIATE THE WORK THAT YOU DO.
YOU DO?
OH, ABSOLUTELY.
JORGE CHAM © 2010
I JUST WISH YOU'D DO MORE OF IT.

I'LL BE OUT OF THE COUNTRY FOR THE NEXT FIVE MONTHS, TAJEL.
MY LOCATION WILL BE UNKNOWN AND MY INTERNET ACCESS WILL BE SPORADIC SO I MAY NOT REPLY TO YOUR E-MAILS.
I ALSO WON'T BE ABLE TO READ YOUR DRAFTS OR ANSWER ANY QUESTIONS FACE TO FACE.
JORGE CHAM © 2010
IN OTHER WORDS, IT'LL BE AS IF I NEVER LEFT.
I MISS YOU ALREADY.

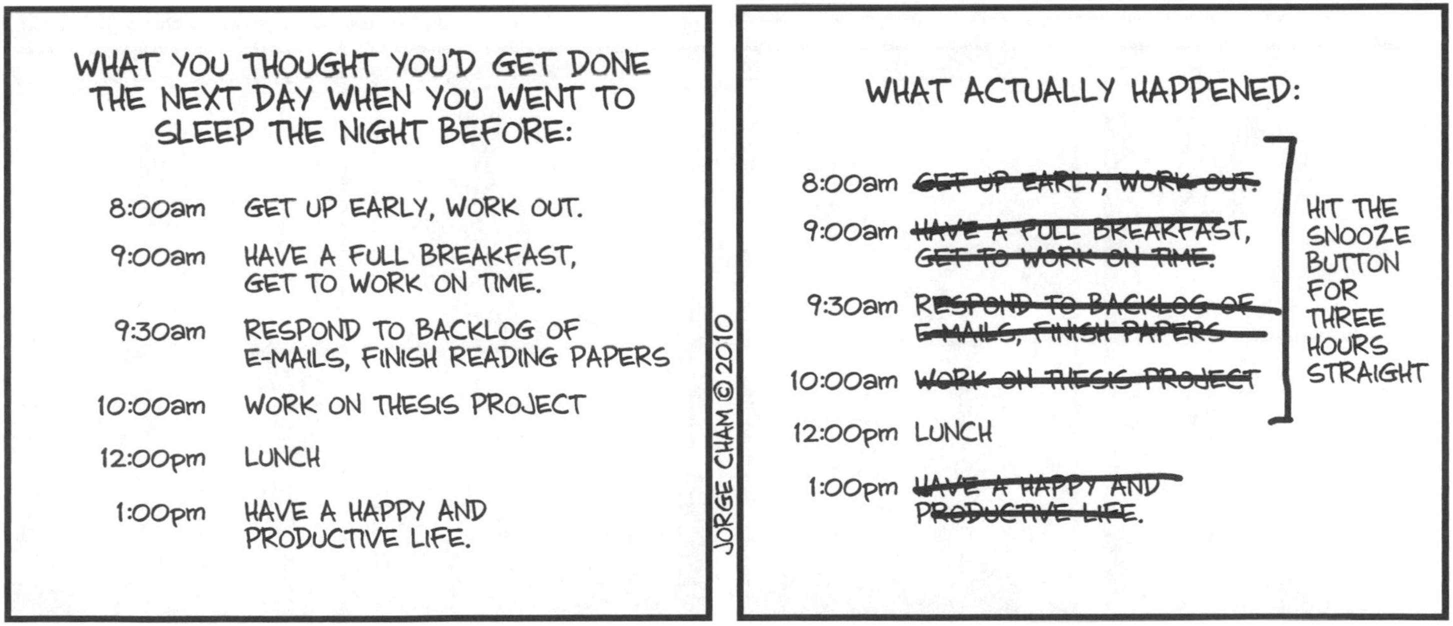
WHAT YOU THOUGHT YOU'D GET DONE THE NEXT DAY WHEN YOU WENT TO SLEEP THE NIGHT BEFORE:
8:00am GET UP EARLY, WORK OUT.
9:00am HAVE A FULL BREAKFAST, GET TO WORK ON TIME.
9:30am RESPOND TO BACKLOG OF E-MAILS, FINISH READING PAPERS
10:00am WORK ON THESIS PROJECT
12:00pm LUNCH
1:00pm HAVE A HAPPY AND PRODUCTIVE LIFE.
JORGE CHAM © 2010
WHAT ACTUALLY HAPPENED:
8:00am ~~GET UP EARLY, WORK OUT.~~
9:00am ~~HAVE A FULL BREAKFAST, GET TO WORK ON TIME.~~
9:30am ~~RESPOND TO BACKLOG OF E-MAILS, FINISH PAPERS~~
10:00am ~~WORK ON THESIS PROJECT~~
HIT THE SNOOZE BUTTON FOR THREE HOURS STRAIGHT
12:00pm LUNCH
1:00pm ~~HAVE A HAPPY AND PRODUCTIVE LIFE.~~

beep beep beep bee-
SIGH...
MY BRAIN IS TELLING ME TO GET UP...
...BUT MY BODY IS TELLING ME TO STAY IN BED.
WHO SHOULD I LISTEN TO??
JORGE CHAM © 2010
ME. GET TO WORK.
MY SUB-CONSCIENCE.

JORGE CHAM © 2010
ZZZ

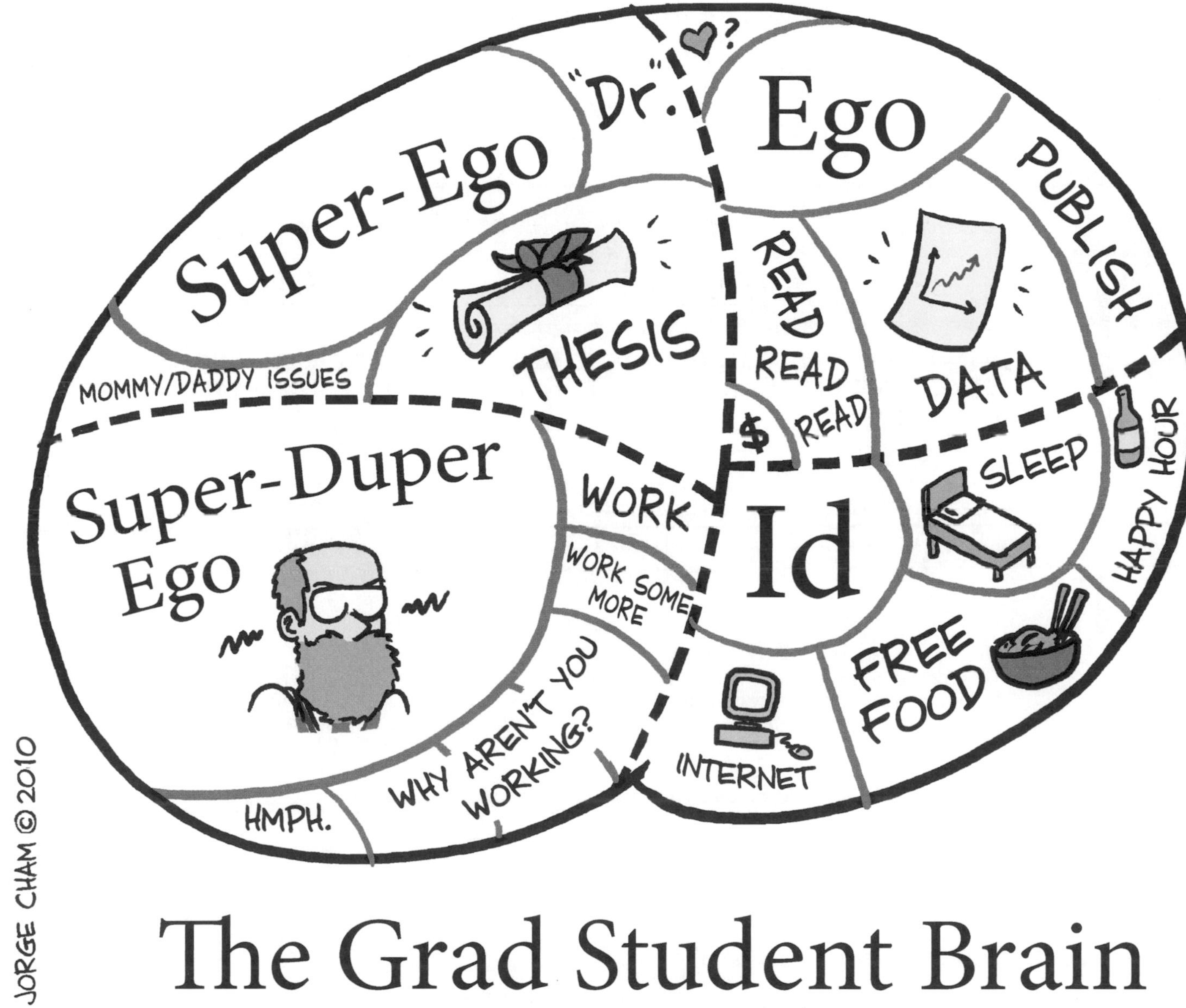

The Grad Student Brain

	Married (or Domestic Partner)	With Kids
Likelihood of stopping out of the Ph.D.:	More likely to stay in Ph.D. Program (odds of stopping = 0.655)	Less likely to stay in Ph.D. Program (odds of stopping = 1.641)
Average time to finish Ph.D.:	Shorter time to graduate (approx. 4 mo. shorter)	Longer time to graduate (approx. 5 mo. longer)

This message brought to you by PROfessors for RESponsible Engagements with Abstinence and/or Retracted CHild-bearing (PRO-RESEARCH). Source: Nettles and Millet, Survey of Doctoral Student Finances, Experiences and Achievements.

IT'S TAKEN ME THREE YEARS, AND I HAD TO START OVER SEVERAL TIMES...
...BUT I THINK I FINALLY HAVE SOME GOOD RESULTS, PROF. SMITH.
HMM, YES.
THIS WILL MAKE A GOOD FIGURE 1 FOR YOUR THESIS.
JORGE CHAM © 2010
JUST 1??
1-A.

YOUR RESULTS ARE UTTERLY LACKING AND INADEQUATE COMPARED TO MY EXPECTATIONS.
WHAT DO YOU HAVE TO SAY FOR YOURSELF?
I... I...
Grad Student
An exception has occured at 09:28:02 in xAdvisorOffice. It is impossible to continue normally.
Press CTRL+ALT+ESC to panic.
You will lose all unsaved dignity.
JORGE CHAM © 2010
GREAT. THE BLUE SCREEN OF DEARTH.
uhh...

YOUR RATE OF PROGRESS IS UNACCEPTABLY SLOW.
FROM NOW ON, I EXPECT YOU TO DOUBLE YOUR EFFORTS.
YOU'RE GOING TO WORK TWICE AS HARD, SLEEP HALF AS MUCH, AND SPEND TWICE AS MUCH TIME IN THE LAB.
JORGE CHAM © 2010
WILL THAT DOUBLE MY CHANCES OF GRADUATING?
THAT'S STILL 50/50.

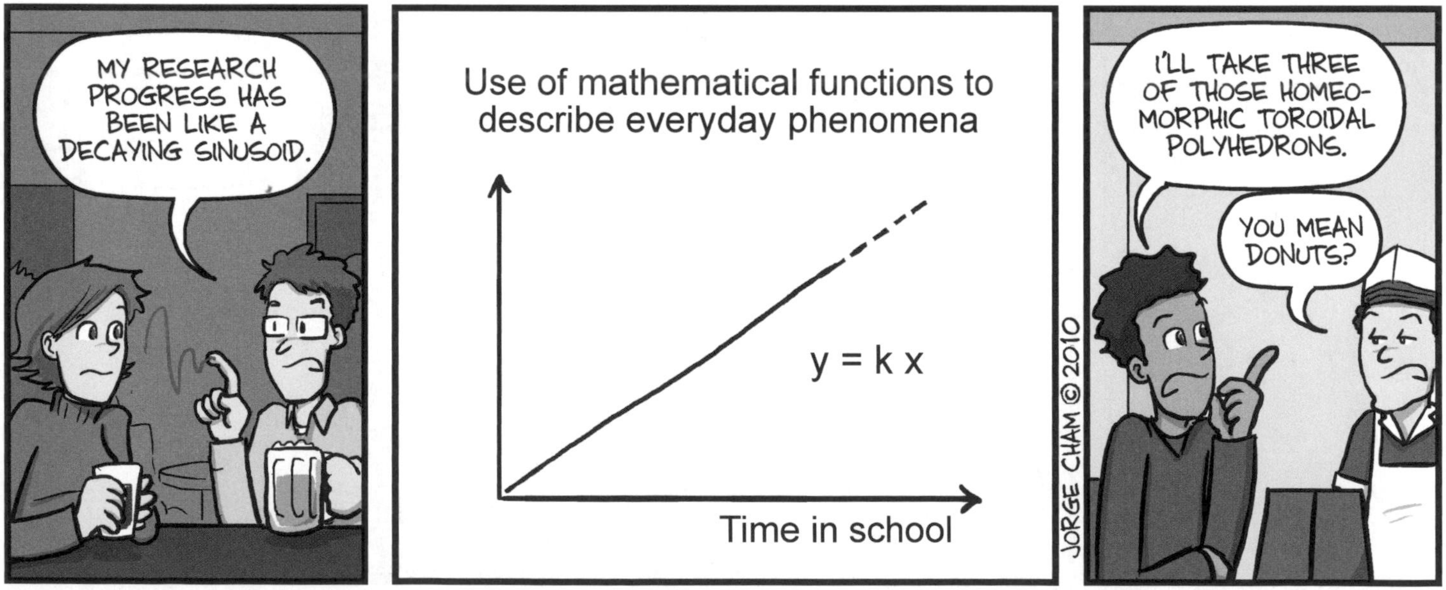
MY RESEARCH PROGRESS HAS BEEN LIKE A DECAYING SINUSOID.
Use of mathematical functions to describe everyday phenomena
y = k x
Time in school
JORGE CHAM © 2010
I'LL TAKE THREE OF THOSE HOMEO-MORPHIC TOROIDAL POLYHEDRONS.
YOU MEAN DONUTS?

SATURDAY MORNING...
OH, WHAT HORRIBLE WEATHER!
YES!!
JORGE CHAM © 2010
NOW I DON'T FEEL SO BAD ABOUT STAYING IN TO GRADE PAPERS.

I WANT YOU TO SEND ME THE LATEST DRAFT OF YOUR PAPER.
UM, OK, BUT... IT'S STILL IN DRAFT FORM. IT'S MISSING SOME FIGURES, THERE'S LOTS OF TYPOS AND IT NEEDS MORE REFERENCES.
YES, YES. I UNDERSTAND.
JORGE CHAM © 2010
BUT HE DIDN'T.
MISSING FIGURES?
TYPOS!
MORE REFERENCES!
WHAT'S WRONG WITH YOU??

Procrastination

Ideally:

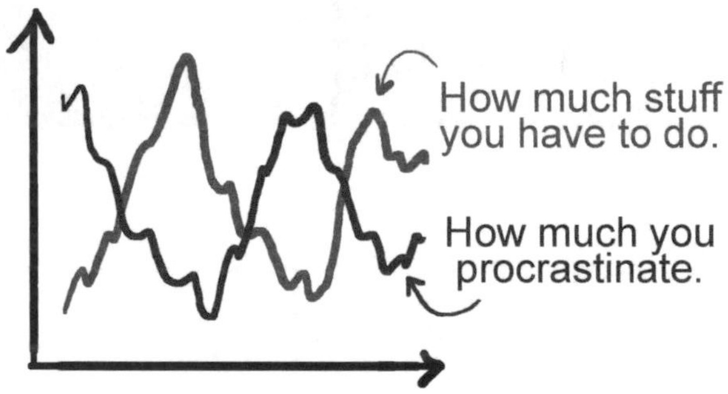

$$\text{Procrastination} \propto \frac{1}{\text{How much stuff you have to do}}$$

In reality:

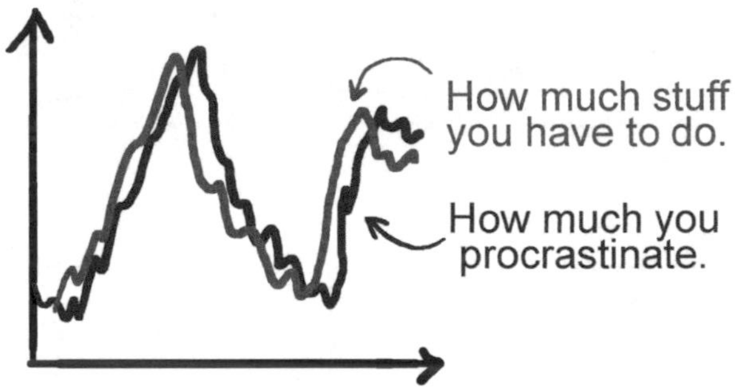

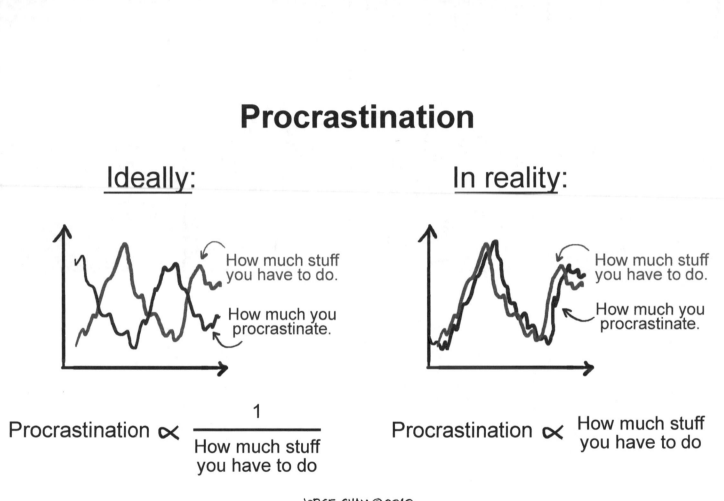

$$\text{Procrastination} \propto \text{How much stuff you have to do}$$

TRICK OR TREAT!!
ding dong!
creeak...
AAAAIIIEEEEEEEE!!!
JORGE CHAM © 2010
A GRAD STUDENT!!
WHAT? I'VE BEEN GRADING ALL WEEKEND!
BEWARE! BEWARE GRAD SCHOOL!

HOW IS YOUR THEORETICAL WORK GOING?
WELL, I PUT ALL THE COMPONENTS OF MY THESIS INTO ONE EQUATION, THEN I SIMPLIFIED ALL THE TERMS.
AND?
I KEEP GETTING Ø = Ø.
JORGE CHAM © 2010
THAT'S AN APT CONCLUSION ABOUT YOU AND YOUR WORK.
SO IT'S ALREADY BEEN DONE?

IF MOVIE SCIENCE WAS MORE LIKE REAL SCIENCE

...SO THEN PROF. SMITH SAID THAT MY DATA IS...
GUYS...
HAVE YOU NOTICED EVERY CONVERSATION WE HAVE REVOLVES AROUND OUR RESEARCH OR OUR ADVISOR?
THAT'S ALL WE TALK ABOUT! IS THERE NOTHING ELSE GOING ON IN OUR LIVES?
JORGE CHAM © 2010
WE COULD TALK ABOUT STUFF WE'VE SEEN WHILE SURFING THE WEB.
THAT'S STILL RESEARCH.

GUYS, FOR ONCE, CAN WE SPEND AN EVENING WHERE WE DON'T TALK ABOUT RESEARCH OR OUR ADVISOR?
SURE.
OF COURSE.
JORGE CHAM © 2010
DO YOU THINK HE EVER TALKS ABOUT US?
...AAAND THAT LASTED TEN SECONDS.

DID YOU KNOW PROF. SMITH USED TO BE A CIRCUS PERFORMER?
WHAT??
IT'S TRUE! I HEARD IT FROM ONE OF THE OLDER STUDENTS BEFORE HE GRADUATED.
HOW DID HE KNOW?
UH, HE HEARD IT FROM ONE OF THE STUDENTS BEFORE HIM.
JORGE CHAM © 2010
SO, IT'S JUST A RUMOR?
WELL, DO YOU WANT TO ASK PROF. SMITH IF HE WAS A CIRCUS PERFORMER??
NOT ME.

OK, WE HAVE TO KNOW IF THESE STORIES ABOUT OUR ADVISOR ARE TRUE.
WHO'S GONNA ASK HIM?
GOLDEN BOY?
I JUST DON'T THINK IT'S ANY OF OUR BUSINESS...
@#%$ GOLDEN BOY.
UNDERGRAD?
NO WAY, I STILL NEED A RECOMMENDATION FROM HIM.
JORGE CHAM © 2010
MIKE?
NO THANKS.
WE'LL BUY YOU LUNCH.
I'LL DO IT.

HE IS...
The Most Unverifiably INTERESTING MAN IN THE WORLD
YOUR ADVISOR.
A FORMER STUDENT ONCE HEARD THAT HE WAS A CIRCUS PERFORMER BEFORE BECOMING AN ACADEMIC.
ONE OF HIS OLD POSTDOCS SWEARS HE HEARD HIS WIFE WAS A MODEL AND EX-EDITOR OF A MAJOR NEWSPAPER.
SOMEONE IN THE NEIGHBORING LAB KIND OF RECALLS ONCE SEEING A PICTURE THAT SHOWED HIM CLIMBING "EL CAPITAN"... POSSIBLY WITHOUT SAFETY GEAR!
ONE OF THE ADMINISTRATIVE ASSISTANTS CLAIMS SHE ONCE HEARD HE PLAYED 6-STRING BANJO FOR A NASHVILLE BAND.
SOMEONE SAID HE ONCE PERFORMED THE HEIMLICH MANEUVER ON THE KING OF NORWAY. TWICE.
JORGE CHAM © 2010
YOU GET E-MAILS FROM HIM AT 2am, 4am AND 6am, WHICH MEANS HE NEVER SLEEPS.
(THIS ONE IS PROBABLY TRUE)
WWW.PHDCOMICS.COM

PROF. SMITH, WE'VE KNOWN EACH OTHER FOR A LONG TIME, RIGHT?
MORE THAN I CARE TO COUNT.
CAN I ASK YOU A PERSONAL QUESTION?
NOT REALLY.
IN ACADEMIA, YOUR PERSONAL LIFE SHOULD HAVE NO BEARING ON YOUR WORK.
IF IT'S NOT ABOUT RESEARCH, I DON'T WANT TO TALK ABOUT IT.
JORGE CHAM © 2010
YOU'RE HURTING MY FEELINGS HERE, PROF. SMITH.
THAT'S NOT RESEARCH, IS IT?

THE PROBLEM IS, IF I TELL YOU ABOUT MY PERSONAL LIFE, YOU MIGHT BE TEMPTED TO DO THE SAME.
PRETTY SOON, EVERYONE WILL BE IN HERE WANTING TO TALK ABOUT NON-RESEARCH RELATED THINGS.
FRANKLY, I JUST DON'T HAVE THE TIME.
JORGE CHAM © 2010
IT'S NOT THAT I DON'T CARE. I JUST FIND IT IRRELEVANT.
GOOD TO MAKE THAT DISTINCTION.

A RESEARCHER'S PERSONAL DETAILS ONLY HELP TO MUDDLE PEOPLE'S PERCEPTION OF HIS/HER ACCOMPLISHMENTS.
IF THE GOAL IS ACADEMIC, DOES IT REALLY MATTER WHO THEY ARE AND WHAT THEY DO?
SAY NO MORE, PROF. SMITH.
YOU'RE ABSOLUTELY RIGHT. IT DOESN'T MATTER AT ALL.
JORGE CHAM © 2010
I WAS ONLY SUPPOSED TO ASK ABOUT HIS PERSONAL LIFE, NOT GET ANSWERS.
AWW, MAN.
IT DOES MATTER! TO US!
WAIT WAIT, DO A SEARCH FOR "SMITH" AND "CIRCUS"...
AHEM.
PROF. SMITH!
WE WERE JUST, UM, GETTING BACK TO WORK!
JORGE CHAM © 2010

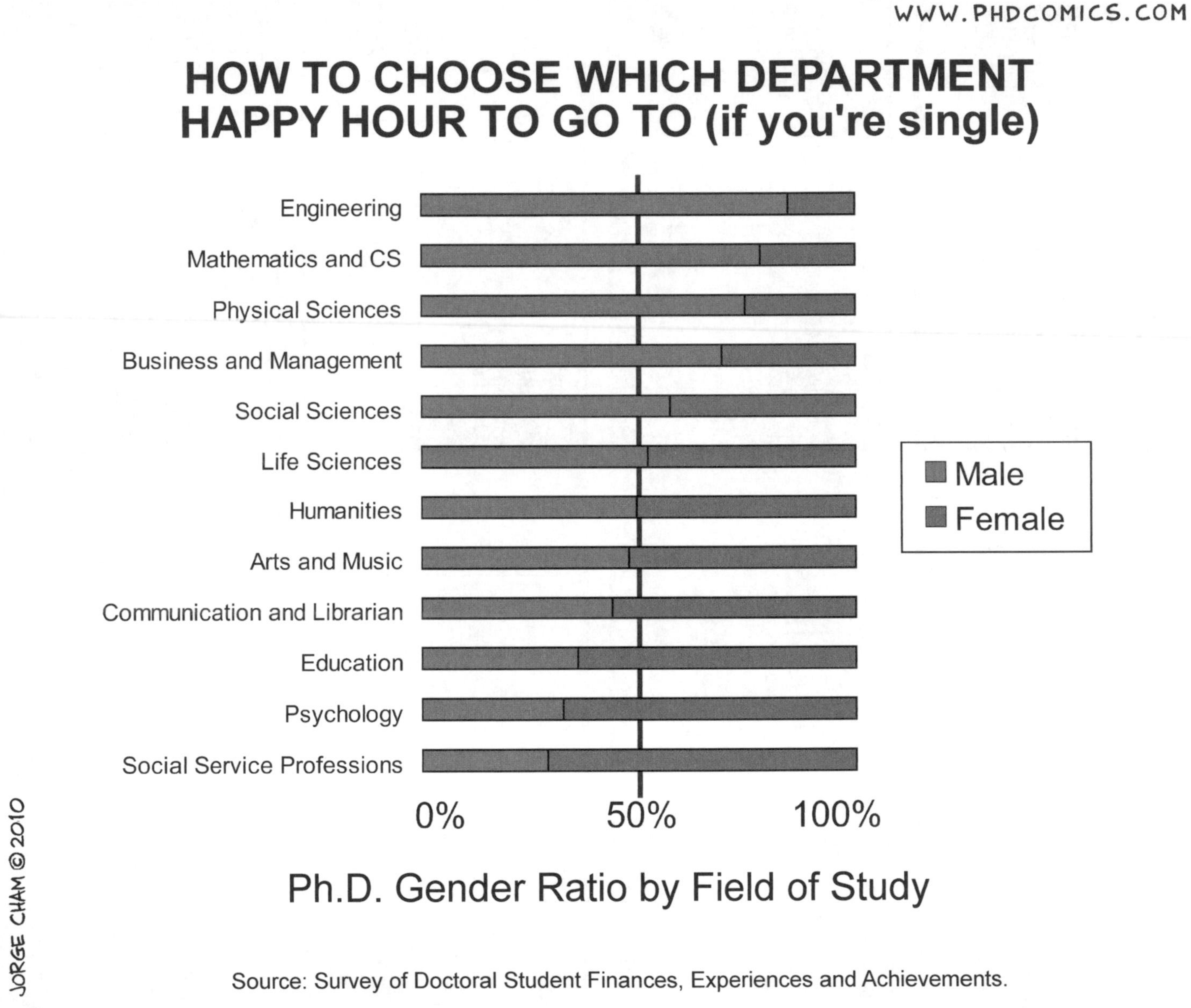
WWW.PHDCOMICS.COM
HOW TO CHOOSE WHICH DEPARTMENT HAPPY HOUR TO GO TO (if you're single)
Engineering
Mathematics and CS
Physical Sciences
Business and Management
Social Sciences
Life Sciences
Humanities
Arts and Music
Communication and Librarian
Education
Psychology
Social Service Professions
Male
Female
0%
50%
100%
Ph.D. Gender Ratio by Field of Study
Source: Survey of Doctoral Student Finances, Experiences and Achievements.
JORGE CHAM © 2010

(GRAD) SCHOOL SPIRIT POP QUIZ!
TEST YOUR DEVOTION TO YOUR ADOPTED ALMA MATER!
WHAT IS YOUR SCHOOL MASCOT'S NAME?
"wolfie d. wolf"? seriously?
1 PT
WHAT ARE THE TEAM COLORS?
yellow and blue?
wrong! it's "golden ochre" and "periwinkle"
1 PT
WHAT IS THE SCHOOL FIGHT SONG?
this is so offensive!
it was written before the civil rights movement.
1 PT
JORGE CHAM © 2010
WHAT NCAA DIVISION AND CONFERENCE DOES YOUR SCHOOL PLAY IN?
what's ncaa?
1 PT
WHO IS THE SCHOOL'S MAIN RIVAL?
booo! state stinks!!
actually, i collaborate with them on research.
1 PT
WHAT'S THE NAME OF THE HEAD COACH?
i need a bigger headset.
he gets paid HOW much??
1 PT
BONUS: 2 PTS IF YOU'VE EVER BEEN INSIDE THE FOOTBALL STADIUM.
2 PT
SCORE:
8 PTS: YOU DID YOUR UNDERGRAD IN THE SAME SCHOOL, DIDN'T YOU?
3-7 PTS: YOU... DATED AN UNDERGRAD?
0-2 PTS: YOU ARE A GRAD STUDENT.
WWW.PHDCOMICS.COM

GRADER TYPES

THESE UNDERGRADS! THESE UNDERGRADS!
THEY'RE SO FRUSTRATING, THESE UNDERGRADS!
WWW.PHDCOMICS.COM
YOU SPEND ALL YOUR TIME TEACHING, BUT THEY NEVER LEARN...
THEY ONLY SEEM TO CARE ABOUT WHAT GRADE THEY EARN!
THEY TEXT DURING CLASS AND SKIP MY REVIEW SESSION...
IF ONLY THERE WAS A WAY...
JORGE CHAM © 2010
...TO TEACH THEM A LESSON?
HMMM...
uh oh.

NET EFFECT OF A VACATION ON WORK PRODUCTIVITY
=
Clearing your mind and recharging your batteries
-
Travel Stress
-
Realizing how much better life would be if you didn't have to work
= 0
sigh.
JORGE CHAM © 2011

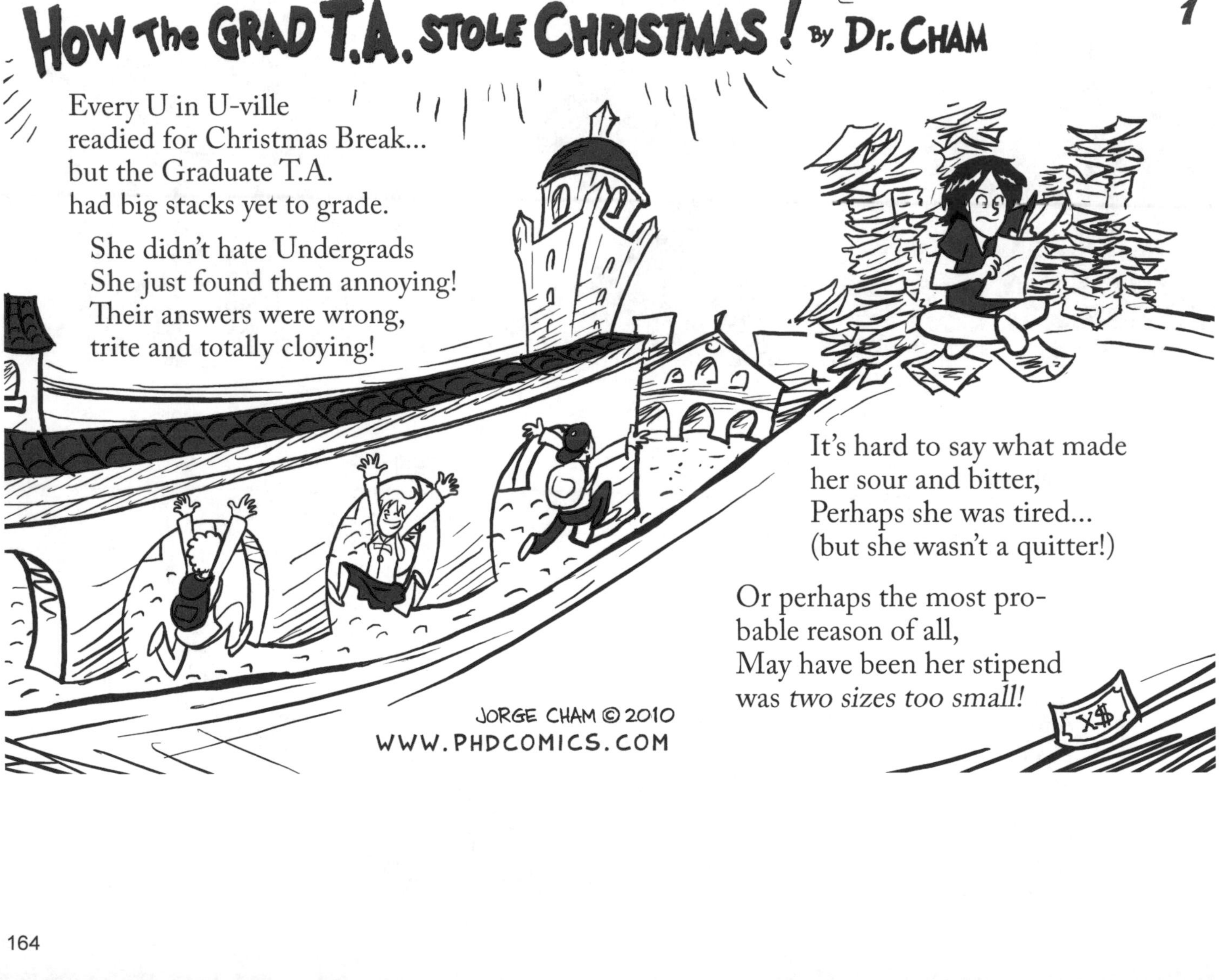
HOW THE GRAD T.A. STOLE CHRISTMAS! By Dr. CHAM
1
Every U in U-ville
readied for Christmas Break...
but the Graduate T.A.
had big stacks yet to grade.
She didn't hate Undergrads
She just found them annoying!
Their answers were wrong,
trite and totally cloying!
It's hard to say what made
her sour and bitter,
Perhaps she was tired...
(but she wasn't a quitter!)
Or perhaps the most pro-
bable reason of all,
May have been her stipend
was *two sizes too small!*
X$
JORGE CHAM © 2010
WWW.PHDCOMICS.COM

HOW THE GRAD T.A. STOLE CHRISTMAS! By Dr. CHAM 2
JORGE CHAM © 2010
WWW.PHDCOMICS.COM
But whatever the reason,
she sat there depressed.
Grading isn't that hard,
but it still caused her stress...
For tomorrow, she knew
all the Undergrads, they'd...
They'd come to her Office
to argue their grade!
...and then! Oh, the whining!
The WHINING! Boo hoo!
"I deserve more points, dude!"
"I tried *really* hard, too!"
Then she got an idea...
a really *awesome* idea...
The T.A. got a wonderful,
awesome idea!
What if... she stopped scoring
with arguable scales?
No more PARTIAL CREDIT!
Let them whine!
Let them wail!

HOW The GRAD T.A. STOLE CHRISTMAS! By Dr. CHAM
3
JORGE CHAM © 2010
WWW.PHDCOMICS.COM
You're a mean one, Grad T.A.!
You really will not budge!
You take points for small mistakes
You would think you had a grudge
Grad T.A....
You're a tough evaluator
and a really harsh judge!
You're a hard one, Grad T.A.
You mark everything that's wrong!
You take points off if its short
You write X's if its long!
Grad T.A...
I would say your fairness
is a little too strong!
You're a stickler, Grad T.A.
You notise every typo!
You mark off for missing units
Use red ink like a psycho
Grad T.A....
Sometimes we're not really sure
you even like us!
NAME??

HOW the GRAD T.A. STOLE CHRISTMAS! By Dr. CHAM 4
JORGE CHAM © 2010
WWW.PHDCOMICS.COM
Three thousand steps up, from her basement abode She carried the freshly marked red ink-stained load...
Soon those Undergrads'll learn... Soon they'll finally get it! When they open their tests, and there's no partial credit!
She knew JUST what they'd say: "Boo hoo HOO! I feel dumber!" "You're ruining our Christmas Break, dude! What a bummer!"
So she watched them with glee, as they picked up their tests, and eagerly waited for them to protest...

HOW THE GRAD T.A. STOLE CHRISTMAS! By Dr. CHAM 5
JORGE CHAM © 2010
WWW.PHDCOMICS.COM
But WAIT!
She-
She couldn't
believe it exactly!
The students reacted
rather matter-of-factly!
How could it be SO?
Was she wrong all along??
Did grading mean more
than just right...
and wrong?
The answer to this became clear as a day,
when she heard a few Undergrads
fearlessly say:
"Who cares! Doesn't matter what score we DESERVE!"
"I can ace this class still, 'cause it's based on a CURVE!"
Well... at least Christmas Break
brings the Holiday Cheer,
of NOT seeing Undergrads
until next YEAR!

SIGH. IT'S HARD TO GET BACK TO WORK AFTER A LONG SCHOOL BREAK.
I SUPPOSE I YEARN FOR THE TIME OFF...
JORGE CHAM © 2011
..WHEN I COULD ACTUALLY WORK WITHOUT ALL THESE PESKY STUDENTS INTERRUPTING ME.

Edit Profile
Relationship Status?
Single?
In a relationship
Engaged?
Married?
In a relationship
with
my thesis
JORGE CHAM © 2011
and:
It's complicated

The Semiotics of Professor E-mail Signatures

Abstract: Professorial types express their mood by a ratio of casualness to effort in how they sign their e-mails. By paying close attention to these variations, you can learn to identify their mood and prepare accordingly.

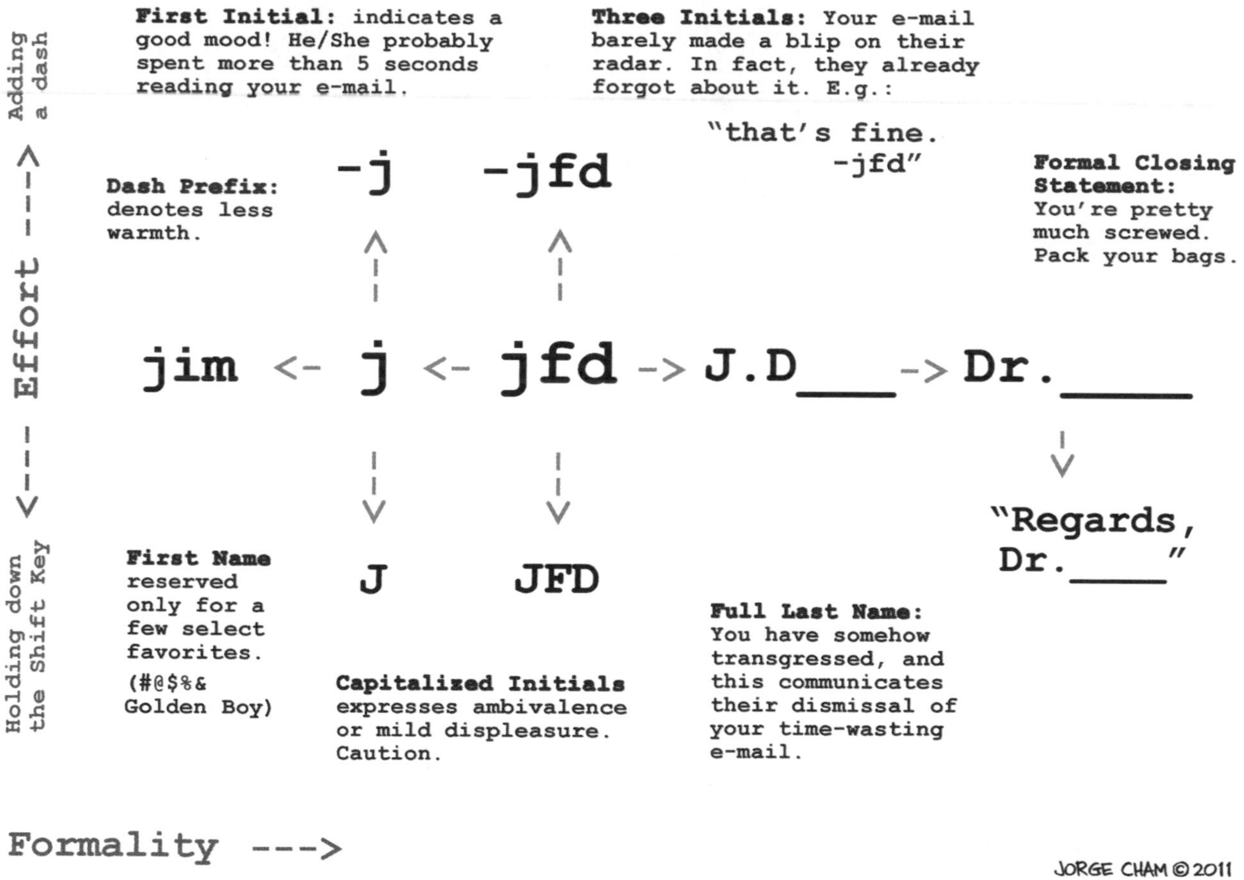
First Initial: indicates a good mood! He/She probably spent more than 5 seconds reading your e-mail.
Three Initials: Your e-mail barely made a blip on their radar. In fact, they already forgot about it. E.g.:
"that's fine. -jfd"
Adding a dash
<--- Effort --->
Holding down the Shift Key
Dash Prefix: denotes less warmth.
-j
-jfd
Formal Closing Statement: You're pretty much screwed. Pack your bags.
jim <- j <- jfd -> J.D___ -> Dr.____
"Regards, Dr.____"
First Name reserved only for a few select favorites. (#@$%& Golden Boy)
J
JFD
Capitalized Initials expresses ambivalence or mild displeasure. Caution.
Full Last Name: You have somehow transgressed, and this communicates their dismissal of your time-wasting e-mail.
Formality --->

(with thanks to Janice from Rice)

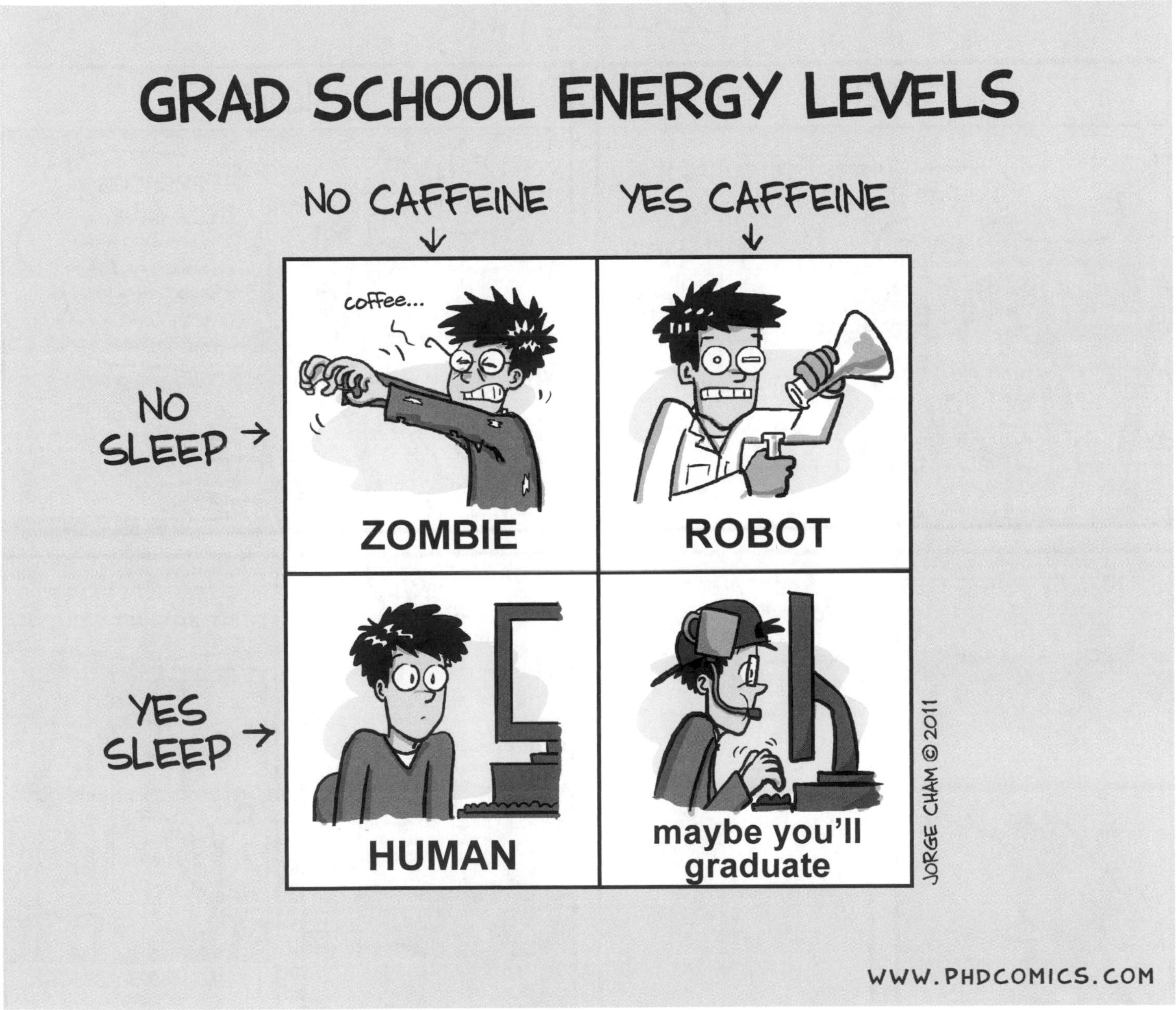
GRAD SCHOOL ENERGY LEVELS
NO CAFFEINE
YES CAFFEINE
NO SLEEP
YES SLEEP
coffee...
ZOMBIE
ROBOT
HUMAN
maybe you'll graduate
JORGE CHAM © 2011
WWW.PHDCOMICS.COM

COLLECTING

THEN
GOT IT.
GOT IT.
NEED IT.
GOT IT.
JORGE CHAM © 2011
NOW
GOT IT.
GOT IT.
NEED IT.
GOT IT.
REFERENCES
OMG, I TOTALLY NEED IT...

Neither snow nor rain...
...nor sleet or gloom of night...
...shall stop grad students from working....
JORGE CHAM © 2011
...lest they face their advisor's might.
THE PROFESSOR'S CREED

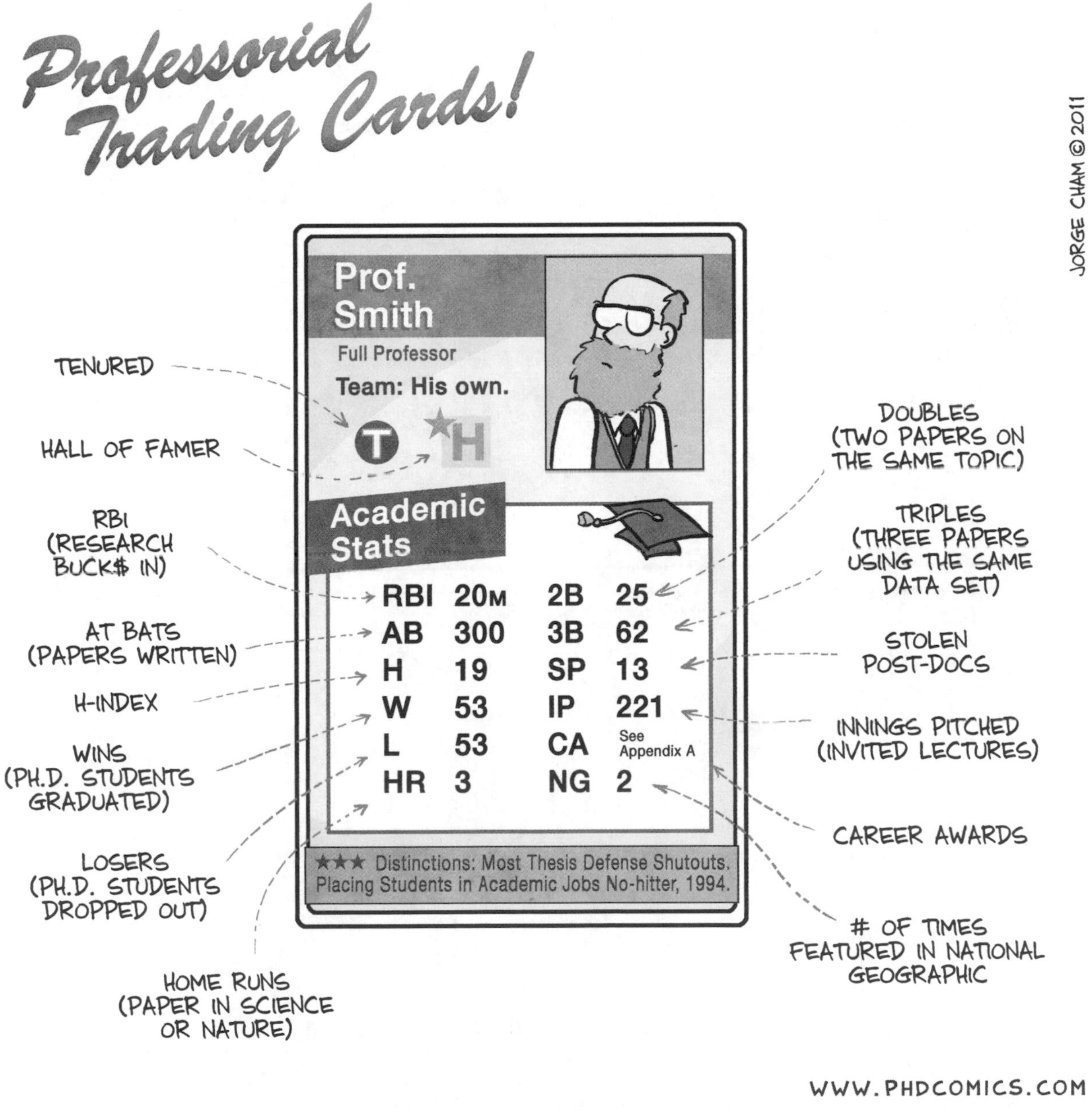
Professorial Trading Cards!
JORGE CHAM © 2011
Prof. Smith
Full Professor
Team: His own.
T
★H
Academic Stats
RBI 20M
AB 300
H 19
W 53
L 53
HR 3
2B 25
3B 62
SP 13
IP 221
CA See Appendix A
NG 2
★★★ Distinctions: Most Thesis Defense Shutouts. Placing Students in Academic Jobs No-hitter, 1994.
TENURED
HALL OF FAMER
RBI (RESEARCH BUCK$ IN)
AT BATS (PAPERS WRITTEN)
H-INDEX
WINS (PH.D. STUDENTS GRADUATED)
LOSERS (PH.D. STUDENTS DROPPED OUT)
HOME RUNS (PAPER IN SCIENCE OR NATURE)
DOUBLES (TWO PAPERS ON THE SAME TOPIC)
TRIPLES (THREE PAPERS USING THE SAME DATA SET)
STOLEN POST-DOCS
INNINGS PITCHED (INVITED LECTURES)
CAREER AWARDS
OF TIMES FEATURED IN NATIONAL GEOGRAPHIC
WWW.PHDCOMICS.COM

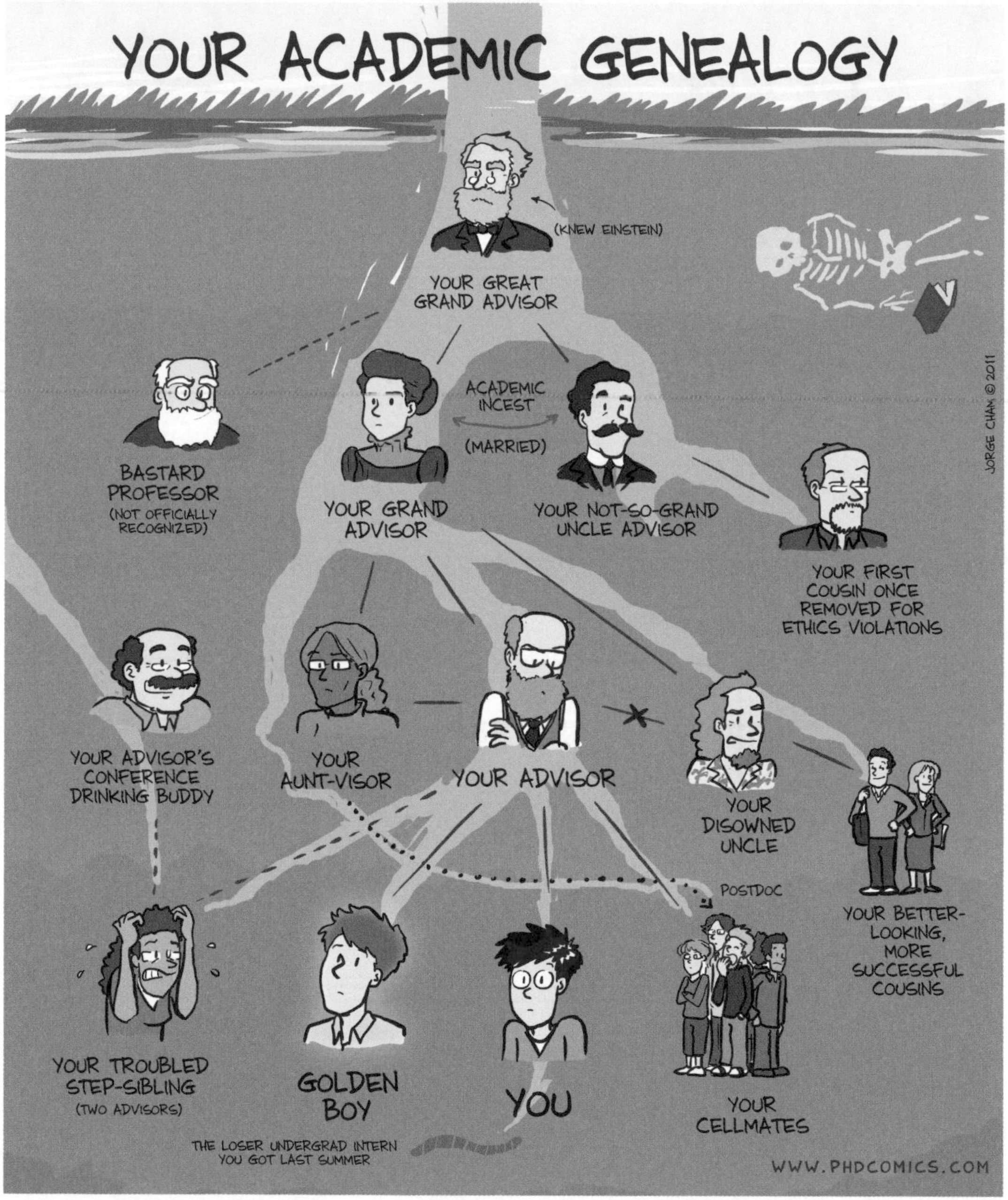
YOUR ACADEMIC GENEALOGY
(KNEW EINSTEIN)
YOUR GREAT GRAND ADVISOR
JORGE CHAM © 2011
ACADEMIC INCEST
(MARRIED)
BASTARD PROFESSOR
(NOT OFFICIALLY RECOGNIZED)
YOUR GRAND ADVISOR
YOUR NOT-SO-GRAND UNCLE ADVISOR
YOUR FIRST COUSIN ONCE REMOVED FOR ETHICS VIOLATIONS
YOUR ADVISOR'S CONFERENCE DRINKING BUDDY
YOUR AUNT-VISOR
YOUR ADVISOR
YOUR DISOWNED UNCLE
POSTDOC
YOUR BETTER-LOOKING, MORE SUCCESSFUL COUSINS
YOUR TROUBLED STEP-SIBLING
(TWO ADVISORS)
GOLDEN BOY
YOU
YOUR CELLMATES
THE LOSER UNDERGRAD INTERN YOU GOT LAST SUMMER
WWW.PHDCOMICS.COM

HOW DO I LOVE YOU, THESIS?
LET ME COUNT THE WAYS...

WWW.PHDCOMICS.COM

THE PHD COMICS GUIDE TO T.A. OFFICE* HOURS
*ASSUMING YOU HAVE AN OFFICE
ATTENDANCE IS EXPONENTIAL:
OFFICE HOUR ATTENDANCE
THE DAY BEFORE THE BIG EXAM
DAY GRADES ARE POSTED
ACADEMIC TERM
JORGE CHAM © 2011
BEST TIMES TO HOLD OFFICE HOURS:*
• FRIDAY AFTERNOONS
• CLASS TIME
• DAY AFTER HOMEWORK IS DUE
*SO NOBODY WILL SHOW UP
BEWARE THE PRE'S:
LIVES WILL DEPEND ON ME.
CAN I GET AN "A" FOR "C" WORK?
MY TUITION PAYS YOU. AS YOUR CUSTOMER, I DEMAND AN "A"!
I CAN'T BE RESPONSIBLE FOR MATERIAL COVERED DURING CLASSES I SKIPPED.
YES, BUT WHY???
PRE-MED
PRE-BUSINESS
PRE-LAW
PRE-PHD
NEVER REVEAL TO STUDENTS...
YOUR CELL-PHONE #
YOUR HOME ADDRESS
YOUR PERSONAL LIFE
YOURSELF
BEING THE "EVIL" T.A. IS IT A BAD THING?
CON
PRO
students won't like you
students won't talk to you
ANSWER: NO.
WWW.PHDCOMICS.COM

I NEED YOU TO EDIT SOMETHING FOR ME.
REALLY?
THAT'S... QUITE AN HONOR.
WHAT IS IT? A TEXTBOOK CHAPTER? A REVIEW ARTICLE? A JOURNAL ISSUE?
NOT QUITE.
JORGE CHAM © 2011
Article
Discussion
Read
Edit
View history
Brian S. Smith (Genius)
From Wikipedia, the online Repository
Contents
1 Awards
2 Sources
3 References
4 External links
2001 MacArthur Fellows Program

PROF. SMITH, I NEED TO MAKE TRAVEL RESERVATIONS FOR THE UPCOMING CONFERENCE.
NO PROBLEM. JUST PAY FOR IT NOW AND THE DEPARTMENT WILL REIMBURSE YOU WHEN YOU COME BACK.
YOU WANT ME TO GIVE THE UNIVERSITY AN INTEREST-FREE LOAN SO I CAN REPRESENT IT AND TELL EVERYONE WHAT A GREAT PLACE THIS IS?
JORGE CHAM © 2011
IT'S NOT INTEREST-FREE IF IT SERVES OUR INTEREST.
that's... interesting.

HI, I NEED TO GET REIMBURSED FOR A TRAVEL EXPENSE.
NO PROBLEM!
ACCOUNTS PAYABLES
JUST FILL OUT THIS SHORT 5-PAGE FORM AND EXPENSE REPORT AND GET IT SIGNED BY YOUR ADVISOR, YOUR PROGRAM DIRECTOR, YOUR FUNDING MANAGER AND YOUR MOTHER AS A CHARACTER REFERENCE.
YOU MUST HAVE THE ORIGINAL, STILL-WARM RECEIPTS, OTHERWISE WE'LL NEED SIGNED AFFIDAVITS FROM THE VENDOR, THREE WITNESSES WHO SAW YOU PAY FOR THE EXPENSE AND YOUR SWORN TESTIMONY.
JORGE CHAM © 2011
HOW MUCH IS IT FOR?
FIVE DOLLARS.
OOH, WE'LL NEED A LONGER FORM.

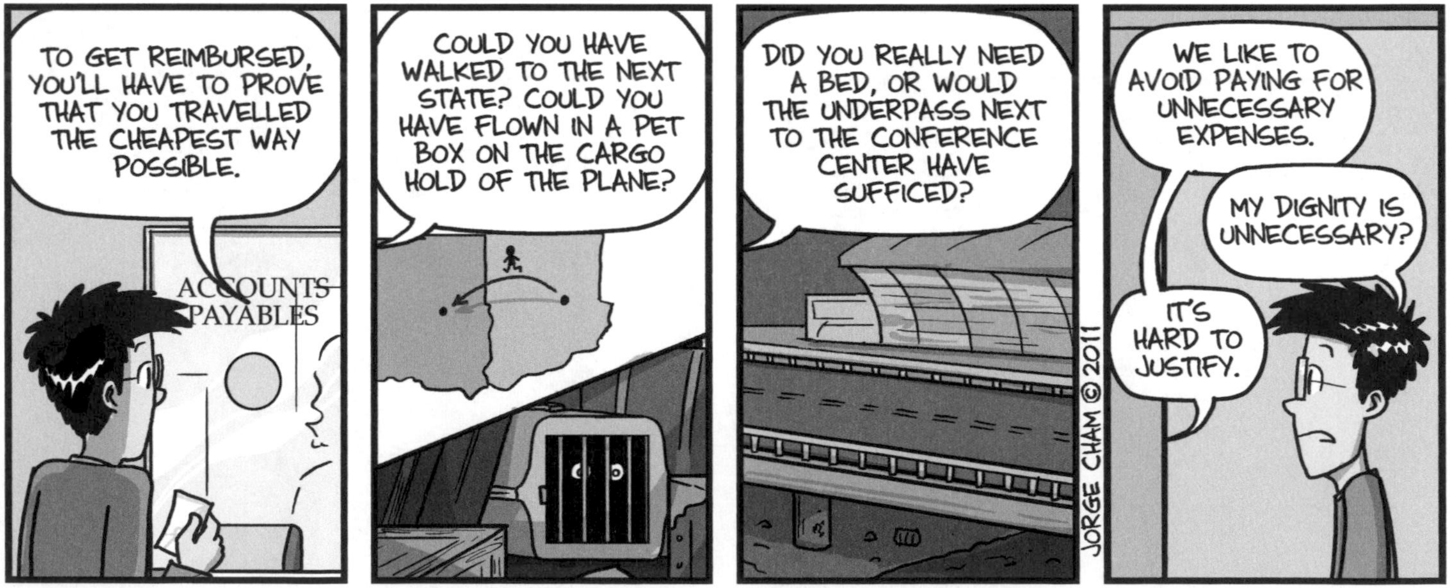
TO GET REIMBURSED, YOU'LL HAVE TO PROVE THAT YOU TRAVELLED THE CHEAPEST WAY POSSIBLE.
ACCOUNTS PAYABLES
COULD YOU HAVE WALKED TO THE NEXT STATE? COULD YOU HAVE FLOWN IN A PET BOX ON THE CARGO HOLD OF THE PLANE?
DID YOU REALLY NEED A BED, OR WOULD THE UNDERPASS NEXT TO THE CONFERENCE CENTER HAVE SUFFICED?
JORGE CHAM © 2011
WE LIKE TO AVOID PAYING FOR UNNECESSARY EXPENSES.
MY DIGNITY IS UNNECESSARY?
IT'S HARD TO JUSTIFY.

PROF. SMITH? I NEED YOUR SIGNATURE ON THIS TRAVEL REIMBURSEMENT FORM.
YES, YES, FINE.
IT WON'T BE THAT EASY FOR YOUR THESIS.
AWW.
JORGE CHAM © 2011

SO HOW LONG BEFORE I GET REIMBURSED?
3 TO 5 WEEKS.
IT'S JUST SHORT ENOUGH THAT YOU THINK YOU'LL GET IT, BUT LONG ENOUGH THAT YOU'LL PROBABLY FORGET ABOUT IT IN CASE WE LOSE YOUR APPLICATION.
SO I MIGHT NEVER SEE MY MONEY?
WAS IT REALLY YOURS TO BEGIN WITH?
I'M A POOR GRAD STUDENT. I NEED TO EAT.
HERE, TAKE THESE FORMS.
JORGE CHAM © 2011

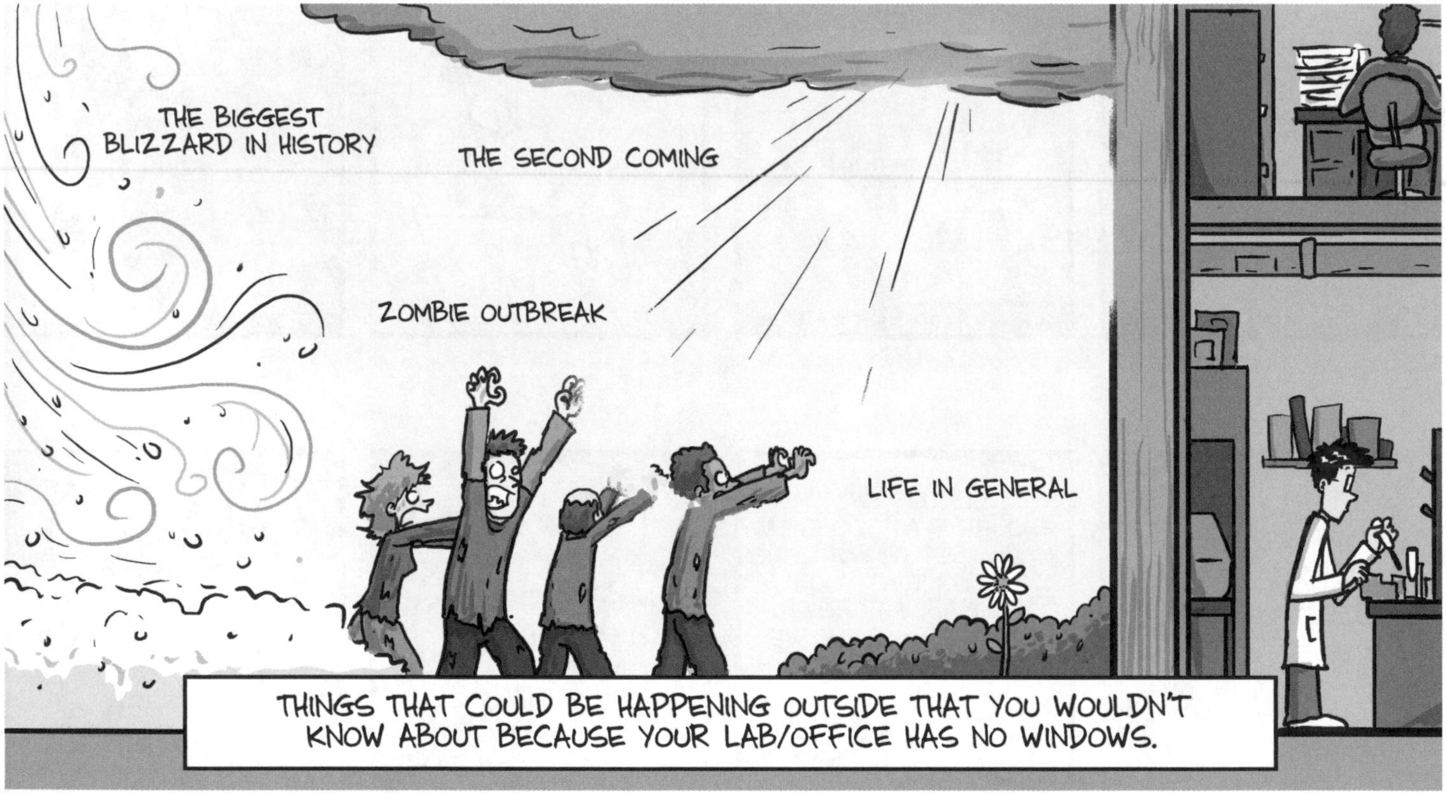
THE BIGGEST BLIZZARD IN HISTORY
THE SECOND COMING
ZOMBIE OUTBREAK
LIFE IN GENERAL
THINGS THAT COULD BE HAPPENING OUTSIDE THAT YOU WOULDN'T KNOW ABOUT BECAUSE YOUR LAB/OFFICE HAS NO WINDOWS.

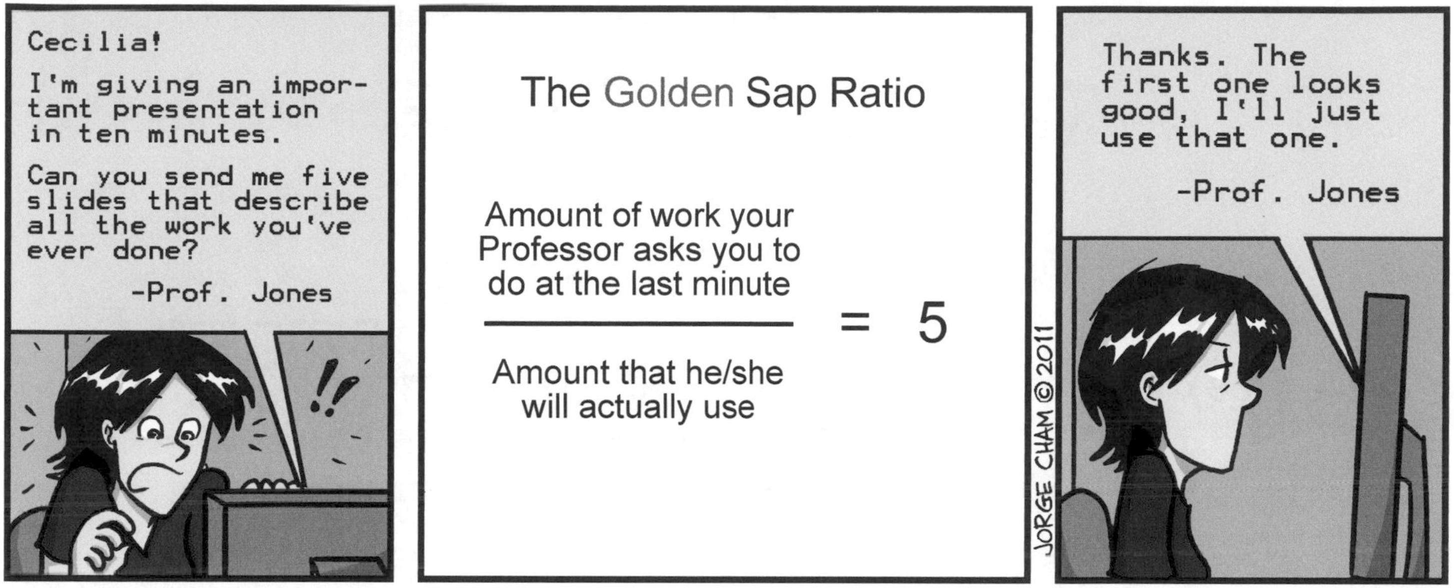

ACADEMIC AUTOCORRECT

WORDS YOUR SMARTPHONE THINKS YOU ARE MISPELLING

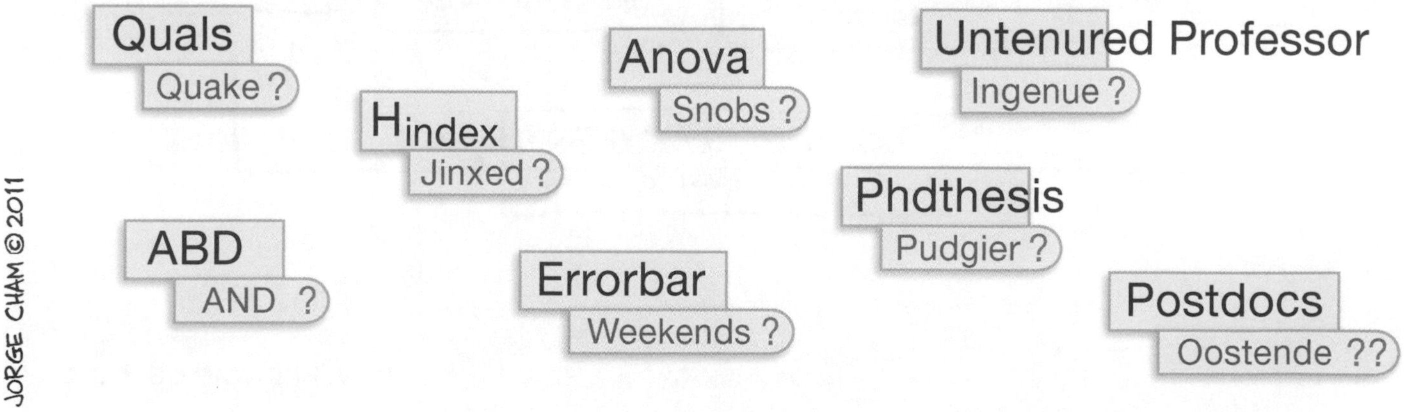

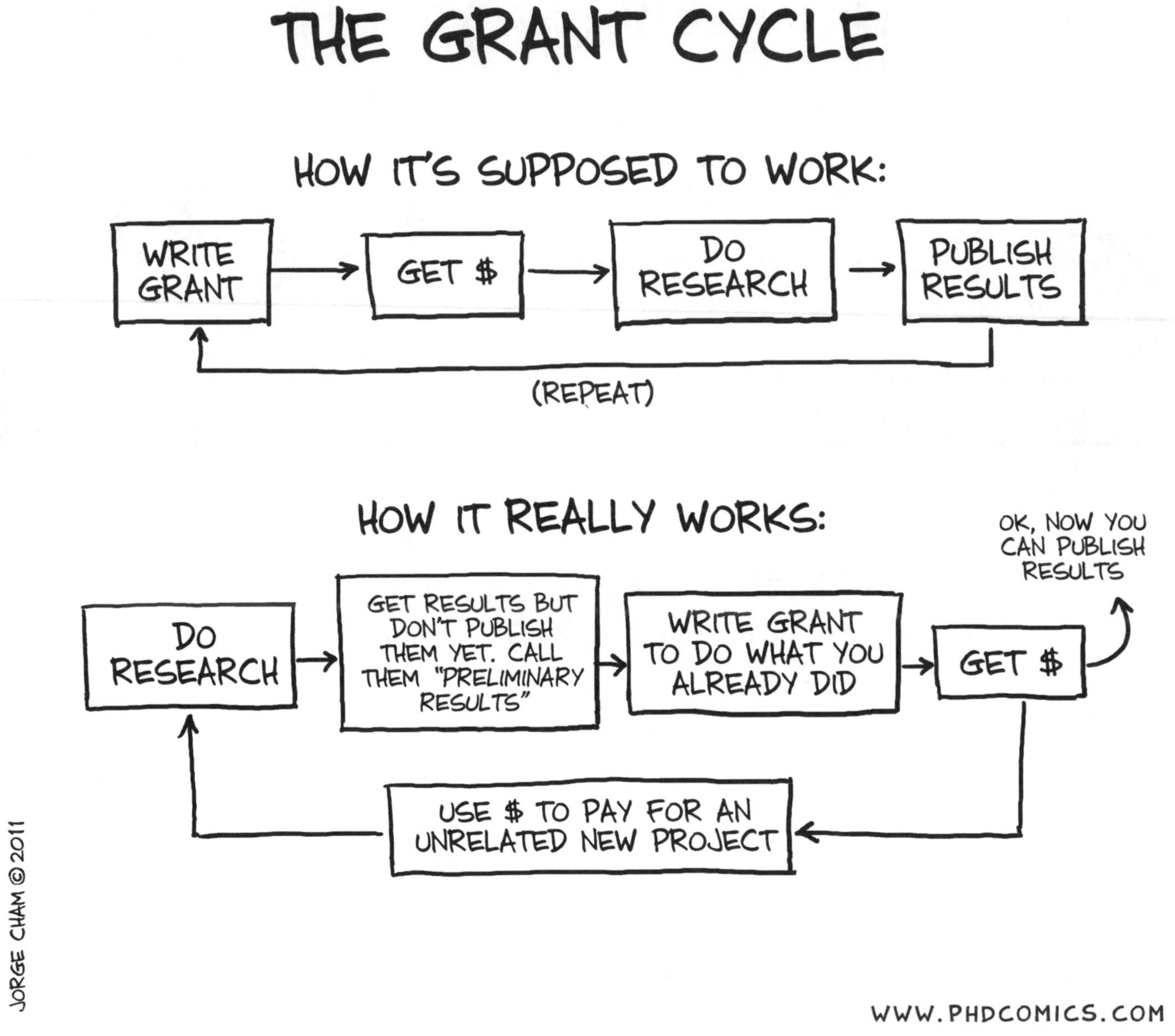
THE GRANT CYCLE
HOW IT'S SUPPOSED TO WORK:
WRITE GRANT
GET $
DO RESEARCH
PUBLISH RESULTS
(REPEAT)
HOW IT REALLY WORKS:
DO RESEARCH
GET RESULTS BUT DON'T PUBLISH THEM YET. CALL THEM "PRELIMINARY RESULTS"
WRITE GRANT TO DO WHAT YOU ALREADY DID
GET $
OK, NOW YOU CAN PUBLISH RESULTS
USE $ TO PAY FOR AN UNRELATED NEW PROJECT
JORGE CHAM © 2011
WWW.PHDCOMICS.COM

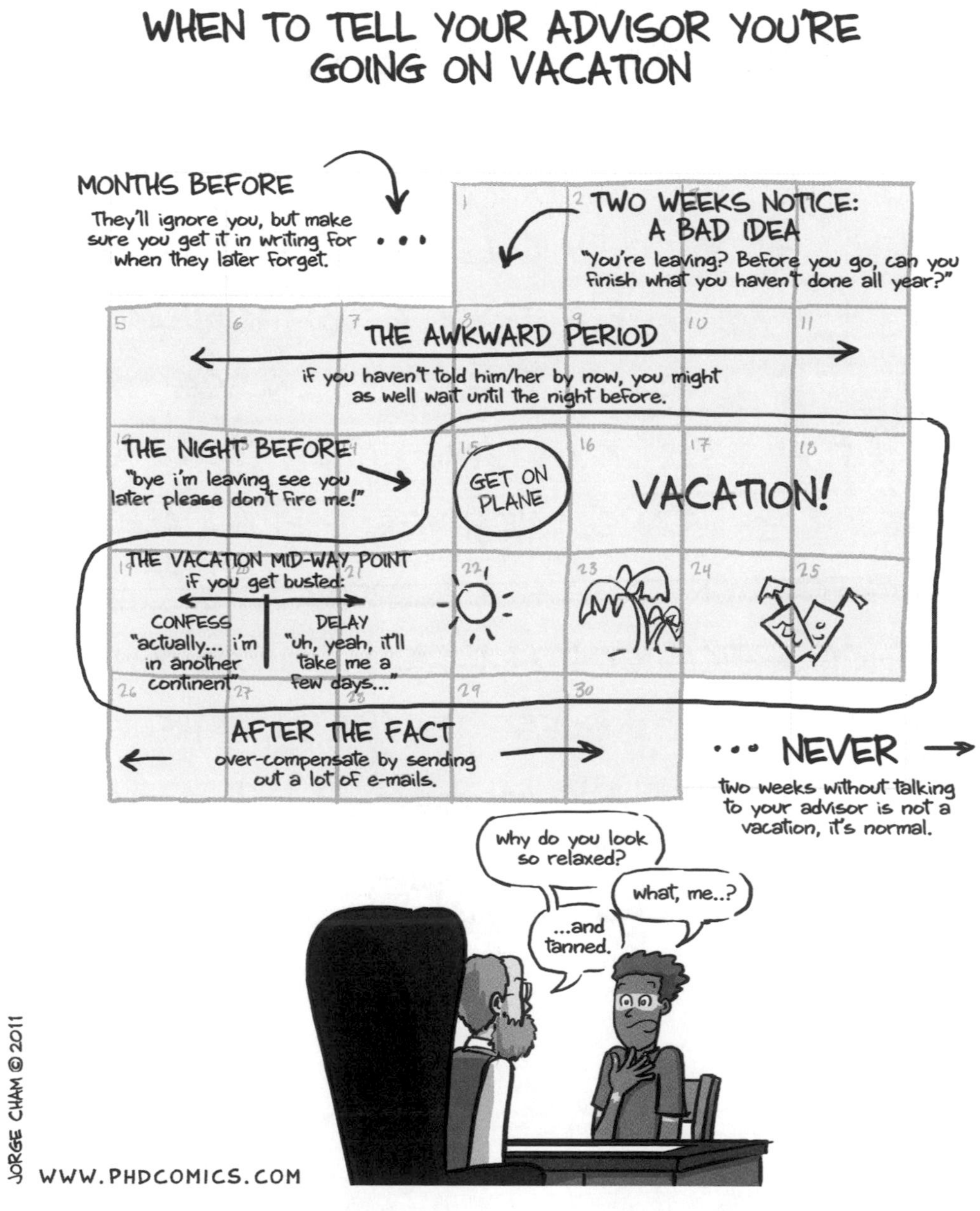
WHEN TO TELL YOUR ADVISOR YOU'RE GOING ON VACATION
MONTHS BEFORE
They'll ignore you, but make sure you get it in writing for when they later forget.
TWO WEEKS NOTICE: A BAD IDEA
"You're leaving? Before you go, can you finish what you haven't done all year?"
THE AWKWARD PERIOD
if you haven't told him/her by now, you might as well wait until the night before.
THE NIGHT BEFORE
"bye i'm leaving see you later please don't fire me!"
GET ON PLANE
VACATION!
THE VACATION MID-WAY POINT
if you get busted:
CONFESS
"actually... i'm in another continent"
DELAY
"uh, yeah, it'll take me a few days..."
AFTER THE FACT
over-compensate by sending out a lot of e-mails.
NEVER
two weeks without talking to your advisor is not a vacation, it's normal.
Why do you look so relaxed?
what, me..?
...and tanned.
JORGE CHAM © 2011
WWW.PHDCOMICS.COM

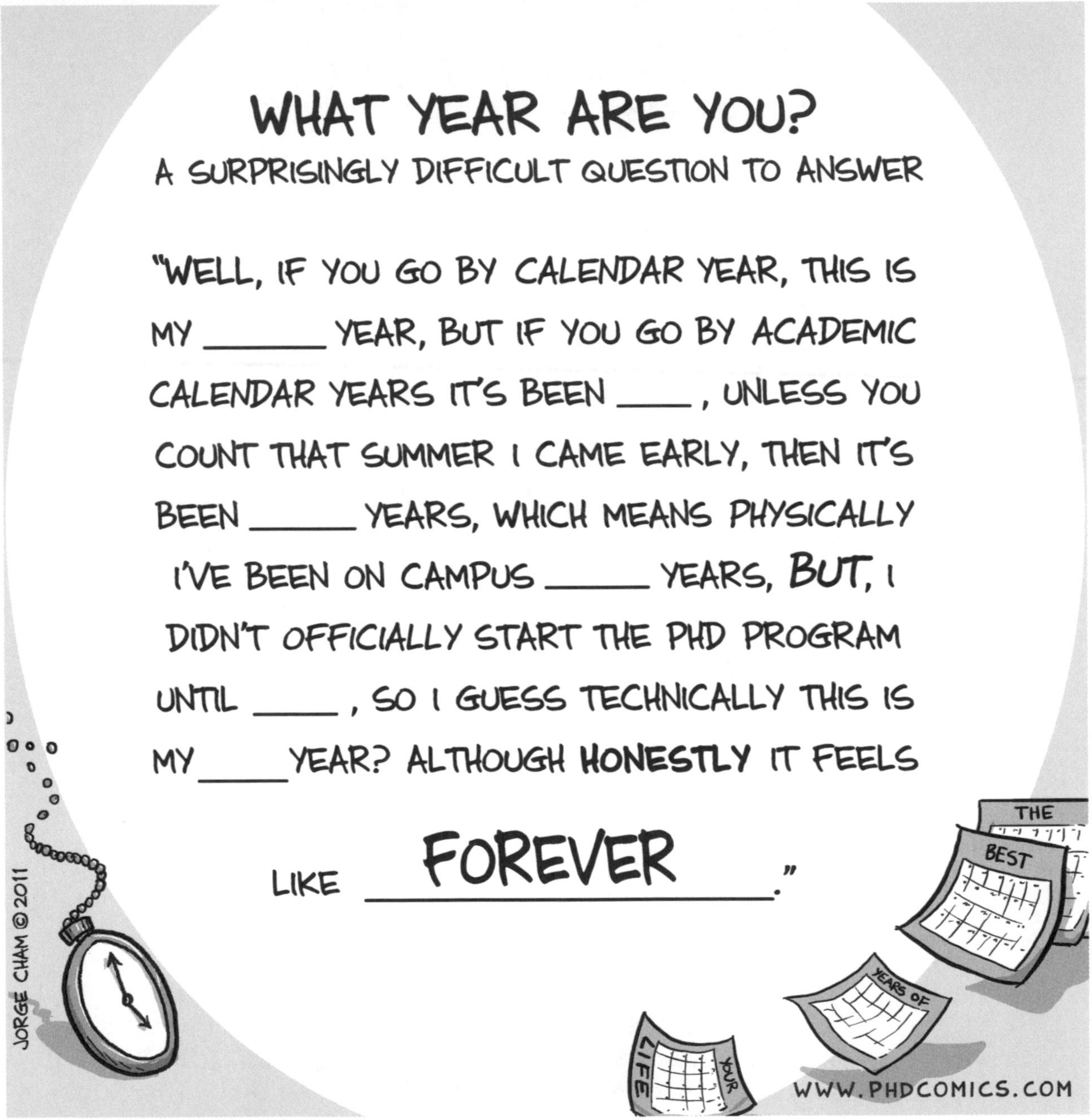
WHAT YEAR ARE YOU?
A SURPRISINGLY DIFFICULT QUESTION TO ANSWER
"WELL, IF YOU GO BY CALENDAR YEAR, THIS IS MY ______ YEAR, BUT IF YOU GO BY ACADEMIC CALENDAR YEARS IT'S BEEN ____ , UNLESS YOU COUNT THAT SUMMER I CAME EARLY, THEN IT'S BEEN ______ YEARS, WHICH MEANS PHYSICALLY I'VE BEEN ON CAMPUS _____ YEARS, BUT, I DIDN'T OFFICIALLY START THE PHD PROGRAM UNTIL ____ , SO I GUESS TECHNICALLY THIS IS MY____YEAR? ALTHOUGH HONESTLY IT FEELS
LIKE FOREVER."
THE
BEST
YEARS OF
YOUR
LIFE
JORGE CHAM © 2011
WWW.PHDCOMICS.COM

A PRAYER FOR GRAD STUDENTS

THE EVOLUTION OF INTELLECTUAL FREEDOM
I'M GOING TO RESEARCH WHATEVER I WANT!
I'M GOING TO RESEARCH WHATEVER MY PROFESSOR WANTS!
I'M GOING TO RESEARCH WHATEVER MY TENURE COMMITTEE WANTS!
I'M GOING TO RESEARCH WHATEVER MY GRANT COMMITTEE WANTS!
I'M GOING TO RESEARCH WHATEVER I-
"Research In Peace"
RIP
JORGE CHAM © 2011
BEFORE GRAD SCHOOL
GRAD STUDENT
ASSISTANT PROFESSOR
TENURED PROFESSOR
EMERITUS PROFESSOR
WWW.PHDCOMICS.COM

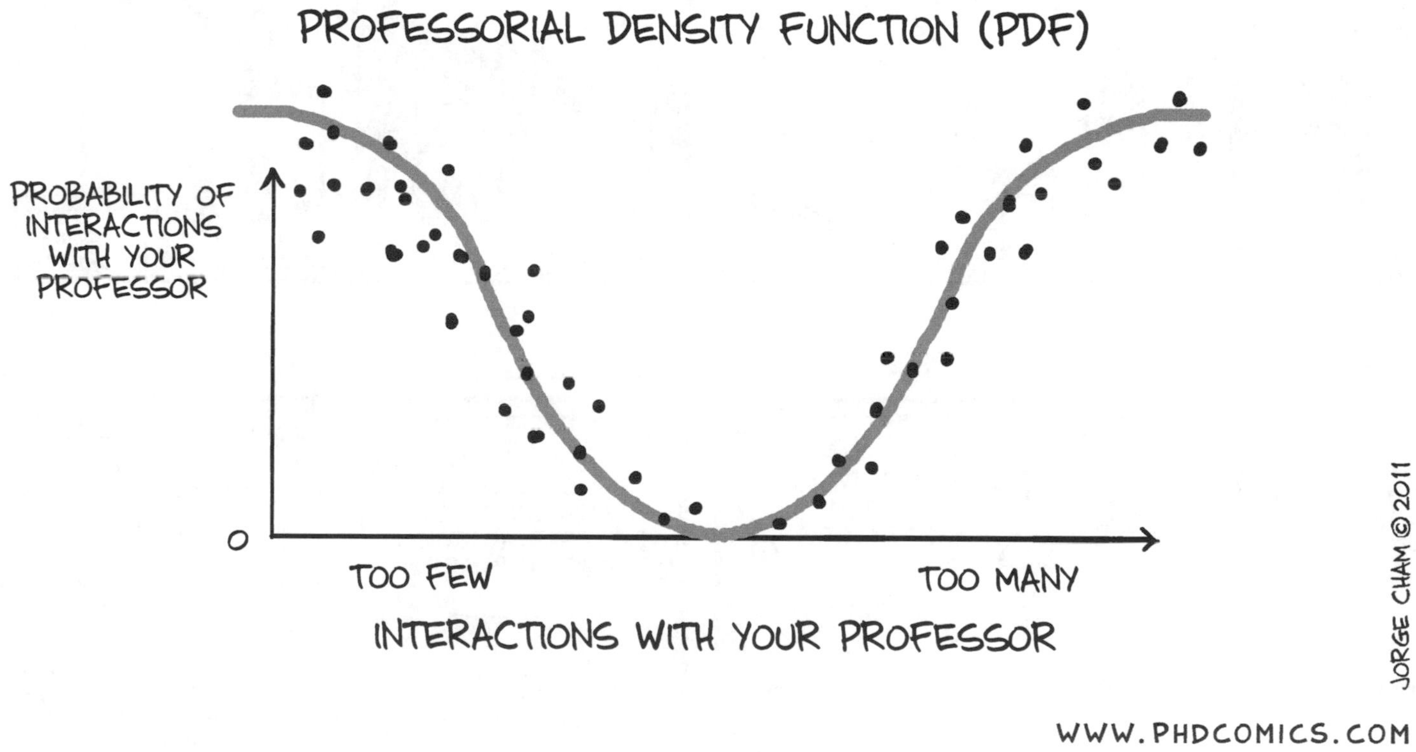
PROFESSORIAL DENSITY FUNCTION (PDF)
PROBABILITY OF INTERACTIONS WITH YOUR PROFESSOR
0
TOO FEW
TOO MANY
INTERACTIONS WITH YOUR PROFESSOR
JORGE CHAM © 2011
WWW.PHDCOMICS.COM

I MADE A FEW TWEAKS TO THE DRAFT PAPER YOU SENT ME.
B. SMITH PROFESSOR
YOU... RE-WROTE THE ENTIRE THING.
YES, IT'S EASIER FOR ME TO RE-WRITE IT THAN TO POINT OUT ALL THE THINGS YOU DID WRONG.
I CALL IT LEARNING BY DEMONSTRATION.
JORGE CHAM © 2011
WHAT ARE WE DEMONSTRATING?
THAT YOU'RE A BAD WRITER.

WHAT IS WRONG WITH MY WRITING?
WELL. FOR STARTERS, YOU USE TOO MANY SENTENCES.
ALSO, YOUR CHOICE OF WORDS IS OFTEN INCORRECT.
AND YOUR PUNCTUATION MARKS ARE STRANGELY PLACED.
REALLY, THE TROUBLE BEGAN WHEN YOU FIRST PRESSED A KEY ON YOUR KEYBOARD.
JORGE CHAM © 2011
ANYTHING ELSE?
YOUR FIGURES ARE UGLY.

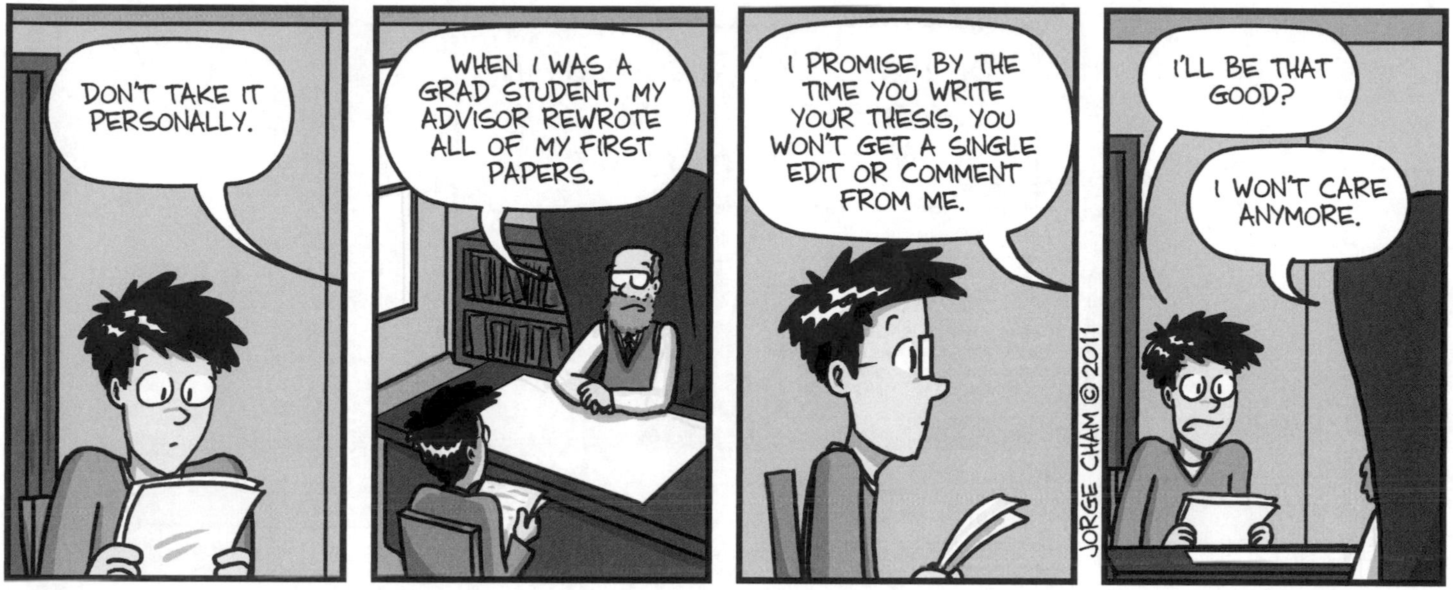
DON'T TAKE IT PERSONALLY.
WHEN I WAS A GRAD STUDENT, MY ADVISOR REWROTE ALL OF MY FIRST PAPERS.
I PROMISE, BY THE TIME YOU WRITE YOUR THESIS, YOU WON'T GET A SINGLE EDIT OR COMMENT FROM ME.
JORGE CHAM © 2011
I'LL BE THAT GOOD?
I WON'T CARE ANYMORE.

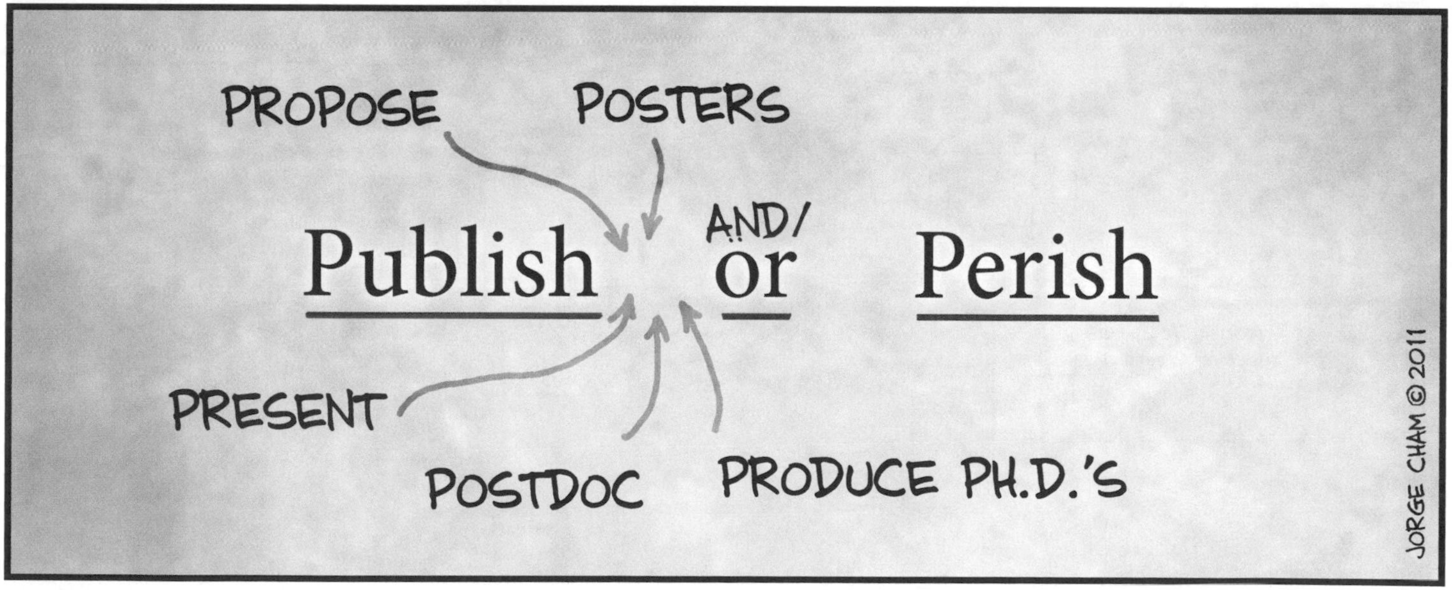
PROPOSE
POSTERS
Publish
AND/
or
Perish
PRESENT
POSTDOC
PRODUCE PH.D.'S
JORGE CHAM © 2011

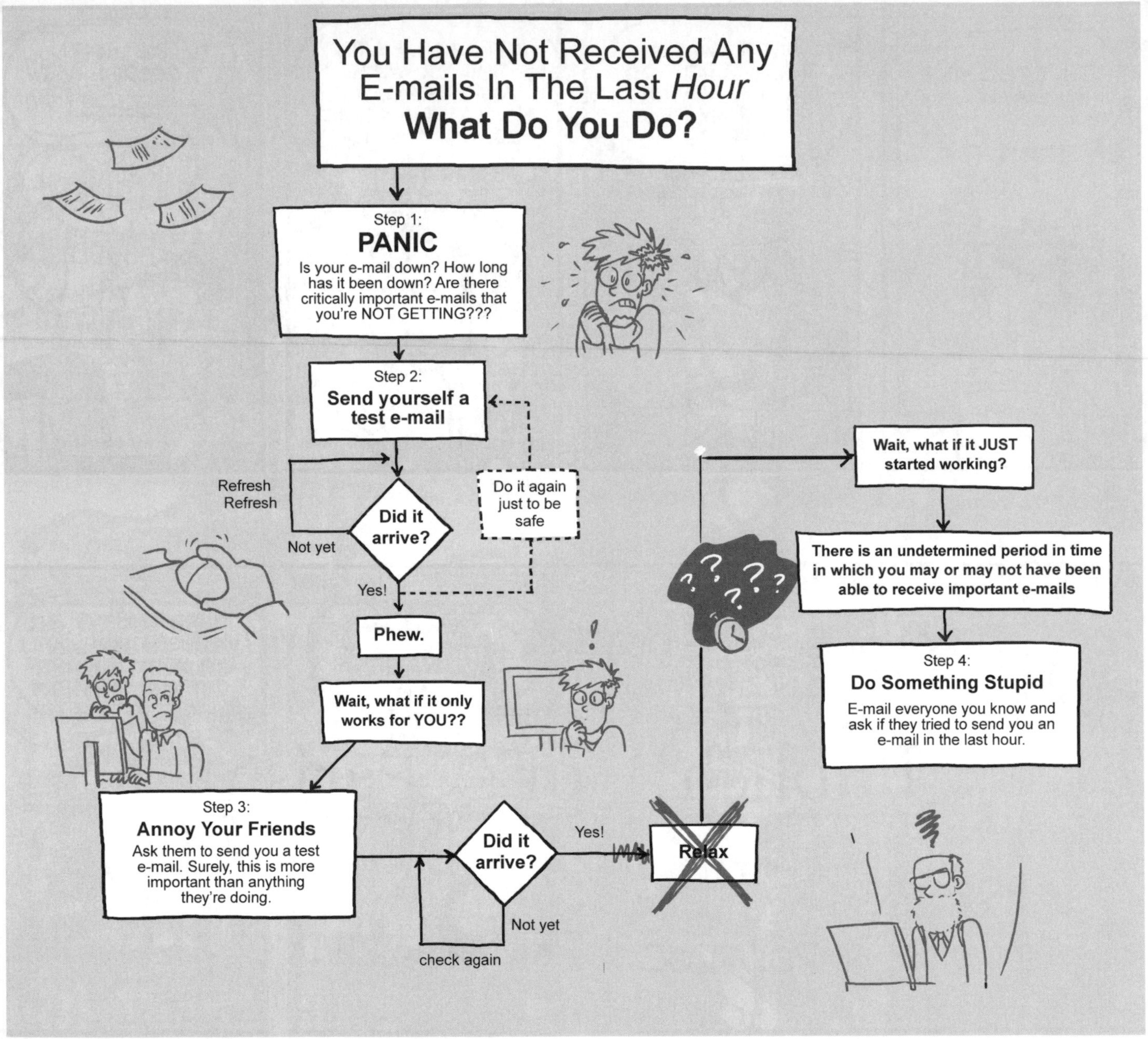

You Have Not Received Any E-mails In The Last *Hour*
What Do You Do?
Step 1:
PANIC
Is your e-mail down? How long has it been down? Are there critically important e-mails that you're NOT GETTING???
Step 2:
Send yourself a test e-mail
Refresh Refresh
Not yet
Did it arrive?
Do it again just to be safe
Yes!
Phew.
Wait, what if it only works for YOU??
Step 3:
Annoy Your Friends
Ask them to send you a test e-mail. Surely, this is more important than anything they're doing.
Did it arrive?
Not yet
check again
Yes!
Relax
Wait, what if it JUST started working?
There is an undetermined period in time in which you may or may not have been able to receive important e-mails
Step 4:
Do Something Stupid
E-mail everyone you know and ask if they tried to send you an e-mail in the last hour.

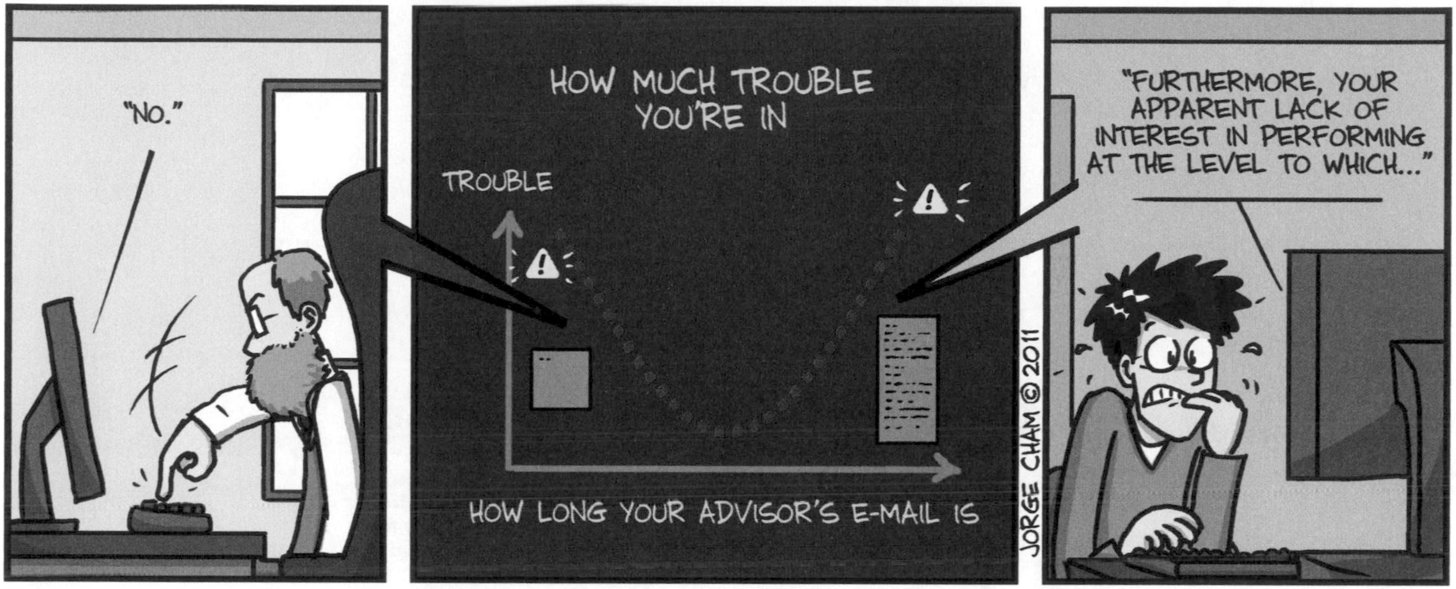
"NO."
HOW MUCH TROUBLE YOU'RE IN
TROUBLE
HOW LONG YOUR ADVISOR'S E-MAIL IS
JORGE CHAM © 2011
"FURTHERMORE, YOUR APPARENT LACK OF INTEREST IN PERFORMING AT THE LEVEL TO WHICH..."

DID YOU GET MY E-MAIL?
WHAT E-MAIL?
THE ONE I SENT LAST WEEK.
LET ME CHECK MY JUNK FOLDER.
AH. HERE IT IS.
...ALONG WITH ALL YOUR EMAILS FROM THE LAST SIX MONTHS.
JORGE CHAM © 2011
MY EMAILS ARE AUTOMATICALLY GOING INTO YOUR JUNK FOLDER??
YOU CAN DO IT AUTOMATICALLY?

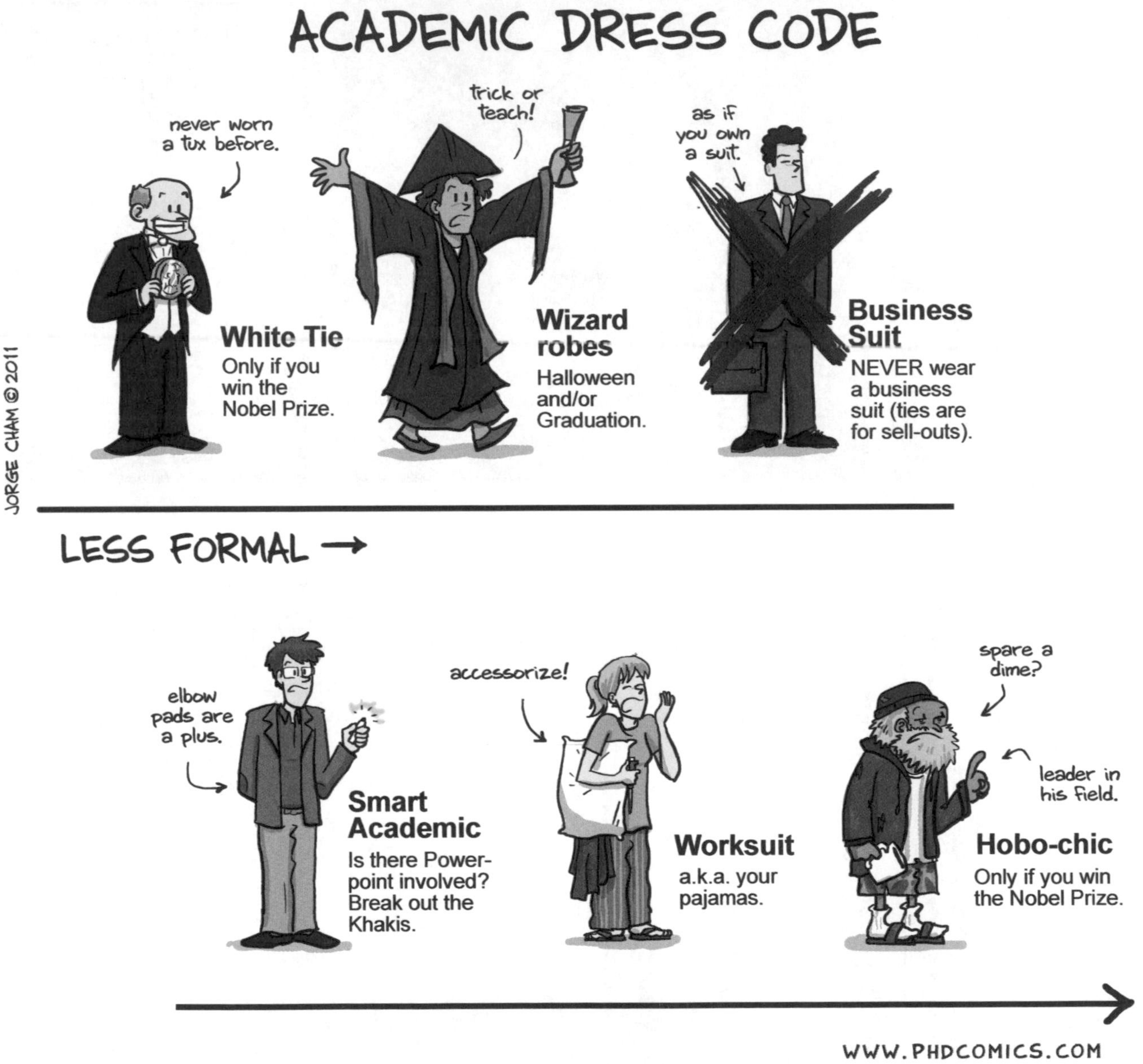
ACADEMIC DRESS CODE
never worn a tux before.
trick or teach!
as if you own a suit.
White Tie
Only if you win the Nobel Prize.
Wizard robes
Halloween and/or Graduation.
Business Suit
NEVER wear a business suit (ties are for sell-outs).
JORGE CHAM © 2011
LESS FORMAL →
elbow pads are a plus.
accessorize!
spare a dime?
leader in his field.
Smart Academic
Is there Power-point involved? Break out the Khakis.
Worksuit
a.k.a. your pajamas.
Hobo-chic
Only if you win the Nobel Prize.
WWW.PHDCOMICS.COM

WELL, I'M OFF TO OCCUPY WALL STREET.
LET ME GET THIS STRAIGHT: YOU'RE PART OF A MOVEMENT THAT IS VOCAL AND FRUSTRATED BUT DOESN'T HAVE CLEAR GOALS, DEMANDS OR A PLAN OF ACTION...
JORGE CHAM © 2011
...AND YOU WANT TO JOIN ANOTHER ONE?
GRAD SCHOOL IS MY BACKUP OCCUPATION.

HALLOWEEN!

BLOOD SUCKING VAMPIRES
boo! investment bankers!
BRAIN-EATING ZOMBIES
grades!
grades!
undergrads.
GHOSTLY APPARITIONS
i see post-docs!
JORGE CHAM © 2011
MAD SCIENTIST
i am not pleased.

"I'VE LOOKED AT IT."

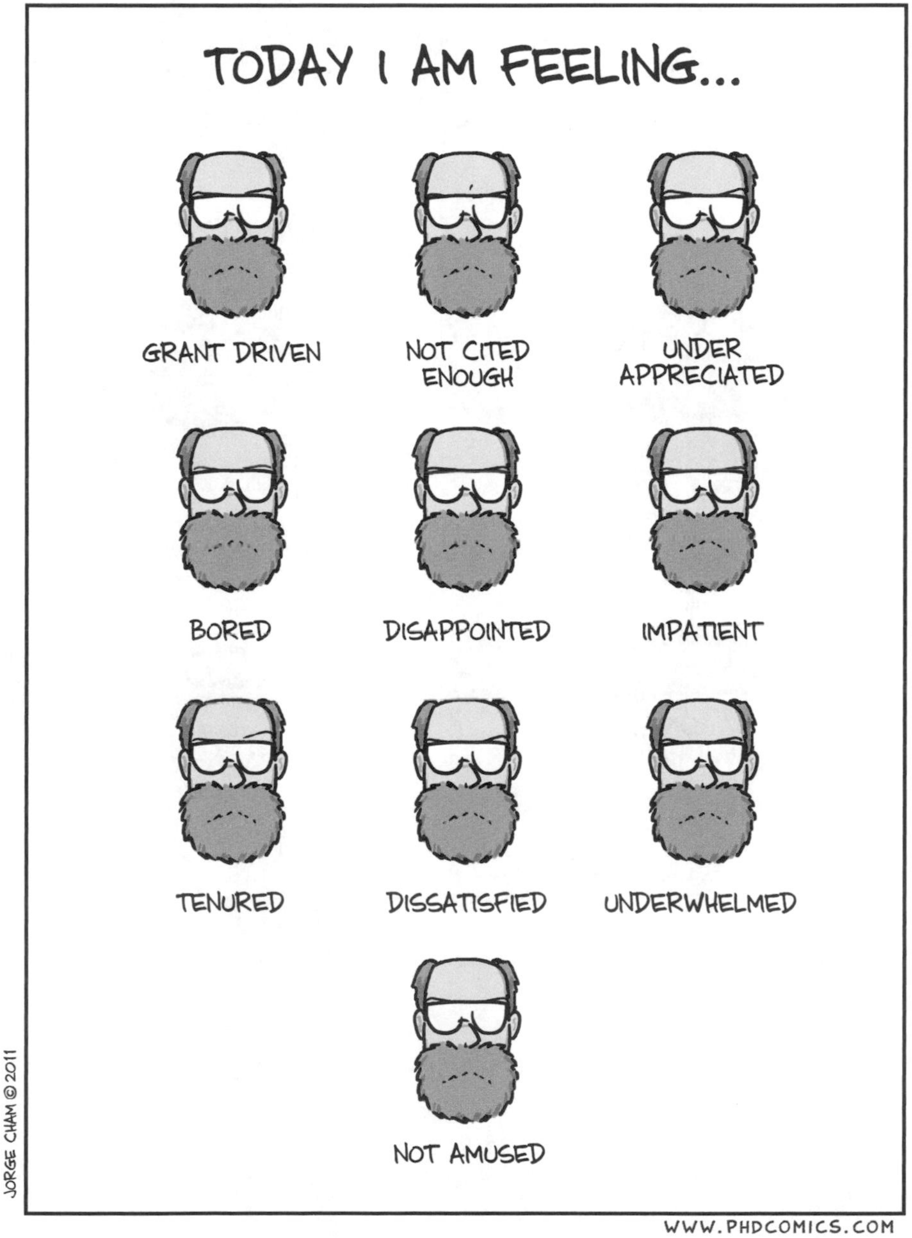

TODAY I AM FEELING...
GRANT DRIVEN
NOT CITED ENOUGH
UNDER APPRECIATED
BORED
DISAPPOINTED
IMPATIENT
TENURED
DISSATISFIED
UNDERWHELMED
NOT AMUSED
JORGE CHAM © 2011
WWW.PHDCOMICS.COM

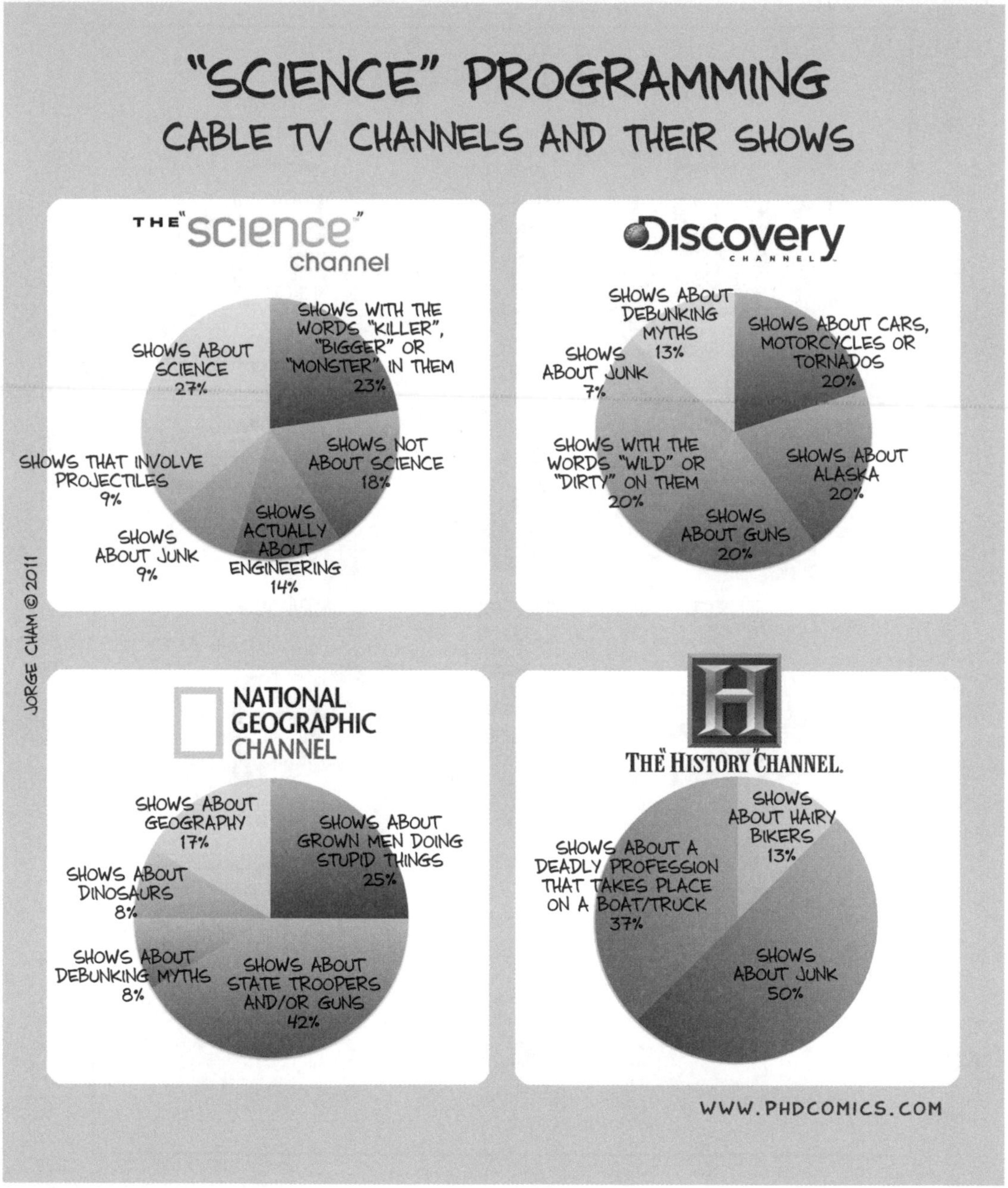
"SCIENCE" PROGRAMMING
CABLE TV CHANNELS AND THEIR SHOWS
THE "SCIENCE" CHANNEL
SHOWS ABOUT SCIENCE 27%
SHOWS WITH THE WORDS "KILLER", "BIGGER" OR "MONSTER" IN THEM 23%
SHOWS NOT ABOUT SCIENCE 18%
SHOWS ACTUALLY ABOUT ENGINEERING 14%
SHOWS ABOUT JUNK 9%
SHOWS THAT INVOLVE PROJECTILES 9%
Discovery CHANNEL
SHOWS ABOUT DEBUNKING MYTHS 13%
SHOWS ABOUT CARS, MOTORCYCLES OR TORNADOS 20%
SHOWS ABOUT ALASKA 20%
SHOWS ABOUT GUNS 20%
SHOWS WITH THE WORDS "WILD" OR "DIRTY" ON THEM 20%
SHOWS ABOUT JUNK 7%
JORGE CHAM © 2011
NATIONAL GEOGRAPHIC CHANNEL
SHOWS ABOUT GEOGRAPHY 17%
SHOWS ABOUT GROWN MEN DOING STUPID THINGS 25%
SHOWS ABOUT STATE TROOPERS AND/OR GUNS 42%
SHOWS ABOUT DEBUNKING MYTHS 8%
SHOWS ABOUT DINOSAURS 8%
THE "HISTORY" CHANNEL.
SHOWS ABOUT HAIRY BIKERS 13%
SHOWS ABOUT JUNK 50%
SHOWS ABOUT A DEADLY PROFESSION THAT TAKES PLACE ON A BOAT/TRUCK 37%
WWW.PHDCOMICS.COM

CECILIA, I WAS LOOKING AT YOUR DATA AND I THINK YOU NEED TO ADD A VARIABLE TO YOUR STUDY.
ANOTHER VARIABLE?? BUT THAT EXPONENTIALLY INCREASES THE AMOUNT OF WORK I HAVE TO DO!
I BARELY UNDERSTAND WHAT'S HAPPENING WITH MY CURRENT VARIABLES!!
JORGE CHAM © 2011
YOU MIGHT NEED A CONTROL VARIABLE TOO.
I DON'T HAVE CONTROL ISSUES!!

8:00AM
9:00AM
JORGE CHAM © 2011
10:00AM
#@$%!!

ping!
Your friend from High School wants to connect with you on **LinkedOut**, the Network for Professionals! Do you accept?
Yes, I accept. My profession is:
Grad Student
click.
JORGE CHAM © 2011
ping!
Your friend has retracted their invitation.
YEP.

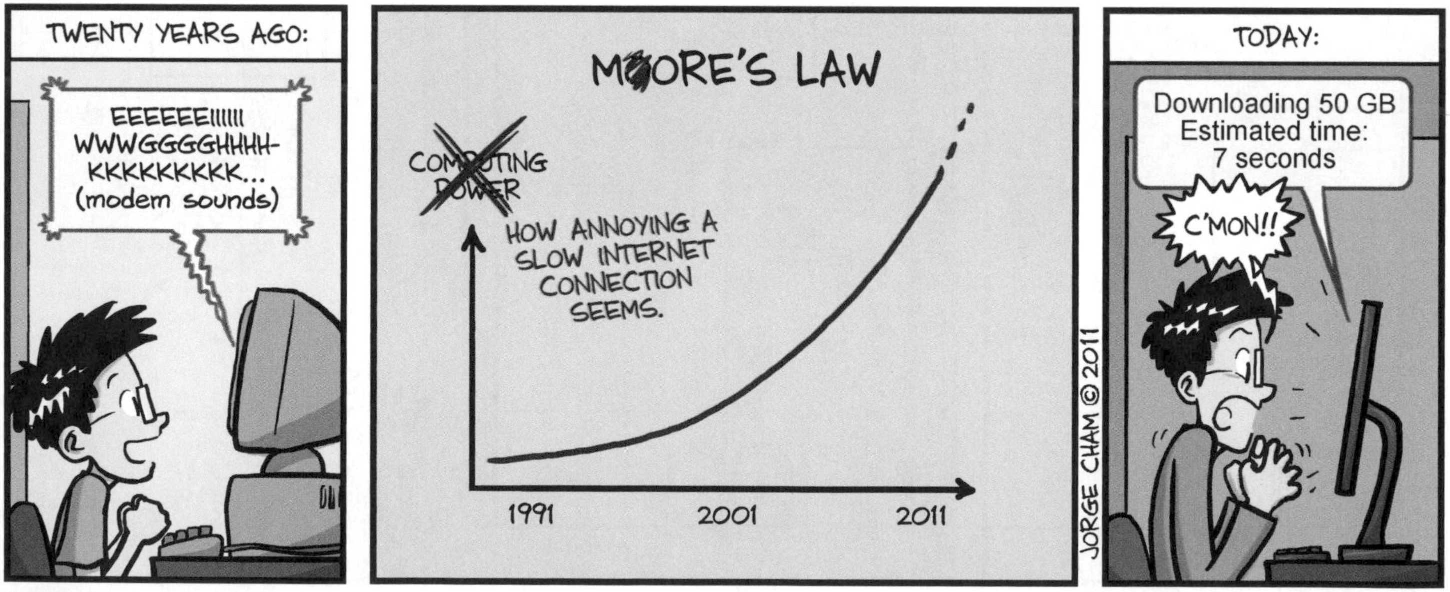
TWENTY YEARS AGO:
EEEEEEEIIIIII WWWGGGGHHHH-KKKKKKKKK... (modem sounds)
MOORE'S LAW
~~COMPUTING POWER~~
HOW ANNOYING A SLOW INTERNET CONNECTION SEEMS.
1991
2001
2011
JORGE CHAM © 2011
TODAY:
Downloading 50 GB Estimated time: 7 seconds
C'MON!!

I'M TELLING YOU, HE KEEPS A LIST OF PEOPLE HE LIKES AND DISLIKES...
HE'S GOT ELVES SLAVING AWAY ALL YEAR DOING MENIAL TASKS FOR LITTLE OR NO PAY...
HE ALWAYS WEARS THE SAME VEST AND HE ONLY SHOWS UP ONCE A YEAR.
JORGE CHAM © 2011
SANTA CLAUS IS A PROFESSOR!!
"H_0 H_0 H_0"? IT'S THE NULL HYPOTHESIS!

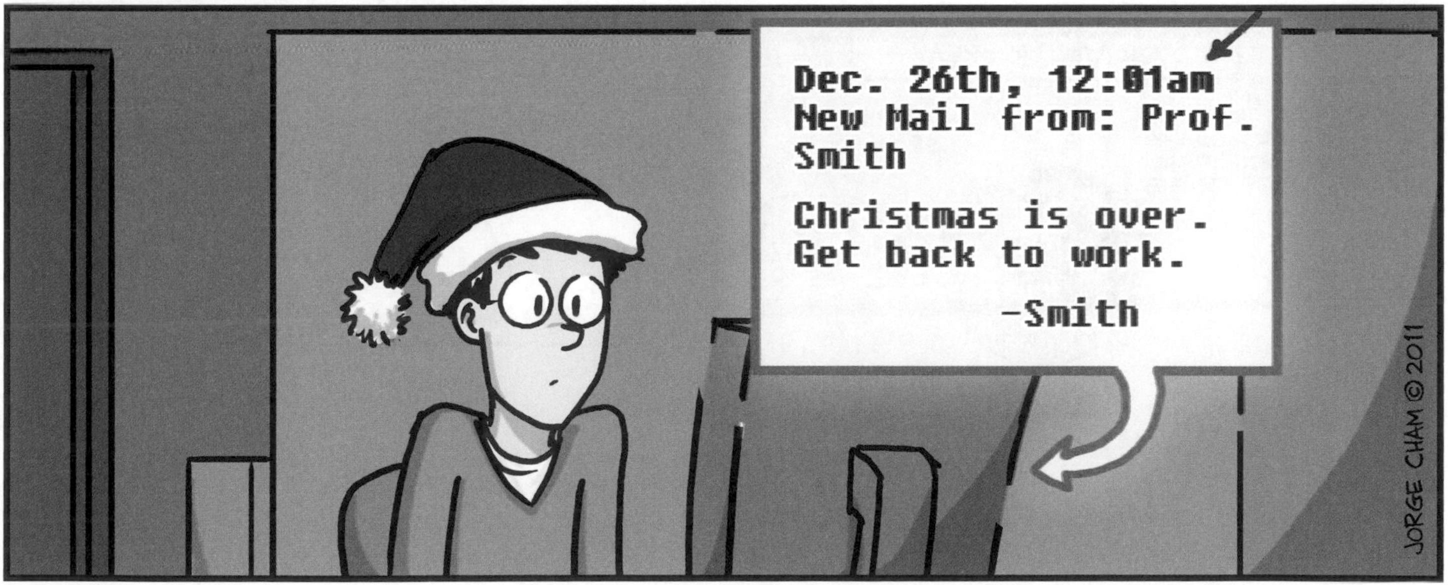
Dec. 26th, 12:01am
New Mail from: Prof. Smith
Christmas is over. Get back to work.
-Smith
JORGE CHAM © 2011

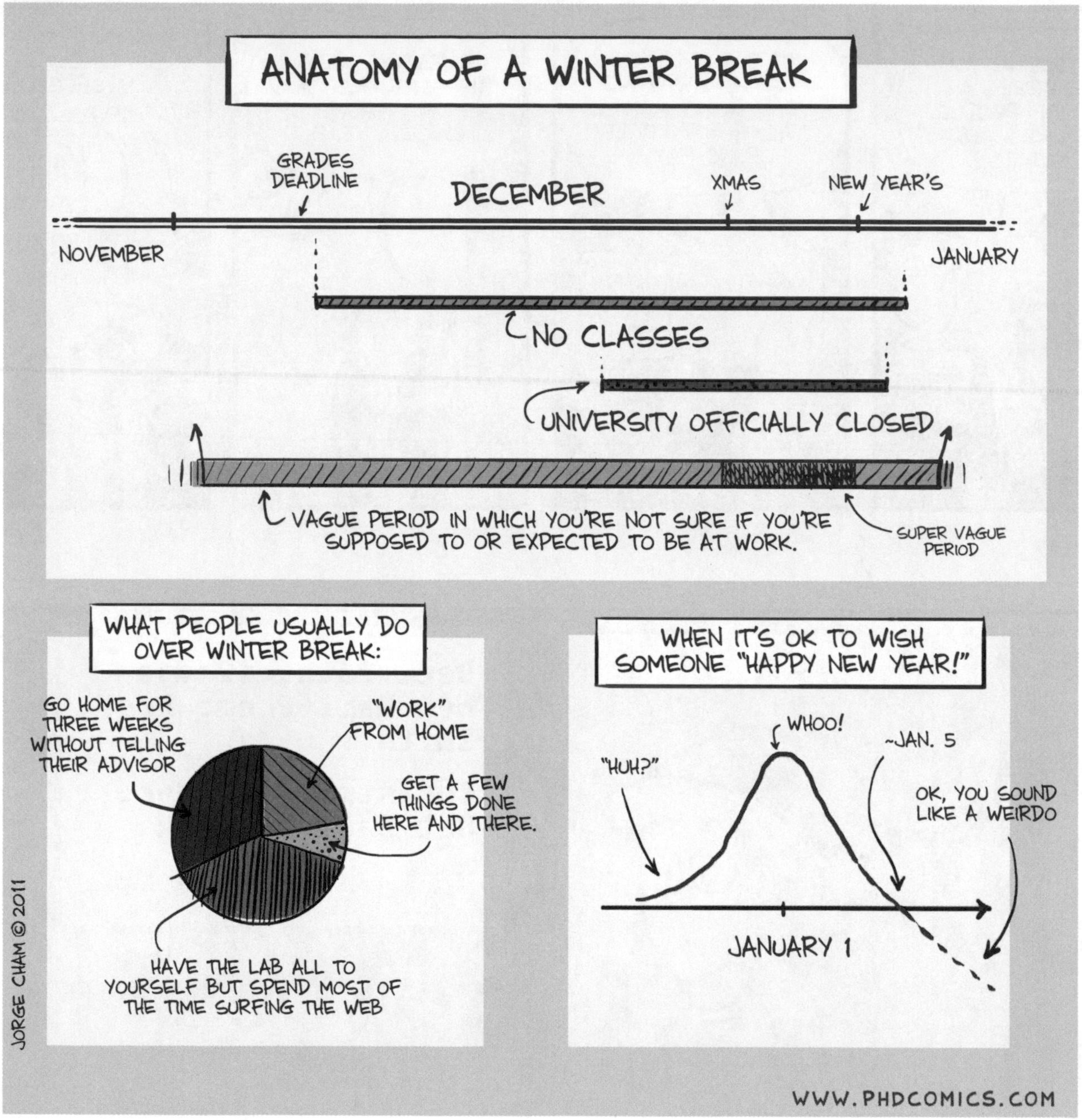
ANATOMY OF A WINTER BREAK
GRADES DEADLINE
DECEMBER
XMAS
NEW YEAR'S
NOVEMBER
JANUARY
NO CLASSES
UNIVERSITY OFFICIALLY CLOSED
VAGUE PERIOD IN WHICH YOU'RE NOT SURE IF YOU'RE SUPPOSED TO OR EXPECTED TO BE AT WORK.
SUPER VAGUE PERIOD
WHAT PEOPLE USUALLY DO OVER WINTER BREAK:
GO HOME FOR THREE WEEKS WITHOUT TELLING THEIR ADVISOR
"WORK" FROM HOME
GET A FEW THINGS DONE HERE AND THERE.
HAVE THE LAB ALL TO YOURSELF BUT SPEND MOST OF THE TIME SURFING THE WEB
WHEN IT'S OK TO WISH SOMEONE "HAPPY NEW YEAR!"
WHOO!
~JAN. 5
"HUH?"
OK, YOU SOUND LIKE A WEIRDO
JANUARY 1
JORGE CHAM © 2011
WWW.PHDCOMICS.COM

!
JORGE CHAM © 2011
THIS ACTUALLY HAPPENS.
IS HE GONE?

THANKS FOR MEETING WITH ME, PROF. RIVERA. I NEED TO DISCUSS A FEW THINGS ABOUT MY THESIS WITH YOU.
NO PROBLEM.
WELL, TO START, THE ARGUMENT I WAS USING FOR-
HOLD ON, HOLD ON. CAN YOU GO BACK A STEP?
OH. UH, WELL IF YOU REMEMBER THE OUTLINE WE DISCUSSED LAST-
NO, NO, GO BACK FURTHER.
JORGE CHAM © 2011
HI, MY NAME IS "TAJEL".
HOW DO YOU SPELL THAT?

More *QUANTUM*
Gradnamics

Feynman diagrams visualize and describe quantum academic interactions. They were first developed by Richard Feynman during his graduate years at Princeton.

Academic Interaction
FEYNMAN DIAGRAMS

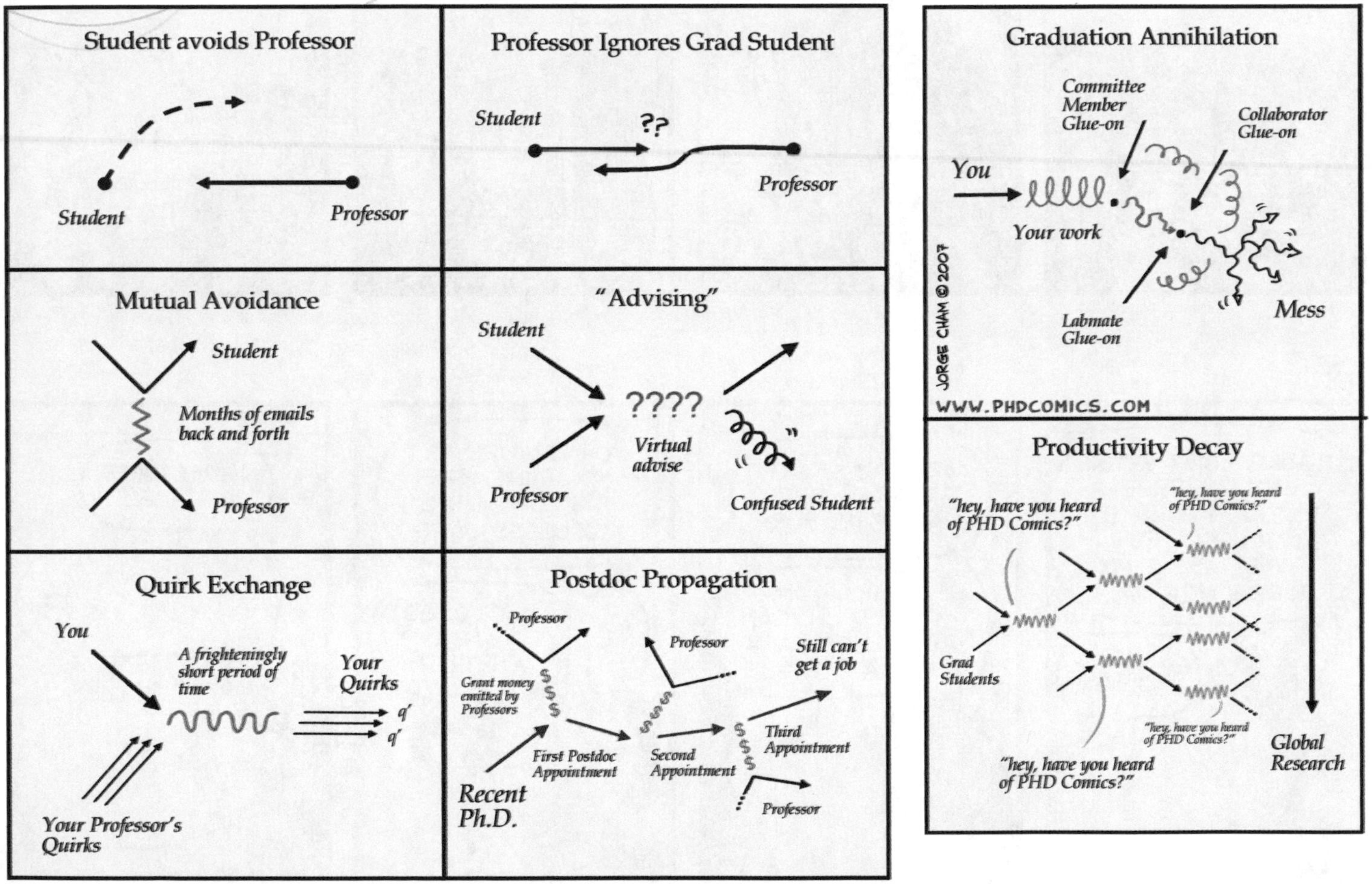

DO YOU THINK THIS WILL BE ENOUGH TO COMPLETE MY THESIS, PROF. RIVERA?
UH, MAYBE.
MAYBE? WHAT DO MEAN "MAYBE"?
I CAN'T REALLY TELL YOU WHAT A FINISHED THESIS WILL LOOK LIKE... I JUST KNOW IT WHEN I SEE IT.
JORGE CHAM ©2011
CAN YOU GIVE ME A CLUE?
IT'S NOT IN THIS ROOM.

SO HOW DO I KNOW WHEN I'VE DONE ENOUGH WORK FOR A THESIS, PROF. RIVERA?
WHEN YOU KNOW YOU'VE DONE ENOUGH, THAT'S WHEN YOU'VE DONE ENOUGH.
IT'S LIKE CLIMBING A MOUNTAIN...
WHEN THE VIEW CHANGES, YOU KNOW YOU'VE REACHED THE TOP.
JORGE CHAM ©2011
UNLESS YOU PASS OUT FROM ALTITUDE SICKNESS.
OR SOMEONE BEATS YOU TO THE TOP.
OR YOU FREEZE TO DEATH.
IT'S A VERSATILE METAPHOR.

OH, BY THE WAY, TAJEL, BEFORE YOU GO...
ANOTHER UNIVERSITY HAS OFFERED ME A POSITION AS CHAIR OF THEIR DEPARTMENT.
WHAT?
I HAVEN'T DECIDED IF I'M GOING OR NOT, BUT I THOUGHT YOU SHOULD KNOW.
wait, wait, let me get this straight...
JORGE CHAM © 2011
YOU'RE LEAVING??
OR NOT. IT'S NOT A BIG DEAL.
maybe i shouldn't have told you.
WELL, YOU HAVE TWO CHOICES, TAJEL. YOU CAN:
A) SWITCH TO A DIFFERENT PROFESSOR AND START YOUR THESIS ALL OVER AGAIN...
OR B) LEAVE EVERYTHING BEHIND, MOVE ACROSS THE COUNTRY AND JOIN ME IN MY NEW RESEARCH GROUP.
HOW ABOUT "C) YOU DON'T TOTALLY MESS UP MY LIFE?"
YOU HAVE A LIFE?
JORGE CHAM © 2011
SO, WHAT'S IT GOING TO BE?

Tales from the Road Comics
2009-2012

HOW LONG CAN HUMANITY SURVIVE ON EARTH?
DO YOU REALLY WANT TO KNOW?
PHD TALES FROM THE ROAD PRESENTS:
SUSTAINABILITY
RECENTLY, I WAS TREATED TO LUNCH AT "SAGE BISTRO"...
WEARING JEANS
...THE ULTRA FANCY RESTAURANT ON THE UNIVERSITY OF BRITISH COLUMBIA CAMPUS.
JOSH, A GRAD IN GEOGRAPHY, JUMPED AT THE CHANCE FOR A FREE MEAL HERE.
SIGN ME UP! IT'S THE BEST FOOD ON CAMPUS!
WHO'S "JORGE CHAM"?
OVERLOOKING THE WATER AND THE BEAUTIFUL MOUNTAINS, THIS WAS CLEARLY WHERE THE CAMPUS "POWER LUNCHES" TOOK PLACE.
UNIVERSITY BIG-WIGS
LITTLE WIGS
JOINING US FOR THE MULTI-COURSE MEAL WERE A COUPLE OF GRAD STUDENTS AND ONE PROFESSOR FROM THE FACULTY OF FORESTRY, ALL EXPERTS ON SUSTAINABILITY.
SO, CAN HUMANS LIVE SUSTAINABLY ON EARTH?
IT DEPENDS ON WHO YOU ASK...
BUT NO.

RIGHT NOW, WESTERN CIVILIZATION USES UP SEVERAL EARTHS FULL OF RESOURCES IN ITS CONSUMPTION...
THE GOOD LIFE
THIS IS BALANCED BY POOR DEVELOPING COUNTRIES WHO DON'T USE MUCH, BUT ONCE THEY CATCH UP...
...IT WON'T BE LONG BEFORE IT ALL COMES CRASHING DOWN.
JORGE CHAM © 2009
EVEN THE SCIENTISTS WHO STUDY THIS ARE PRONE TO EXCESS: AT A RECENT SUSTAINABILITY CONFERENCE, THE PROF. AT THE TABLE PUT UP A SLIDE WITH THE NUMBER OF TREES CONSUMED BY JUST FLYING EVERYONE TO THE CONFERENCE:
THIS CONFERENCE = 60,000 TREES
YES, BUT WE'RE WORTH IT.
IN FACT, MANY SAY WE ALREADY REACHED THE POINT OF NO RETURN.
YOU MEAN IT'S TOO LATE?
OH, THE HUMAN RACE WILL SURVIVE...
JUST NOT EVERYONE IN IT.
IN ADVANCE OF THE IMPENDING COLLAPSE OF CIVILIZATION, JOSH SAYS HE KEEPS A 6-MONTH SUPPLY OF CANNED BEANS IN HIS GARAGE.
YOU CAN USE THE ENSUING METHANE AS BIO-FUEL!
BEANS
BEANS
ONLY A SEVERE CRISIS LIKE THIS, THEY SAY, WILL FINALLY CAUSE PEOPLE AND CORPORATIONS TO UNDERGO RADICAL CHANGE:
FEWER CARS
SMALLER HOMES
MINIMAL WASTE
A LOT OF WHAT WE SEE TODAY IS JUST SUPERFICIAL "GREEN WASHING"...
NEW! ECOHUMMER
IT'S EGO-FRIENDLY!

IS THIS REALLY IT FOR HUMANITY? I BEG THEM FOR A GLIMMER OF HOPE:
PLEASE! GIVE ME SOME HOPE!
THE PROFESSOR THERE TRIES HIS BEST:
WHAT GIVES ME HOPE FOR THE FUTURE ARE THESE GUYS...
THE NEXT GENERATION OF GRAD STUDENTS WHO ARE BRINGING FRESH THINKING AND NEW IDEAS TO OUR PROBLEMS.
YEAH, WE'RE ALL DOOMED.
MORE WINE?
WWW.PHDCOMICS.COM

LAST YEAR I WAS INVITED TO SPEAK AT THE M.D. ANDERSON CANCER RESEARCH CENTER.
WATCHING THE AUDITORIUM FILL TO CAPACITY, I COULDN'T HELP BUT ASK...
DON'T YOU PEOPLE HAVE BETTER THINGS TO DO??
LIKE FINDING THE CURE FOR CANCER??
PROCRASTINATION
OVER DINNER AT THE HOUSTON AQUARIUM, THE GRAD STUDENTS LET ME IN ON THE GREAT SECRET OF CANCER RESEARCH...
THERE WILL NEVER BE A CURE FOR CANCER.
DON'T TELL OUR SPONSORS.
PHD "TALES FROM THE ROAD" TALKS ABOUT...
CANCER
WWW.PHDCOMICS.COM
YOU SEE, CANCER IS NOT ONE DISEASE...
IT'S NOT AN OUTSIDE AGENT ATTACKING YOUR BODY...
...OR SOMETHING IN YOUR BODY FAILING...
THERE ARE MANY, MANY TYPES OF CANCER: IT CAN CHANGE FROM PERSON TO PERSON...
...AND EVEN WITHIN THE SAME PERSON.
JORGE CHAM © 2009

ULTIMATELY WHAT WE SEEK ARE PROTOCOLS FOR A SERIES OF TESTS THAT ASCERTAIN WHAT THE BEST DRUG FOR EACH PATIENT IS AT A GIVEN TIME IN THE DEVELOPMENT OF THE DISEASE.
EXCUSE ME?
EXACTLY.
WHEN WE LOOK FOR DONATIONS, "GIVE US A MILLION $$'S TO FIND A CURE FOR CANCER"...
...SOUNDS A LOT BETTER THAN "GIVE US A MILLION $$'S TO FIND A MILLION CURES FOR A MILLION TYPES OF CANCERS"
??
THE PROBLEM IS THAT CANCER IS NOT A SINGLE MUTATION...
IT'S A WHOLE BUNCH OF POSSIBLE MUTATIONS OR DISRUPTIONS THAT, TOGETHER, ALLOW THE CELL TO:
DEACTIVATE PROGRAMMED LIMITS IN LIFESPAN AND HOW MANY TIMES ITS DNA CAN BE COPIED
CIRCUMVENT MECHANISMS FOR DETECTING AND REPAIRING DAMAGED DNA.
RECRUIT BLOOD VESSELS TO BRING IN NUTRIENTS
MAKE ITS OWN GROWTH SIGNALS AND IGNORE INHIBITORS FROM THE REST OF THE BODY
...SEPARATE AND ATTACK OTHER PARTS OF THE BODY.
IT'S A PROCESS THAT CAN OCCUR IN MANY DIFFERENT WAYS AND THROUGH MANY DIFFERENT MEANS, WHICH MAKES IT DIFFICULT TO FIND A COMMON CURE.
CANCER CELLS HAVE FIGURED OUT HOW TO CHEAT DEATH IN ALL ITS FORMS...
...EXCEPT ONE: THEIR HOST CANNOT SUSTAIN THEM.

I ASK MY HOST IF WORKING ON SOMETHING LIKE CANCER MAKES IT EASY TO FEEL MOTIVATED ABOUT YOUR RESEARCH.
YEAH, THAT WEARS OFF AFTER THE FIRST LAB EXPERIMENT.
WHEN YOUR PROJECT IS A SMALL ASPECT OF A SUB-PROBLEM OF SUCH A COMPLEX PHENOMENON, IT'S EASY TO THINK,
SIGH... WHAT'S THE POINT?
BUT SEEING PATIENTS HERE EVERYDAY REMINDS YOU WHAT YOU'RE DOING IS IMPORTANT.
FOR SOME, THE DISEASE HAS STRUCK CLOSE TO HOME:
MY FRIEND WAS DIAGNOSED AND 12 MONTHS LATER HE WAS GONE.
FOR OTHERS, EVEN CLOSER: AT THE END OF THE BOOKSIGNING, A YOUNG WOMAN ON HER WAY TO RADIO-THERAPY TELLS ME SHE WENT FROM BEING A PH.D. STUDENT IN CANCER RESEARCH TO BEING A PATIENT HERSELF.
I DECIDED NOT TO FINISH MY THESIS.
I DIDN'T WANT TO SPEND MY DAYS WORKING IN A LAB.
ANYWAYS, THANKS FOR MAKING US LAUGH.
I GUESS WE ALL DO WHAT WE CAN.

nature vs. Science PT. 2
A PHD Tales from the Road
www.phdcomics.com
AT A RECENT CONFERENCE IN CAMBRIDGE, I MET NATURE'S ONLINE PUBLISHING DIRECTOR, TIMO HANNAY.
YOU GUYS RUN MY COMICS ON YOUR WEBSITE.
WE DO?
IN HIS PRESENTATION, TIMO CANDIDLY DESCRIBES THE BUSINESS OF NATURE:
1 BASICALLY, SCIENTISTS GIVE US THEIR WORK FOR FREE...
2 ...THEN WE HAVE VOLUNTEER SCIENTISTS REVIEW IT FOR US FOR FREE...
3 ...THEN WE BUNDLE IT ALL UP AND SELL IT BACK TO THEM FOR A PROFIT.
$
JORGE CHAM © 2009
IT SOUNDS OUTRAGEOUS, BUT SCIENTISTS WILL DO IT BECAUSE THEY WANT TO BE PUBLISHED.
WE CAN CHARGE WHATEVER WE WANT. IT'S ESSENTIALLY A MONOPOLY,
nature genetics
nature medicine
GO TO PNAS

WELL, ALMOST. DOWN THE STREET, I VISIT THE OFFICES OF THE EUROPEAN BUREAU OF SCIENCE MAGAZINE:
IT'S A PRETTY SPIRITED RIVALRY.
LIKE TIME VS. NEWSWEEK.
JOHN TRAVIS, NEWS EDITOR
SO, WHICH ONE ARE YOU?
TIME. ONLY BECAUSE WE'RE BETTER.
nature
GALLERY OF EMBARRASSING NATURE GAFFES.
THERE'S EVEN AN ANNUAL CRICKET MATCH (THE BRITS USUALLY WIN)
TOTAL 272
WKTS 7
OVERS 47
INNS 156
RETRACTIONS 3
IMP. FACTOR 29.045
WE'RE PLAYING BASEBALL NEXT YEAR!
THE STAKES ARE HIGH.
WHAT EXACTLY DO YOU COMPETE FOR? SUBSCRIBERS? SALES?
THE BEST PAPERS.
OUR GOAL IS TO PUBLISH THE MOST INTERESTING, MOST PROVOCATIVE SCIENCE OF THE DAY.
PROVOCATIVE?
WHIZ! BANG!
COMPETITON IS SO FIERCE, EACH MAGAZINE EVEN SENDS SCOUTS TO RESEARCH CONFERENCES TO RECRUIT POTENTIAL PUBLICATIONS.
YOU GOT TALENT, KID.
HAVE YOU THOUGHT ABOUT PUBLISHING IN SCIENCE?

SOME SCIENTISTS WILL EVEN PLAY UP THE RIVALRY, IF THEY KNOW THEY'RE SITTING ON SOMETHING HOT.
YOU KNOW, NATURE IS OFFERING ME THE COVER IF I GO WITH THEM...
STILL, TIMO BELIEVES PRINT JOURNALS WILL LIKELY DISAPPEAR WITHIN THE NEXT 10 YEARS.
THE WEB IS WHERE IT'S AT.
SO I HEAR.
THE STIGMA OF THE INTERNET IS FADING. PEOPLE DON'T CARE ANYMORE IF SOMETHING ISN'T ACTUALLY PUBLISHED ON PAPER.
WELL, EXCEPT MONEY.
IT IS NATURE.COM *
* SOMEWHAT PARAPHRASED.

nature vs. Science PT. 3
A PHD Tales from the Road
www.phdcomics.com
HOW DOES A PAPER GET PUBLISHED IN A JOURNAL LIKE SCIENCE OR NATURE?
MARIA, A JUNIOR EDITOR AT SCIENCE, EXPLAINS THE PROCESS...
I'M A BIG PROCRASTINATOR.
WHEN PAPERS COME IN, EDITORS LIKE MARIA PERFORM "TRIAGE", PICKING OUT THE PAPERS THEY FEEL ARE APPROPRIATE FOR SCIENCE.
OOH.
THEY THEN HAND IT OFF TO AN EXTERNAL BOARD, WHICH COORDINATES PEER REVIEWS.
IN ALL, ABOUT 10% OF PAPERS SUBMITTED MAKE IT TO PRINT.
I HAVE A 10% CHANCE OF GETTING INTO SCIENCE?
WELL, MAYBE NOT YOU.
200 submissions/week
30%
10%
BONUS!
AT A RECENT EVENT CO-SPONSORED BY NATURE, I MEET A FEW OF THEIR TOP EDITORS:
I LEFT A TENURED JOB AT A TOP UNIVERSITY.
I ALWAYS WANTED TO BE AN EDITOR.
TERRY, NATURE CHEMICAL BIOLOGY.
200 PAPERS IS NOT A LOT. MOST SCIENTISTS SELF-SELECT THEMSELVES OUT.
THROUGHOUT THE PROCESS, EACH EDITOR TAKES OWNERSHIP OF A PARTICULAR PAPER.
WE WORK WITH THE AUTHORS TO MAKE THE PAPER CLEARER AND MORE CONCISE.
SCIENTISTS TEND TO OVER-REACH.
YOUR "DECIPHERING ACADEMESE" COMIC HELPS A LOT.
WE DON'T JUST PUBLISH THE PAPER. WE MAKE IT BETTER.

WE TRY TO SELECT PAPERS THAT ARE INFLUENTIAL OR THAT CAUSE PEOPLE TO THINK IN NEW WAYS.
NICOLA, CANCER REVIEWS
DOESN'T SELECTING IT HELP IT BECOME INFLUENTIAL?
THE THOUGHT HAS CROSSED OUR MINDS.
GOOGLE
THE LAST PAPER MARIA TOOK TO PRINT PRESENTED THE FIRST PLANET EVER DETECTED OUTSIDE OUR SOLAR SYSTEM.
IT MUST BE COOL TO SEE A PAPER YOU COACHED GO TO PRINT.
IMAGINE HOW THE AUTHORS FEEL!
IS IT WEIRD BEING ONE OF THE KEEPERS OF THE PEARLY GATES OF SCIENCE?
THIS IS THE PERFECT JOB FOR ME. I LOVE TO READ.
I GET TO BE AT THE CENTER OF SCIENCE WITHOUT ACTUALLY HAVING TO DO IT!
JORGE CHAM © 2009

nature VS. Science VS OPEN ACCESS??? PT. 4
A PHD Tales from the Road
www.phdcomics.com
SO WHAT DOES THE FUTURE HOLD FOR SCIENTIFIC PUBLISHING? TIMO EXPLAINS:
THE FUNDAMENTAL DEBATE OF OUR TIME IS OPEN ACCESS.
OPEN ACCESS?
WHO OWNS THE RIGHT TO PUBLISHED RESEARCH? AND MORE IMPORTANTLY,
WHO'S GONNA PAY FOR IT?
I DIDN'T KNOW A LOT ABOUT THIS TOPIC, SO I DID WHAT ANY HARD-HITTING INTERNET JOURNALIST (READ: BLOGGER) DOES TO GET TO THE TRUTH:
I SURFED THE WEB. (IN MY PJ'S)
HERE IS WHAT I FOUND OUT:
IN 2001, SEVERAL PROMINENT SCIENTISTS PUBLISH AN OPEN LETTER THAT PROCLAIMS:
"SCIENTIFIC RESEARCH AND IDEAS SHOULD NEITHER BE OWNED NOR CONTROLLED BY PUBLISHERS. THEY SHOULD BELONG TO THE PUBLIC AND BE FREELY AVAILABLE."
34,000 SCIENTISTS SIGN THE PETITION.
SHORTLY BEFORE, VITEK TRACZ, FOUNDER OF BIOMED CENTRAL, ENVISIONS AN ONLINE OPEN REPOSITORY OF PAPERS:
SCIENCE CAN'T FUNCTION EFFICIENTLY ANYMORE WITHOUT OPEN, UNRESTRICTED ACCESS. IT IS INEVITABLE.
IN 2005, THE NATIONAL INST. OF HEALTH MANDATES THAT ALL NIH-FUNDED RESEARCH BE FREELY ACCESSIBLE WHEN PUBLISHED.
NATIONAL INSTITUTES OF HEALTH
IN 2007, A LOBBYING GROUP IS FORMED BY CERTAIN PUBLISHERS, PROFESSIONAL SOCIETIES AND SOME ACADEMICS, HERALDING OPEN ACCESS AS THE END OF SCIENTIFIC INTEGRITY.
PRISM
NUMBER OF OPEN ACCESS JOURNALS
1000
2000
4000
1980
1990
2000
Source: Directory of Open Access Journals

USING MY EXTENSIVE CONTACT NETWORK (READ: TWITTER), I LAND AN INTERVIEW WITH PETE BINFIELD, MANAGING EDITOR OF "PLOS ONE", CURRENTLY THE LARGEST OPEN ACCESS JOURNAL ON EARTH.
THIS ISN'T "GOTCHA" JOURNALISM, IS IT?
YOU'RE NOT GONNA QUOTE ME OUT OF CONTEXT, ARE YOU?
PEOPLE ARE AFRAID TO TALK TO ME?
PETE IS A 15 YEAR VETERAN OF THE PUBLISHING BUSINESS.
ALL THAT TIME, I FELT THERE WAS SOMETHING WRONG WITH THE CURRENT SYSTEM.
"THERE IS SO MUCH WASTE IN THE SUBMISSION PROCESS AND IN THE MARKETING AND SALES DEPARTMENTS OF JOURNALS...
...THERE HAS TO BE A MORE INTELLIGENT WAY TO DO THINGS."
SCIENCE?
JOURNALS
PLOS ONE TAKES A STEP FURTHER AND ONLY PEER-REVIEWS FOR TECHNICAL CORRECTNESS, NOT "IMPACT". THEY USE THE WEB TO RANK EACH PAPER.
THE #1 PAPER THIS YEAR IS...
KEYBOARD CAT?
WHY SHOULD A FEW INDIVIDUALS AT THE TOP JOURNALS HAVE ALL THE POWER?
LET THE WORLD DECIDE WHAT IS SIGNIFICANT!
WILL SUBSCRIPTION JOURNALS SURVIVE? CAN OPEN ACCESS PUBLISHERS STAY AFLOAT? WHAT'S GONNA HAPPEN TO SCIENTIFIC PUBLISHING??
To download the full story, please sign-in to your subscription account or make a payment.
Login Required
User Name:
Password:
GO ›
Forgotten username or password?
Don't really care? Sign out Here
JORGE CHAM © 2009

I JUST GOT DEPORTED BY THE BRITISH GOVERNMENT!
WELL, ALMOST.
[DETAINED!]
A PHD TALES FROM THE ROAD HEATHROW DETENTION FACILITY
AFTER TRAVELS TO ALASKA, NETHERLANDS, HUNGARY AND GERMANY, I END UP HERE IN THE U.K. FOR A 7-LECTURE TOUR.
WHERE AM I AGAIN?
PLEASE STATE YOUR PURPOSE.
WWW.PHDCOMICS.COM
NOW, IT USED TO BE THAT I'D TRY TO EXPLAIN TO THE BORDER AGENTS MY COMPLICATED CAREER:
uh, well, i have a Ph.D. but i draw comics and get invited to give lectures about procrastination...
COME AGAIN?
IMMIGRATION
BUT AT SOME POINT I FIGURED OUT IT'S BEST TO KEEP THINGS SIMPLE:
I'M A CARTOONIST!
HAHA, REALLY? COME ON IN!
OR SO I THOUGHT...
PLEASE FOLLOW ME.
EXIT
SIR, YOU'RE BEING DETAINED BY U.K. BORDER CONTROL, PENDING FURTHER INVESTIGATION.
LOOK HERE.
JORGE CHAM © 2009
SIGN HERE.
WAIT HERE.
FREAK OUT HERE.
!!

THE OFFICER ASSIGNED TO MY CASE EXPLAINED THE PROBLEM:
WE DON'T THINK YOU QUALIFY AS AN ACADEMIC VISITOR.
BUT I HAVE A PH.D.! I'M GIVING LECTURES AT UNIVERSITIES! I HAVE A PH.D.!
SORRY.
THE RULES SAY DOCTORS ARE ALLOWED IN, BUT YOU'RE NOT A REAL DOCTOR, ARE YOU?
* HE ACTUALLY SAID THIS.
WHILE WAITING, I STARTED TO CHAT WITH SOME OF THE OTHER DETAINEES:
RASHID
ABDUL
I'M JUST HERE TO VISIT MY FAMILY!
posters of superman, batman, marilyn monroe, puppies
everything is bolted down.
ALL MEN, ALL NON-WHITE
IS THERE A MR. MOHAMMED..?
YES?
YES?
* THIS ACTUALLY HAPPENED.

OK, TO BE FAIR, THERE WAS ONE WHITE GUY.
WHAT THE F*@#!!
AFTER HOURS IN DETENTION (AT LEAST THERE WAS FREE FOOD) I WAS GIVEN THE NEWS:
YOU'RE BEING DEPORTED.
BUT, BUT... I HAVE A PH.D.!
"WE'VE PUT YOU ON THE FIRST FLIGHT OUT TOMORROW. REPORT BACK THEN."
Welcome to the U.K.
HMM, NOW WHAT?
TO BE CONCLUDED!
I CHECK INTO A HOTEL THAT NIGHT AND SEND FRANTIC EMAILS TO ALL SEVEN LECTURE ORGANIZERS.
OH MAN, I HOPE SOMEBODY IS CHECKING THEIR EMAIL!
SUNDAY NIGHT AT 9pm
PING! REPLY!
PING!
PING!
THANK GOODNESS FOR WORKAHOLIC ACADEMICS!
ARMED WITH LETTERS OF SUPPORT, I GO THE NEXT MORNING AND BEG THEM TO REVIEW MY CASE.
"DR. CHAM IS A HIGHLY-REGARDED EXPERT IN POST-GRAD RESEARCH?"
IT'S NOT UNTRUE.

TWO HOURS BEFORE MY DEPORTATION FLIGHT, I AM UNCEREMONIOUSLY HANDED BACK MY PASSPORT:
TAKE CARE.
THAT'S IT?
SINCE I WROTE THESE COMICS, I'VE BEEN HEARING MORE AND MORE STORIES FROM PEOPLE WITH SIMILAR EXPERIENCES NOT JUST IN THE U.K., BUT THE U.S. AS WELL.
i was detained for 24 hours!
our speaker was sent back to his country!
the postdoc in my lab is being forced to leave!
THIS IS WHAT IT'S LIKE FOR US WITH (muslim/latin-american/non-european/non-US) BACKGROUNDS!
AT ONE OF THE UNIVERSITIES I SPOKE AT, THE GRADUATE DEAN TELLS ME THINGS HAVE GOTTEN WORSE IN RECENT YEARS.
IT'S STARTING TO RESTRICT OUR ABILITY TO DO RESEARCH.
THE U.K. NOW REQUIRES THAT DEPARTMENTS CLOSELY TRACK THEIR INTERNATIONAL STUDENTS:
june 15, meeting with student whats-his-name.
THERE HAVE TO BE AT LEAST 10 RECORDED INTERACTIONS WITH THEM A YEAR.
AS YOU CAN IMAGINE, THIS CAN BE DIFFICULT WITH PH.D. STUDENTS.
THEY TEND TO... DRIFT.
SO, IT LOOKS LIKE WE'LL HAVE A HAPPY ENDING: THE LECTURES HAVE GONE WELL AND EVERYONE HAS BEEN WONDERFUL.
STILL, I KEEP LOOKING OVER MY SHOULDER FOR SOME REASON.
JORGE CHAM © 2009
WWW.PHDCOMICS.COM

RECENTLY, I TRAVELLED TO FRANCE TO GIVE MY "POWER OF PROCRASTINATION" TALK AT THE FAMOUS ÉCOLE POLYTECHNIQUE (AKA "X") NEAR PARIS.
a tech school? have they heard of an elevator??
PHD TALES FROM THE ROAD:
ÉGALITÉ DE CHANCE
OPPORTUNITY, ELITISM AND POLITICS IN ACADEMIA, PART 1 OF 2
MY OPENING ACT? NONE OTHER THAN FRENCH PRESIDENT NICOLAS SARKOZY HIMSELF!
OK, IT'S MORE LIKE THEY HAD TO POSTPONE MY TALK BECAUSE HE DECIDED TO GIVE A LAST-MINUTE POLITICAL SPEECH ON CAMPUS.
SACRE BLEU! WHO DOES HE THINK HE IS?
UH, LE PRÉSIDENT?
WWW.PHDCOMICS.COM
JORGE CHAM © 2010
WHEN I ARRIVED, THE SCHOOL WAS IN COMPLETE CHAOS: SECURITY EVERYWHERE, LARGE CROWDS, PROFESSORS STAGING PROTESTS!
RECHERCHE EN PERIL!!
(PROTESTS ARE DE RIGEUR IN FRANCE)
SARKOZY'S SPEECH WAS ON "EQUALITY OF OPPORTUNITY", THE LATEST IN A SERIES OF REFORMS HIS RIGHT-LEANING (FOR FRANCE) GOVERNMENT HAS ENACTED.
MY "PERSONAL" INVITATION:
Monsieur Nicolas Sarkozy
Président de la République
THE GOAL: TO REDIRECT POWER AWAY FROM PROFESSORS, UNIONS AND THE CNRS (FRANCE'S NSF) AND INTO THE HANDS OF UNIVERSITY ADMINISTRATORS, .
SO THEY CAN BE MORE "STRATEGIC" WITH THEIR RESEARCH.
BASICALLY, WE ARE COPYING THE U.S. SYSTEM.

I TRIED TO GET IN THE LECTURE, BUT WAS CRUSHED BY THE HUGE MOB FIGHTING THEIR WAY IN. UNFORTUNATELY, SOME FRENCH STEREOTYPES ARE TRUE:
PUSHY!
SMELLY!
I HAD TO SETTLE FOR A SEAT IN THE OVERFLOW ROOM.
SUBTITLES, PLEASE!
IN HIS SPEECH, SARKOZY RE-ITERATED CRITICISM OF FRANCE'S "GRANDE ÉCOLE" SYSTEM OF PUBLIC HIGHER EDUCATION AS BEING TOO ELITIST.
"HOW CAN WE TALK ABOUT A REPUBLIC WHEN SUCCESS DOES NOT DEPEND ON MERIT?"
LATER THAT NIGHT, AT PARIS' SUPPOSEDLY OLDEST BAR, A GROUP OF "X'ERS" TRY TO EXPLAIN TO ME THIS COMPLEX SYSTEM:
WE'RE GOING TO NEED PEN AND PAPER.
AND MORE BEER.
BASICALLY, THE FRENCH SYSTEM FUNNELS YOU AFTER HIGH SCHOOL INTO ONE OF TWO TRACKS:
HIGH SCHOOL
(WHAT NOW??)
EASY NO PRESSURE
90%
BAC EXAM
10%
VERY HARD WORK
UNIVERSITY
(CRAPPY)*
PREPA
(TOUGH TIME)
3yrs
2yrs
LICENCE
MASTERS
(NOT SO BAD)
2yrs
GRANDES ÉCOLES
3YRS
90%
(NO WORK) EASY
CRAPPY JOB**
10%
PHD
GOOD JOB
€€€€
???YRS
CNRS
(WILL IT LAST LONG?)
???
(MAYBE)
* EXCEPT LAW, MEDICINE
** EXCEPT IF YOU ARE SMART + MOTIVATED

GETTING INTO THE ÉCOLE SYSTEM ESSENTIALLY GUARANTEES YOU ONE OF THE TOP PAYING JOBS, SINCE EMPLOYERS USE IT AS A BLACK AND WHITE FILTER:
YOU'RE FROM AN ÉCOLE? ME TOO! YOU'RE HIRED.
ALEXANDRE, A PHYSICS PHD, SAYS HIS FATHER NEVER GOT A PROMOTION SIMPLY BECAUSE HE WAS NOT FROM AN ELITE SCHOOL.
IT'S A 200 YEAR OLD DISCRIMINATION SCANDAL, IS WHAT IT IS.
SO, A TEST IN HIGH SCHOOL DETERMINES WHETHER YOU'LL GET A GOOD OR BAD JOB FOR THE REST OF YOUR LIFE?
MERDE!
OR YOU CAN GET A PH.D.
FIN DE PART 1

PHD TALES FROM THE ROAD:
EGALITE DE CHANCE
PART 2 OF 2
MANY SEE THE GRANDES ÉCOLES SYSTEM AS UNFAIR, BUT WHERE IS THE INJUSTICE?
IS IT ONLY FOR RICH PEOPLE?
UH, NO, IT'S FREE.
IS ADMISSION BASED ON RACE OR CONNECTIONS?
UH, NO, IT'S BASED ON A TEST.
THE PROBLEM, THEY TELL ME, IS NOT RACIAL, ETHNIC OR FINANCIAL, IT'S...
...SOCIAL.
WHAT IF YOU GROW UP IN A BAD NEIGHBORHOOD OR ENVIRONMENT WHERE NO ONE EVER ENCOURAGES YOU, OR PREPARES YOU OR EVEN TELLS YOU THIS DUAL SYSTEM EXISTS?
U
ÉCOLES
STUDENTS FROM THE WORKING CLASSES ARE FIVE TIMES LESS LIKELY TO MAKE IT TO A GRANDE ÉCOLE.
TEK, AN ENGINEERING PH.D. AND THE SON OF CAMBODIAN REFUGEES, TELLS ME THAT GROWING UP IN A BANLIEUE, THE ÉCOLES SEEMED UNATTAINABLE.
I THOUGHT YOU HAD TO BE A GENIUS TO GET IN.
THEN HE MET US.
INSTEAD, HE WENT ALONG WITH EVERYONE ELSE TO A UNIVERSITY.
EXPECTATIONS WERE SO LOW, IT ACTUALLY TAUGHT ME TO BE SELF-MOTIVATED AND TO LEARN BY MYSELF.
IT'S A USEFUL SKILL IN RESEARCH.

THE ÉCOLE SYSTEM, THEY ALL AGREE, MOSTLY WEEDS OUT BASED ON ONE SKILL:
BEING GOOD AT TAKING TESTS.
IN THIS WAY, THE PH.D. IS A GREAT EQUALIZER.
THERE IS NO DIFFERENCE HERE BETWEEN PEOPLE FROM EITHER SYSTEM.
WE'RE ALL SAD! GEEKS
IN HIS SPEECH, SARKOZY PROPOSED REQUIRING THAT ÉCOLES ADMIT 30% OF THEIR STUDENTS FROM LOW-INCOME BACKGROUNDS. THE ÉCOLES WERE OUTRAGED:
"THIS WILL INEVITABLY LEAD TO LOWER STANDARDS."
HEY!
CONFERENCE DES GRANDES ECOLES
PRESIDENT OF THE CONFERENCE OF GRANDE ECOLES
FLORIAN, WHO JOINED IN THE PROFESSOR PROTEST, EXPLAINS THE UNDERLYING ISSUE HERE:
PROFESSORS DON'T OBJECT SO MUCH TO THE CHANGES...
BUT RATHER HOW THEY ARE BEING PUSHED THROUGH WITHOUT THEIR CONSULTATION.
IT'S A VICIOUS CYCLE:
WHY BOTHER?
PROFESSORS SAY NO BECAUSE THEY ARE NOT CONSULTED.
(AND THEY DON'T LIKE CHANGE)
THE GOVERNMENT DOESN'T CONSULT THEM BECAUSE EVERYONE KNOWS PROFESSORS WILL SAY "NO"
DON'T BOTHER ME.
JORGE CHAM © 2010

AFTER THE TALK WAS OVER, I TRIED TO GET A PEEK AT FRANCE'S CONTROVERSIAL PRESIDENT.
ALAS, I ONLY SAW THE TOP OF HIS HEAD.
WWW.PHDCOMICS.COM
LATER AT THE BOOKSIGNING, I ASKED ONE OF THE GRADS, SALIM, WHAT HE THOUGHT OF THE BIG SPEECH:
IT WAS NICE. BUT THERE'S A BIG DIFFERENCE BETWEEN WHAT PEOPLE SAY AND WHAT THEY DO.
WAIT, WHOSE SPEECH ARE WE TALKING ABOUT? YOURS OR SARKOZY'S?
FIN!

ONE OF MY FAVORITE MOVIES OF ALL TIME IS "CONTACT" STARRING JODIE FOSTER AND BASED ON THE NOVEL BY CARL SAGAN.
PHD TALES FROM THE ROAD
CONTACT
NEW MEXICO TECH AND THE VLA - PART 1 OF 2
IT'S ABOUT SCIENCE AND RELIGION AND ONE WOMAN'S QUEST TO ANSWER THE QUESTION:
CONTACT
ARE WE ALONE?
I FIRST SAW THIS MOVIE IN GRAD SCHOOL WITH THE FILM MAKERS' PROBABLE WORST NIGHTMARE: SIGNAL PROCESSING PHD'S.
NO WAY INVERTING THE SIGNAL POLARITY WOULD HAVE BOOSTED FIELD COHERENCE!
THE ALIENS WERE COOL, THOUGH.
SO YOU CAN IMAGINE MY EXCITEMENT WHEN I WAS OFFERED A TOUR OF THE RADIO TELESCOPES FEATURED IN THE FILM DURING A RECENT VISIT TO NEW MEXICO TECH:
THE (IMAGINATIVELY NAMED) VERY LARGE ARRAY (VLA)
LEADING THE TOUR WAS CRYSTAL, A PHD STUDENT IN ASTRONOMY:
READY?
I'M OK TO GO! OK TO GO!*
* MOVIE REFERENCE

YOU THINK YOUR SCHOOL IS IN A REMOTE LOCATION? TRY SOCORRO, NM, A DESERT TOWN SO SMALL IT ONLY HAS ONE THEATER.
ACTUALLY, IT CLOSED DOWN.
THERE ISN'T EVEN A STARBUCKS!
GASP!
THE ISOLATION, THOUGH, MAKES IT A PERFECT PLACE FOR WATCHING THE SKIES.
AND FOR GETTING RESEARCH DONE?
WE FIND OTHER WAYS TO PROCRASTINATE.
MOST PEOPLE FIND OUT ABOUT THE VLA AND NEW MEXICO TECH THROUGH THE MOVIE.
IT'S GREAT PUBLICITY, BUT...
"...SOMETIMES IT'S HARD TO UNDO THAT PUBLIC PERCEPTION."
HAS E.T. CALLED YET?
WE DO REAL SCIENCE HERE, NOT SCIENCE FICTION!
AWWW...
CAN YOU CALL THEM?
I'M HANGING UP NOW, MOM.
WWW.PHDCOMICS.COM

"CONTACT" PHD TALES FROM THE ROAD: NEW MEXICO TECH AND THE VLA, PART 2 OF 2
CRYSTAL EXPLAINS HER RESEARCH:
"I LOOK AT THE X-RAYS EMITTED IN REGIONS WHERE HIGH-MASS STARS ARE BORN."
"THE RADIATION CAPTURED BY THE TELESCOPES GIVES US AN IDEA OF THE COMPOSITION AND DISTRIBUTION OF THE PROCESSES INVOLVED."
THE ARRAY OF 27 GIANT MOVABLE 25m-DIAMETER ANTENNAES ARE SO SENSITIVE, MICROWAVE OVENS ARE PROHIBITED ON SITE.
HOW DO YOU HEAT UP THE RAMEN??
CELL PHONES OFF TOO!
OTHER DANGERS INCLUDE:
WALKING TOUR
CAUTION
WATCH OUT FOR SNAKES
SNAKES!
ACTING LIKE A FAN BOY
V L A
OBLIGATORY "VLA" POSE PHOTO

LIKE JODIE FOSTER'S CHARACTER IN THE MOVIE, CRYSTAL WAS HOOKED ON ASTRONOMY FROM AN EARLY AGE.
"I'D CAMP OUT IN MY BACKYARD AND LOOK UP AT THE STARS....
WE LIVED IN THE MIDDLE OF NOWHERE."
THE PUBLIC EDUCATION SHE HAD ACCESS TO WASN'T GREAT, SO WHEN SHE FINALLY GOT TO TAKE AN ASTRONOMY CLASS AT A LOCAL COMMUNITY COLLEGE, SHE WAS ECSTATIC.
GLEE!
JORGE CHAM © 2010
DOES SHE STILL FEEL THE SAME WAY, YEARS INTO GRAD SCHOOL?
WELL, THE HARD PART IS NOT KNOWING HOW LONG YOUR THESIS WILL TAKE.
ASSUMING YOU'RE ALLOWED TO USE THE TELESCOPES, YOUR PROJECT MAY NOT EVEN WORK!
AFTER MY LECTURE, I SIGN A BOOK FOR PROFESSOR BARRY CLARK, THE MAN IN CHARGE OF APPROVING TIME ON THE TELESCOPES.
YOU'RE STILL...
ALIVE?
WORKING?
CLARK WAS ONE OF THE ORIGINAL DESIGNERS OF THE VLA.

WHEN YOU GET INTO THE NITTY GRITTY OF ASTRONOMY RESEARCH, CRYSTAL TELLS ME, YOU DON'T WORK WITH THE PRETTY COLOR PICTURES THAT GOT YOU HOOKED AS A KID.
I20S and N1-N2 (Chandra source 109)
Ca?
Ca?
Fe
Normalized counts s^-1 keV^-1
Energy (keV)
BUT I STILL LOVE IT. IT'S NOT WHAT THE STARS LOOK LIKE THAT MATTERS.
IT'S WHAT THEY'RE MADE OF.
RECENTLY, I STARTED ASKING FANS WHO THEIR FAVORITE PHD CHARACTER IS. AT THE SIGNING HERE IN NEW MEXICO, A FAN TELLS ME:
CECILIA! SHE'S JUST LIKE ME!
IT MAKES ME FEEL LESS ALONE.
WWW.PHDCOMICS.COM

YES, THE LASER* TURNS FIFTY THIS YEAR.
*Light Amplified by Stimulated Emission of Radiation
ON A RECENT VISIT TO U. LAVAL IN QUEBEC, CANADA, PROF. MICHEL PICHE CHARACTERIZES THE LASER'S HISTORY.
IT WASN'T A COHERENT STRAIGHT LINE.
A NEAR-PERFECT COPY OF PROF. SMITH (BUT NICER!)
TO ILLUSTRATE, THE NOBEL PRIZE, THE FIRST PROTOTYPE AND THE PATENT FOR THE LASER ARE ALL CREDITED TO DIFFERENT PEOPLE.
IT'S A FASCINATING STORY, FUELED BY COLD WAR PARANOIA, A PUBLIC FASCINATED BY ITS SCI-FI IMPLICATIONS AND PURE SCIENTIFIC HARD WORK.
PICHE EXPLAINS TO ME HOW THE LASER WORKS:
ATOMS CAN EXIST IN DIFFERENT ENERGY LEVELS.
KIND OF LIKE GRAD STUDENTS.
ZZZ
ACCORDING TO EINSTEIN THERE ARE THREE WAYS AN ATOM CAN TRANSITION BETWEEN LEVELS:
THE ATOM ABSORBS A PHOTON AND GOES UP A LEVEL.
THE ATOM DROPS A LEVEL AND EMITS A PHOTON.
THE ATOM GETS HIT BY A PHOTON, EMITS AN EXTRA PHOTON IDENTICAL TO THE ONE THAT HIT IT, AND DROPS A LEVEL.

IT'S THIS LAST EFFECT, CALLED "STIMULATED EMISSION" THAT IS USED IN THE LASER.
JORGE CHAM © 2010
STIMULATION
THE STIMULATED ATOM CREATES A PERFECTLY SYNCHRONIZED COPY OF THE ORIGINAL PHOTON.
BY PLACING A MEDIUM (IT CAN BE ANYTHING: RUBY, GAS, JELLO...) BETWEEN TWO MIRRORS AND EXCITING IT TO A HIGHER STATE, A SORT OF CHAIN-REACTION RESONANT ECHO CHAMBER FORMS:
MIRROR
HALF-MIRROR
STIMULATION
COINCIDENTALLY, THIS WEEK IS ALSO THE FIFTH YEAR ANNIVERSARY OF THE PHD LECTURES.
(is this guy sleeping??)
IT WAS FIVE YEARS AGO THAT I GAVE MY FIRST TALK AT M.I.T. (ORGANIZED BY MY SISTER)
SEEING HOW MANY PEOPLE CAME OUT REALLY HELPED INSPIRE ME TO LEAVE ACADEMIA AND DO THESE COMICS FULL TIME.
200 LECTURES LATER, I AM MOST GRATEFUL TO THE FANS THAT ALLOW ME TO DO THIS FOR A LIVING.
IN THE ECHO CHAMBER OF ACADEMIA, IT IS THEM THAT SPREAD THE WORD ABOUT PHD COMICS.
have you heard of phd comics?
have you heard of phd comics?
have you heard of phd comics?
have you heard of phd comics?
AT THAT FIRST BOOK-SIGNING, A GIRL NAMED CHRISTINA DROVE IN FROM OUT OF TOWN TO GET A BOOK SIGNED.
I LOVE PHD!
AND LASERS?
I ♥ LASERS

I RECENTLY RAN INTO HER DURING A VISIT TO THE U. OF CENTRAL FLORIDA.
HEY, I ♥ LASERS, RIGHT?
IT'S BEEN YEARS! HOW DO YOU REMEMBER???
HER FAVORITE MOVIE GROWING UP WAS "REAL GENIUS".
IT MADE ME WANT TO STUDY LASERS.
AND MARRY VAL KILMER.
VAL KILMER
DURING A TOUR OF HER LAB, I ASK HER SOMETHING THAT'S BEEN BOTHERING ME ABOUT HOW THE LASER WORKS:
WHY DOES THE ATOM EMIT THE SECOND PHOTON (AND WHY IS IT IDENTICAL?)
AH, THAT'S THE SECRET SAUCE.
YOU'LL HAVE TO ASK EINSTEIN.*
WWW.PHDCOMICS.COM
*THEY DON'T KNOW.

TRUE TALES OF PROCRASTINATION!!
APPROVED BY THE INTERNET
PHD
FREE! 0¢
JORGE CHAM © 2010
WWW. PHD COMICS .COM
1
Behold... the PHD GUY takes on... COMIC-CON!
THIS IS SO PATRIARCHAL HEGEMONIC.
FEAR NOT! I AM A DOCTOR!
Featuring!
GRAD STUDENTS IN COSTUME!
COMIC ART SCHOLARS!
SOCIOLOGISTS!
GEEKINESS OVERLOAD!
FREE FOOD SENSE... TINGLING!!
PART 1 OF 3
1ST ISSUE!

LAST YEAR, I ATTENDED COMIC-CON, ONE OF THE LARGEST COMIC BOOK CONVENTIONS IN THE WORLD.
OVER 120,000 PEOPLE FLOCK TO THIS INSANE MECCA OF FANTASY, SCIENCE FICTION AND POP CULTURE.
I EVEN HAD A BOOTH, COURTESY OF THE "UNSHELVED" GUYS...
A GRAD STUDENT COMIC AND A LIBRARY COMIC... WE'LL CORNER THE EXTRA-NERD MARKET!
I HAD NO IDEA WHAT TO EXPECT.
WOULD ANYONE RECOGNIZE OR EVEN CARE ABOUT MY COMICS HERE?
PHD COMICS!
HEY, IT'S PHD COMICS!
I WAS PLEASANTLY SURPRISED!

WE'RE BIOLOGY GRAD STUDENTS! WE LOVE YOUR COMIC!
THERE ARE GRAD STUDENTS HERE AT COMIC-CON?
OF COURSE! FANTASY, ESCAPING REALITY...
IT'S IN KEEPING WITH THE WHOLE THEME OF GRAD SCHOOL!
JORGE CHAM © 2010
LATER...
DR. CHAM!
WHO..? SAL!?
CALTECH
SAL WORKED FOR ME AS A T.A. AT CALTECH. HE'S NOW GETTING A PH.D. WITH MY OLD ADVISOR AT STANFORD.
ACTUALLY, HE DOESN'T KNOW I'M HERE. HE THINKS I'M IN THE LAB!
UH, YOU KNOW HE READS THIS COMIC, RIGHT?
GULP!

PART 2 OF 3
MEANWHILE...
UPSTAIRS FROM THE MAIN CONVENTION FLOOR IS THE ANNUAL "COMIC ARTS CONFERENCE"...
A GATHERING OF SERIOUS SCHOLARS WHO STUDY COMICS AND COMICS CULTURE.
LET ME BEGIN THIS MEETING BY SAYING...
ACADEMICS ASSEMBLE!
I SAT IN ON SOME OF THE SESSIONS:
IN THAT THEY ARE BOTH ORPHANS, I POSTULATE THERE ARE FOLKLORIC PARALLELS BETWEEN THE ORIGIN STORIES OF SUPERMAN AND BATMAN.
HOLY SECRET ORIGIN, BATMAN!
MY TRANSLINEAR MODEL OF TEMPORALITY IN COMICS UTILIZES BIFURCATED IDENTIFIERS OF RHYTHMS EMBLEMATIC OF...
zzz zz
SUPERHEROES AS MYTHOLOGY? I DON'T THINK SO.
THEY AREN'T GODS OF OLD. NOBODY ARGUES WHETHER SUPERMAN EXISTS.
huh

IT'S A PRETTY FORMAL AFFAIR...
YES, THIS IS A TWO PART QUESTION.
CAN YOU ELABORATE ON THE INDETERMINACY IN YOUR POST MODERNIST STORYTELLING THEORY?
ALSO, WHO'D WIN IN A FIGHT, PIKACHU OR HULK?
...GIVEN THE SETTING.
JORGE CHAM © 2010
AFTERWARDS, I TALK TO NEIL COHN, A PERENNIAL FIXTURE AT THE CONFERENCE AND A GRAD STUDENT AT TUFTS UNIVERSITY.
COMIC-CON ISN'T ABOUT COMICS ANYMORE.
IN HIS RESEARCH, HE MEASURES PEOPLE'S BRAIN WAVES WHILE THEY READ COMICS.
YOU CAN READ THEIR THOUGHT BALLONS!?

NEIL EXPLAINS...
HUMAN BEINGS COMMUNICATE IN THREE WAYS:
VERBAL
MOVEMENT
GRAPHICAL
COMICS ARE A THIRD LANGUAGE, BUT NO ONE HAS FORMALLY STUDIED ITS LINGUISTICS!
NOW YOU CUT THAT OUT!
NEIL SPENT FIVE YEARS TRYING TO FIND A PH.D. PROGRAM THAT WOULD TAKE HIM SERIOUSLY.
SLAM
COMICS!? GET OUTTA HERE!
FINALLY, A FORMER STUDENT OF NOAM CHOMSKY TOOK HIM IN.
I TOLD HIM THIS IS GROUND ZERO FOR A NEW FIELD!

WWW.PHDCOMICS.COM NEXT: A CONCLUSION!

PART 3 OF 3
COMIC-CON IS IN FULL SWING AND I'M FOLLOWING SOCIOLOGIST DAN PERKEL THROUGH THE BUSY CROWDS.
MOST SOCIOLOGISTS GET TO GO TO EXOTIC LOCATIONS.
I GET COMIC-CON.
IT'S BEEN AN EXHAUSTING COUPLE OF DAYS: WORKING THE BOOTH...
HOW MUCH FOR THE SHIRT?
$18.
I'LL GIVE YOU $10.
CRASHING IN PEOPLE'S HOTEL ROOMS...
ZZzz!
EATING CONVENTION CENTER "FOOD"...
$8 FOR A PRETZEL!??

DAN IS AT COMIC-CON DOING AN ETHNOGRAPHIC STUDY OF COMIC ARTISTS.
CAN I INTERVIEW YOU?
CAN I INTERVIEW YOU?
JORGE CHAM © 2010
HE AGREES TO LET ME FOLLOW HIM AS HE CONDUCTS HIS FIELD WORK.
OK, BUT... BE COOL.
WHAT?
HI, I'M A SOCIOLOGIST. CAN I ASK YOU A FEW QUESTIONS?
(JUST IGNORE THE GUY BEHIND ME)
WHO WATCHES THE WATCHMEN?

DAN'S RESEARCH IS ON HOW ARTISTS USE ONLINE COMMUNITY FORUMS TO PROMOTE THEIR WORK.
SOCIOLOGY IS NOT ABOUT DEFINING WHAT'S "NORMAL."
IT'S ABOUT GETTING DIFFERENT PEOPLE'S PERSPECTIVE.
YOU LISTEN TO THEM, AND YOU FIND PATTERNS.
WE EACH LIVE IN A DIFFERENT SOCIAL WORLD.
AND EACH OF OUR EXPERIENCES ARE DIFFERENT.
OVER DINNER THAT NIGHT, I ASK CAR-TOONIST FRIENDS AMY AND KAZU WHY THEY COME TO COMIC-CON EACH YEAR.
I THINK IT'S EXCITING! PEOPLE DRESS UP.
IT'S LIKE NERD PROM.
IT'S NOT ABOUT SELLING AND PROMOTING YOUR WORK...
IT'S THIS RIGHT HERE. HANGING OUT WITH YOUR FRIENDS AND FELLOW ARTISTS.

AS I PACK UP TO LEAVE, I GET A LAST-MINUTE GIFT FROM COMIC-CON...
JORGE CHAM © 2010
...A STAN LEE CAMEO!
EXCELSIOR!
WWW.PHDCOMICS.COM
THE END!

About the Author

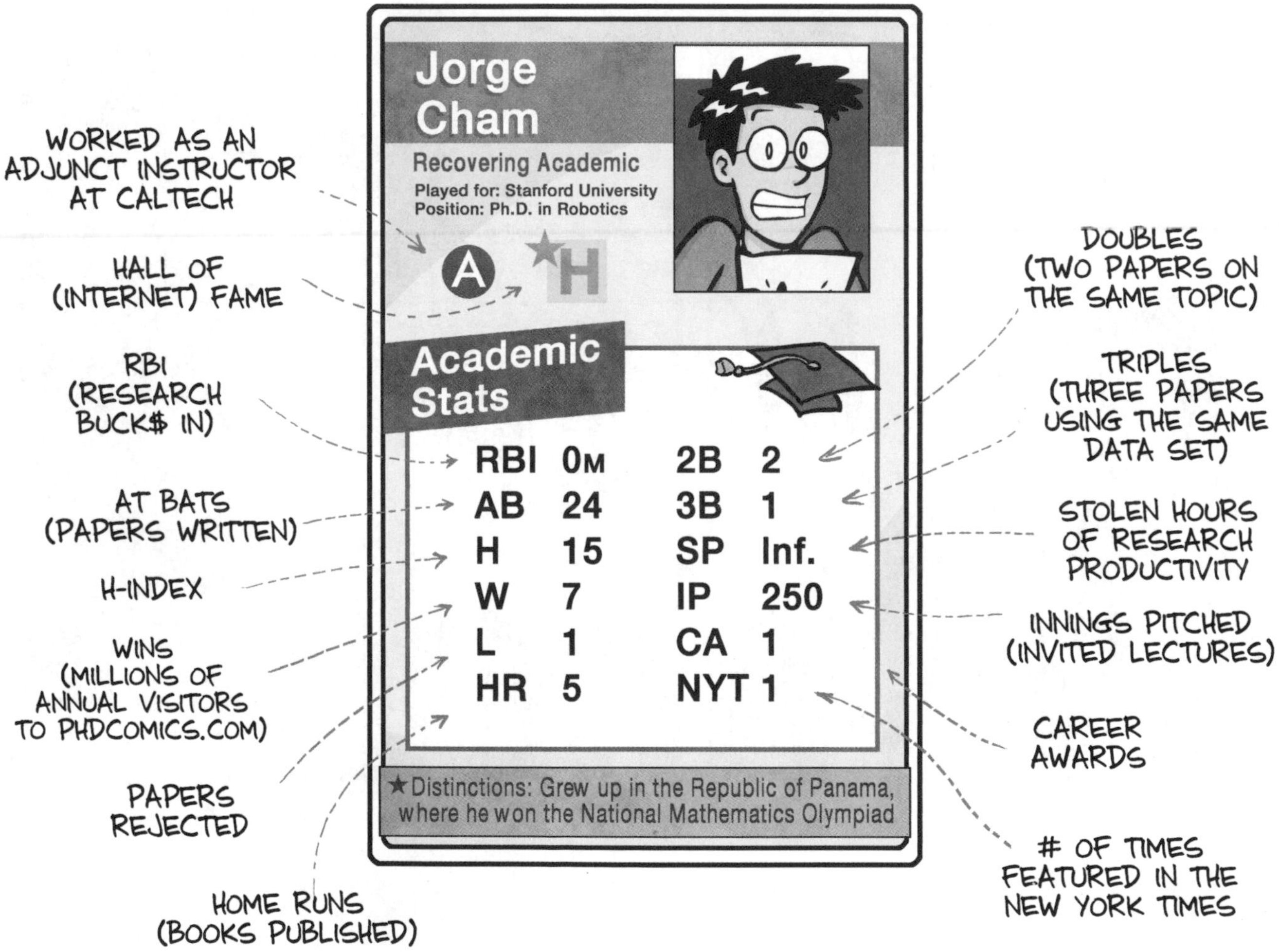

Jorge Cham
Recovering Academic
Played for: Stanford University
Position: Ph.D. in Robotics
A
H
Academic Stats
RBI 0M
AB 24
H 15
W 7
L 1
HR 5
2B 2
3B 1
SP Inf.
IP 250
CA 1
NYT 1
★Distinctions: Grew up in the Republic of Panama, where he won the National Mathematics Olympiad
WORKED AS AN ADJUNCT INSTRUCTOR AT CALTECH
HALL OF (INTERNET) FAME
RBI (RESEARCH BUCK$ IN)
AT BATS (PAPERS WRITTEN)
H-INDEX
WINS (MILLIONS OF ANNUAL VISITORS TO PHDCOMICS.COM)
PAPERS REJECTED
HOME RUNS (BOOKS PUBLISHED)
DOUBLES (TWO PAPERS ON THE SAME TOPIC)
TRIPLES (THREE PAPERS USING THE SAME DATA SET)
STOLEN HOURS OF RESEARCH PRODUCTIVITY
INNINGS PITCHED (INVITED LECTURES)
CAREER AWARDS
OF TIMES FEATURED IN THE NEW YORK TIMES